# Art Psychothera

Art psychotherapy groups offer clients the opportunity for an alternative form of self-expression and communication within a psychodynamic group context. This form of therapy raises some theoretical isues which are as yet unexplored.

Contributors to this book discuss the significance of enactment through the use of space and materials and ask whether a model can be applied universally to art therapy group work with diverse client groups. Through case studies they explore the challenges encountered in practice, and the tensions and dilemmas inherent to art therapy groups. They discuss work with children, forensic patients, patients on acute psychiatric wards, the cognitively impaired elderly, institutionalised patients moving into the community, and drug and alcohol abusers. The book also introduces a model of an introductory workshop to art therapy.

*Art Psychotherapy Groups* is a valuable resource for practising and trainee art therapists, group therapists and all professionals working psychodynamically with clients who have severe mental health problems.

**Sally Skaife** and **Val Huet** are both Lecturers in Art and Group Psychotherapy at Goldsmiths' College, London.

**Contributors**: Angela Byers, Sarah Deco, Jane Dudley, Andrea Gilroy, Val Huet, Frances Prokofiev, Jane Saotome, Nicholas Sarra, Sally Skaife, Neil Springham.

# Art Psychotherapy Groups

## Between pictures and words

Edited by
Sally Skaife and Val Huet

London and New York

First published 1998 by Routledge
11 New Fetter Lane, London EC4P 4EE

Simultaneously published in the USA and Canada
by Routledge
29 West 35th Street, New York, NY 10001

Typeset in Times by Keystroke, Jacaranda Lodge, Wolverhampton
Printed and bound in Great Britain by Biddles Ltd, Guildford and King's Lynn

*British Library Cataloguing in Publication Data*
A catalogue record for this book is available from the British Library

*Library of Congress Cataloging in Publication Data*
Art psychotherapy groups / edited by Sally Skaife and Val Huet.
        Includes bibliographical references and index.
        1. Art therapy. 2. Group psychotherapy. I. Skaife, Sally
    II. Huet, Valerie
        [DNLM: 1. Art Therapy. 2. Psychotherapy, Group. WM 450.5.A8
A78386 1998]
    RC489.A7A765 1998
    616.89'1656–dc21
    DNLM/DLC
    for Library of Congress                                          97–42738

ISBN 0–415–15072–8 (hbk)
ISBN 0–415–15073–6 (pbk)

# Contents

# Figures

# Contributors

**Angela Byers** is currently an art therapist for an N.H.S. trust in South London. She has recently completed a Diploma in Group Psychotherapy at Goldsmiths' College, University of London, where she also trained in art therapy in 1983–5.

**Sarah Deco** is an art therapist and group analyst. She worked for twelve years in the N.H.S. and for Social Services and taught for several years on the art therapy course in St Albans/Hatfield. She now works in private practice and in organisational consultancy.

**Jane Dudley** currently works part-time as an art therapist and group psychotherapist in adult psychiatry. She also teaches on the Art Psychotherapy Diploma at Goldsmiths' College, University of London. Prior to training as an art therapist she worked for some years at the Henderson Therapeutic Community as a charge nurse.

**Andrea Gilroy** teaches at the Art Psychotherapy Unit, Goldsmiths' College, University of London. Her publications include *Pictures at an Exhibition. Selected Essays on Art and Art Therapy* (with Dalley, T., 1989, Routledge), *Art Therapy. A Handbook* (with Waller, D., 1992, Open University Press) and *Art and Music. Therapy and Research* (with Lee, C., 1995, Routledge).

**Val Huet** has worked in community psychiatric services and in a large psychiatric hospital, where she headed an Arts Therapies department. Since 1992, she has taught on the Art Therapy foundation and diploma courses at Goldsmiths' College, University of London. She trained as a group psychotherapist and teaches on the diploma course at Goldsmiths' College. She also works as a private supervisor.

**Frances Prokofiev** has worked as an art therapist in mainstream primary schools for five years and has a particular interest in group work. She has published several papers for teachers on the use of art therapy in mainstream education. She also ran an art therapy group for terminally ill cancer patients for five years.

**Jane Saotome** qualified as an art therapist in 1975. She has an MA in Art Psychotherapy from Goldsmiths' College, University of London. She currently works for the N.H.S in adult and adolescent psychiatry.

**Nicholas Sarra** is an art therapist and group analyst. He lived and worked in Africa, China and the Middle East before moving to London, where he worked at Sutton and Guy's Hospitals, and part-time at Goldsmiths' College. He now lives in Devon and works both for the N.H.S and in private practice. He has a particular interest in organisational dynamics.

**Sally Skaife** has worked in Adult Psychiatry for twelve years and has been teaching at Goldsmiths' College, University of London, on Art Therapy courses since 1986, and on the Diploma in Group Psychotherapy since 1995. She has an MA in Art Psychotherapy, is a past chairperson of the British Association of Art Therapists, and is a member of the editorial board of *Inscape*, the journal of the British Association of Art Therapists.

**Neil Springham** works for an N.H.S. trust in Surrey and specialises in work with drug and alcohol dependent clients. He has an MA in Art Psychotherapy and is a visiting tutor at Goldsmiths' College, University of London.

# Chapter 1

# Introduction

*Sally Skaife and Val Huet*

Art therapy group practice is part of most art therapists' clinical work. This has been the case since the beginning of the profession when art therapists worked with groups of patients from large psychiatric institutions within art studios. Yet, considering the amount of experience developed in group work, there is a dearth of literature about it in comparison to the amount of publication on work with individuals. That is not to say that practice has not been developing, as is shown in the chapters in this book, which we feel is long overdue since it describes art therapy groups in a number of settings with different client groups.

Two main factors have influenced the development of models of art therapy group: the context in which they have been practised, which historically has been within adult psychiatry, and the parallel development of group analytic psychotherapy, which has occurred chiefly in the private sector but also within therapeutic communities, and in the 1970s within psychiatric units in general hospitals. To start with, art therapists practised what are now called studio-based art therapy groups within large psychiatric hospitals. With the development of psychiatric departments within general hospitals, art therapists became influenced by other professionals' use of groups often working alongside occupational therapists and a theme-based, or projective, art group developed as a form of practice. In more recent times group analytic art therapy and group interactive models (McNeilly, 1983, 1987, 1990; Waller, 1993) have developed and this has paralleled the move of art therapy practice to within the community, and to a widening client group. This evolution has happened within a very short time span, and the work of most art therapists who have written about groups encompasses this development.

Other issues have also been at play. As Klein (1995) states, 'ideas do not usually become accepted and disseminated purely for reasons of logic or evidence. Style of presentation, personal and political influences, the thirst for new and tasty experiences, chance factors, all play their part' (Klein, 1995: 217).

These various factors have been significant in the development of art therapy group practice. We are aware that various 'ingredients' such as personal interest, political leanings, work experience, chance meetings, friendships, etc., have played their part here too. Through editing this book and writing our chapter, we have become aware that our respective professional development reflects the evolution of art therapy practice and of the profession itself: at the time of writing this, art therapists, along with music and drama therapists, have just been granted State Registration, a prospect that certainly felt out of reach when we both began our careers.

Sally Skaife first undertook art therapy training when it was an option available as part of a post-graduate art teaching certificate at Goldsmiths' College in 1975 (for further description of training, see Waller, 1991: 219). On placement in a therapeutic community, she encountered the 'projective art group' in which the focus was on the end product of the art work and how it related to the clients' problems. She experienced this as quite a culture shock, as her own interest in art therapy stemmed from a belief in the therapeutic possibilities of art making. She later understood that art therapy was influenced by the occupational therapy department of which it was part. Later, when working in a psychiatric unit, she experimented with various types of art therapy groups with the intention that art making should be at the centre of the therapy. Some of these included discussion of well-known art works, taking patients out to art galleries and craft making. In 1977 she undertook post-graduate study in art therapy, which was becoming established as an independent training (Waller, 1991: 232). Group work was not then formally taught as part of the curriculum although students participated in art therapy groups. These introduced different art-based exercises and themes.

A noticeable change had taken place by the time Val Huet trained at Goldsmiths' College in 1984: the profession had aligned itself more closely with psychotherapy practice. The training addressed group work, which was increasingly perceived as important. Three staff members, Diane Waller (Head of Unit), Gerry McNeilly and Joan Woddis had undergone, or were completing, group trainings. Hence, there was a clear sense of a coherent approach to groups amongst staff. A mainly non-directive psychodynamic model was used in the experiential art therapy workshops. Mostly, no themes or time boundaries were set and the group was responsible for determining the content of the sessions. Verbal experiential groups were also conducted; these were the precursors to 'the large group' which later became part of the training. Although interest in, and commitment to, group work was strong, the length of art therapy training (a one-year intensive course until 1992) did not allow for the in-depth teaching of art therapy group work and trainees learnt about group dynamics mainly within experiential workshops and with client groups on their placements. Art therapists interested in working with groups often undertook group psychotherapy training and, as Waller (1991: 14) points out, an increasing number of art therapists are doing so. It is worth noting that this was the case for most of the contributors to this book. It will be interesting to evaluate whether a longer training time helps students to be better equipped for group work, or if they feel the complexity of such work still calls for the grounding of a purely group-oriented course. This complexity is further compounded by the fact that art therapy group practice has always been in a state of evolution as a review of the literature shows.

We have chosen to review the British literature only, as we feel the practice described in this book was chiefly informed by this. We refer the reader to Waller (1993: 8) and Prokofiev in this book for some discussion of the American literature.

## DEVELOPMENT OF ART THERAPY GROUP PRACTICE IN BRITAIN: REVIEW OF THE LITERATURE

Waller (1991, 1993) writes on the historical development of the art therapy profession and of art therapy groups. She discusses the evolution of the open studio model within psychiatric hospitals, which mirrored the art school setting. Patients were then encouraged to use art materials within an individual space in the room and work was discussed privately in 'whispered conversations in a corner of a room to the exclusion of other patients' (Waller, 1993: 8). Waller traces the departure from this model to the late 1960s, when new ideas about groups began to influence art therapy group practice. From then on many art therapists seemed to develop a stronger sense of group dynamics and of the need for formal boundaries such as time, space and frequency of meetings. It is interesting to note that this process happened whilst the British Association of Art Therapists (BAAT) was becoming established as a professional body for art therapy and focusing on criteria for registration and training (see Waller, 1991). There seems to be a similar move away from informality and *ad hoc* arrangements in order to define and strengthen both practice and professional identity.

Until the early 1980s, British literature on art therapy groups is sparse. In 1982, Liebmann published a compilation of *Art Games and Structures for Groups* following a survey involving forty-two art therapists. There is a paucity of theoretical material in this initial pamphlet, apart from a brief introduction focusing on the meaning and importance of games. Liebmann assumes a directive and theme-centred approach as the group leader is responsible for selecting the right game and making it work. Following this initial pamphlet, a book on *Art Therapy for Groups: a Handbook of Themes, Games and Exercises* was published by Liebmann (1986). Mainly a practical description of art-based exercises, the book straddles the boundaries between art therapy groups and 'projective' or 'therapeutic' art groups run by many occupational therapists and teachers. It is offered for use by any interested professionals who may follow the exercises detailed in the book.

Reactions to the publication of this book were mixed: some art therapists saw it as a threat to their still fragile professional identities and as a disappointment because it did not address in-depth theoretical issues encountered within theme-based groups, others welcomed it as a source of practical ideas (see McNeilly, Thornton and Molloy below).

Inspired by the work of Foulkes on Group Analysis, McNeilly (1983) challenged this directive, theme-centred approach. In 1983, whilst training in Group Analysis, McNeilly published an article on 'Directive and non-directive approaches in art therapy' in which he challenges the use of themes as creating a risk of uncovering material too quickly and of taking away from the interactions between group members by focusing too much on the group leader. McNeilly warns that 'with a non-directive approach the attacks can be intense' (McNeilly, 1983: 215) and wonders if by setting themes the art therapist may be evading transference issues. This paper stimulated a debate within the profession concerning art therapists' practice in groups: Thornton (1985) defends the use of themes in art therapy groups and Molloy (1988) warns of their potentially invasive quality.

In 'Further Contributions to Group Analytic Art Therapy' (1987), McNeilly addresses some of the criticism made of his previous article. This concerns an apparent lack of space for in-depth work and the diminishing importance of the art work which appears left at the background. McNeilly states that he does not see the need for giving his own comment to all images, feeling that 'communication is more important than interpretation' (McNeilly, 1987: 9). He stresses again the potential dynamic quality of a non-directive approach and that providing themes may be a means of allaying the anxiety of the art therapist as well as of the patients. McNeilly refers to the 'Group Matrix' as defined by Foulkes (1964), which comprises all the shared conscious and unconscious knowledge, interactions and experiences in the group. He feels that the art therapist needs to be able to tolerate uncertainty and to let the group evolve in the matrix, until some shared theme emerges from the material brought by the group members.

Greenwood and Layton (1987) describe a community-based art therapy group for people with severe mental health problems which seems to integrate a loose theme-centred approach with an awareness of group dynamics. The therapists ensure the maintenance of basic boundaries such as regularity of time, safety of space, consistency of therapists' presence and warning of any changes such as breaks. Greenwood and Layton comment that although basic practice for many psychotherapists, these boundaries are often overlooked by art therapists.

Non-threatening themes are offered to group members for optional use by the therapists, although often themes emerge from the group discussion which takes place in the first ten minutes of the group. Greenwood and Layton mention agreeing with McNeilly's views on the danger that setting themes might meet the therapist's needs rather then the clients. However, they feel that themes offer some containment for the anxieties of clients who find any increase in stress difficult to cope with. They describe a process during which the art therapist picks up the theme from the group discussion and gives it back to the group in a moderated form. They feel that 'it is as if the "intolerable" is put into the therapist in the form of a theme' (Greenwood and Layton 1987: 14).

The therapists make images themselves during the group and Greenwood and Layton describe this as a 'side-by-side' approach. Refuting criticism that exposure to the therapist's unconscious might be harmful for the patient or the therapist and that it might minimise transference, and therefore the process of therapy, they write:

> Our concept of *side-by-side* therapy describes how sharing the experience of working on pictures together gives opportunity for servicing boundaries and feeling relationships between individuals. Showing the work and talking about the pictures together provides additional opportunities for development of self in relation to others and sharing and modifying anxieties.
>
> (Greenwood and Layton, 1987: 14)

They use Bion's concept of 'containment' (1962) and describe the group as a container both during the verbal and the art-making part. They see the art work as providing the three phases of containment: projection, digestion and re-introjection. Material is projected and represented in the image. It is then digested within the process of art making and during the group discussion.

Greenwood and Layton (1991) later describe a form of humour, 'Taking The Piss' (TTP), which has a 'dual function of deflating tension and promoting growth' (Greenwood and Layton, 1991: 7). Although they discuss the uses of TTP generally in art therapy, they also describe its effect within an outpatient art therapy group for psychotic clients and in mixed diagnosis and non-psychotic groups.

An approach similar to Greenwood and Layton's may be found in Skailes' work (1990) with psychiatric patients. Skailes describes two art therapy groups: one runs in the day hospital, the other is 'outward-bound' (Skailes, 1990: 68) and based in the community. Both are for clients who may become caught in the 'Revolving Door' effect of psychiatric treatment (Skailes, 1990: 58). In both groups Skailes, like Greenwood and Layton, mixes a non-directive approach with the use of loose themes and story-telling.

Significantly, Waller (1990) edited a special section on 'Group Analysis and the Arts Therapies' in *Group Analysis: The Journal of Group Analytic Psychotherapy*: this seems to reflect a stronger link between the arts and group psychotherapies, and Waller mentions the incorporation of group psychotherapy training at the Goldsmiths' Art Psychotherapy Unit (Waller, 1990: 211). McNeilly, Skaife and Strand are among the contributors to this special section.

McNeilly (1990) discusses his personal process in training in group analysis and art therapy. He concludes that both are 'two sides of my own theoretical/technical coin' (McNeilly, 1990: 224) and advocates further work on cross-fertilisation.

Skaife writing on 'Self-determination in Group Analytic Art Therapy' (1990) describes a group in which she does not fix time boundaries for art-making and talking, and the group is left to make such decisions themselves. She discusses how existential material that emerges, such as the fear of taking risks, of being alone (with the art work), can be analysed and much gained from the feelings brought up in the process.

Although Strand (1990) works with institutionalised clients with learning difficulties, her approach to an art therapy group run within a hospital differs from Greenwood and Layton's (1987) and Skailes's (1990). No themes are given to the group and the two co-conductors do not use art; the only structure in the group seems to be a set allocation of time for art-making and talking. Strand describes the group as 'closed' with seven members and feels that this helps provide a sense of security and value within an environment characterised by high staff turnover and sudden, unexplained changes. An initial task is to encourage interaction between members who are used to seeking praise and validation by staff but who rarely talk to each other. There is at first a certain amount of direction given by the therapists to the group which Strand describes as 'social skills teaching' (Strand, 1990: 259). It involves showing people how to listen and be listened to, and also encouraging the use of people's names. Strand notes that the need for some degree of direction from the art therapists decreased as people gained confidence in themselves and she comments on their high level of motivation to participate. One of the predominant group themes to emerge is the one of loss:

> Loss was discussed in terms of the loss of family or friends; a sense of abandonment or rejection; the realization of difference and not being 'normal'; the fear of one's death.
>
> (Strand, 1990: 261)

Strand's approach seems to straddle directive and non-directive stances and to give emphasis to the importance of interaction between group members.

Case and Dalley (1992) write on different approaches to art therapy group work. Highlighting some of the historical background given above, they identify and illustrate different models such as the studio-based, the group analytic and the theme-centred groups. They also describe phases of development in groups, and transference and projective processes. Although Case and Dalley gather some of the most relevant points on art therapy group practice and its link with group psychotherapy, the chapter being part of an introductory handbook to art therapy, is necessarily brief and does not enter into an in-depth discussion.

A group interactive art therapy model is developed in a book by Waller (1993). This book is significant in that it is the first publication solely concerned with art therapy group practice. Waller defines her approach by drawing on the work of Yalom (1975, 1983), Bloch and Crouch (1985), Aveline and Dryden (1988), Ratigan and Aveline (1988) and Agazarian and Peters (1989) who all emphasise the importance of interaction between members (including the conductor) in group psychotherapy. The roots of such an approach are firmly in existentialism and Waller states that 'the concept of responsibility, freedom and choice are central to the interactive model' (Waller, 1993: 23).

The emphasis is on the 'here-and-now', which is where all feelings and interactions are analysed and worked through, shifting the emphasis of the group from the historical narrative to interpersonal learning. Waller stresses that although transference is no longer the only tool, many practitioners often use both psychoanalytic and interactive models, and that there is much of an overlap in practice.

Waller identifies curative factors which are usually present within psychotherapy groups and some of the most notable ones are: giving and sharing of information, installation of hope, alleviation of loneliness, catharsis, group cohesiveness and interpersonal learning (Waller, 1993: 36). She then lists and discusses thirteen further curative factors found in interactive art therapy groups. These are: a greater atmosphere of trust in the group once the 'performance fear' of art making has been confronted, art as an alternative to words and a media for play, image-making resembling 'free association', and the art work containing symbolic meaning as well as a reflection of the 'here-and-now' material of the group. The art object may be used to enact feelings towards the conductor, and is the focus of projection as well of interaction. Art-making also gives the group a structure which some clients may find less threatening than a purely verbal group. The images provide a reminder to the members and the conductor of the events of the sessions. Waller feels that at times, art quickens group processes and the conductor may need to regulate the pace of the group if this happens. She stresses the value of creative activity and sees a link between the ability to experiment with art materials within the group and a greater openness in life outside (Waller, 1993: 40).

Waller discusses the role of the conductor within an interactive art therapy group. She describes how, even when themes are introduced, the art therapist continues to pay close attention to group dynamics and encourages the group members to do likewise, instead of working with people individually within the group. Quoting Aveline and Dryden (1988), she makes a comparison with psychodrama groups where the conductor has 'an uncommon blend of extroversion and sensitivity, as well as energy and the ability to think on one's feet and to tolerate the scrutiny of the group in the prominent role of director' (Aveline and Dryden, 1988: 149; in Waller, 1993: 49). She also stresses that attending to practical matters is an important task for the art therapist, and she discusses issues regarding suitability and availability of space and materials.

Waller describes how themes may be usefully introduced in an inter-active art therapy group, an approach which she finds particularly useful when conducting time-limited workshops. She also discusses short-term interactive art therapy groups and pays particular attention to ward-based groups. The rapid turnover of patients often creates confusion for practitioners since there is 'no coherent, commonly accepted method for running in-patient groups' (Waller, 1993: 73). She advocates adapting the interactive art therapy group model to work more effectively with short-term groups. She also feels this model is particularly suited to work with children and adolescents, since it offers an arena to explore peer relationships, an important issue for adolescents. Waller further illustrates the model in practice through the use of case examples.

Another publication on groups by Campbell on *Creative Art in Group Work* concerns itself mainly with the use of art-based themes in groups (Campbell, 1993). Interestingly, this book does not meet with the level of controversy raised by Liebmann (1982), although there are many similarities in the listing and description of art-based exercises which may be used in groups.

More recently, Skaife (1997) and Huet (1997) have written on women's art therapy groups. Skaife explores transference and countertransference in an art therapy group in which she, the therapist, was pregnant and compares it with similar groups discussed in the verbal group analytic literature. The clients appear less involved in pre-oedipal material in the art therapy group, which she felt might be due to the physical act of painting, which allowed members to identify with the creativity of her pregnancy, rather than become regressed. Also, feelings could be released and expressed in an alternative and more neutral arena than directly to the therapist, allowing for expression of aggressive feelings to be held in the images and returned to at a time when there was less fear of damaging the therapist or her baby.

Huet writes on a community-based art therapy group with older women referred through psychiatric resources. She discusses socio-cultural perceptions of ageing and of older women. She adapts a mainly non-directive model by introducing some time structure to alleviate a high level of anxiety. She describes dynamics particular to a younger art therapist working with older women in a group and the effect of a double transference regarding mothers and daughters. She feels that art offers a valuable mode of expression for older women who are often made to feel invisible. Huet also advocates greater awareness from therapists of issues encountered when working with this client group.

Models of art therapy group practice discussed in the literature can be

distinguished by the relationship of pictures to words or verbal interaction within them, hence the title of this book. In the studio-based
model the process of art making is given a prominent role, but verbal
interaction is mainly between individual and art therapist. In theme-
centred art therapy groups, the focus is also on the art work, but mainly
in its contribution to understanding the individual client's problems.
Since it is generally the art therapist's task to introduce the themes, the
conductor has a leader-like role. The verbal interaction tends to be
mainly between the conductor and individual clients in the group rather
than amongst the whole group. Group analytic or interactive art therapy
understands image making as part of the group dynamics, and interaction
is between all members of the group including the conductor.

All these different models are used within contemporary art therapy
group practice. In a way, this variety means that art therapists are able to
adapt to the needs of different client groups and offer a therapeutic
resource to people who otherwise would be unable to use purely verbal
therapy. It is to be noted that, although an approach inspired by the
studio model is still in use, the disappearance of large institutions has
meant a loss of permanent studio space where art was at the forefront
of the art therapy process. The consequences of this loss have not yet
been fully realised by the care system, although one suspects they have
been heartily felt by clients and art therapists alike. There are also
implications for models of art therapy group practised.

## WHAT IS NEW IN THE BOOK

This book follows on from the work of McNeilly (1984, 1987, 1990)
and that of Waller (1993) in extending a model of art therapy group by
theoretical exploration and application of it to different client groups.
Our own chapter explores particular areas of theory in art therapy
groups. Containment of primitive and regressive behaviour always
amplified in groups and in art therapy groups potentially even more so,
is described by Prokofiev, Sarra, Saotome and to a certain extent Deco
and Byers. Prokofiev gives a thorough resumé of management issues
involved in running children's art therapy groups, and amongst her case
presentations, gives an original case description of a group co-run with
the class teacher. Deco describes a model of art therapy group for
patients on acute wards, a very welcome addition to the literature. She
calls for a 'return to the studio-based model', but one with clearly
defined boundaries. She describes her own process of setting out to
achieve this. Sarra, Saotome and Byers discuss theoretical issues

involved in providing psychodynamic art therapy groups for, respectively, highly disturbed patients on a forensic ward, chronically psychotic institutionalised patients and the cognitively impaired elderly. Springham introduces an original theory in describing why art therapy groups in particular can be so helpful to clients in a drug and alcohol dependency unit. Saotome's chapter is in two parts, describing first her MA research into art therapy groups provided in long-term psychiatry, and second giving a moving case study of a group of chronically psychotic patients about to move into the 'community'. Last, Dudley, Gilroy and Skaife describe introductory workshops for people interested in finding out about art therapy. They describe using a model of experiential group which allows for the development of an art therapy group process, whilst simultaneously using this to teach about art therapy.

## THEORETICAL ISSUES IN THE BOOK

Our own chapter addresses theoretical issues in art psychotherapy groups and is divided into two sections; one addresses dilemmas about the relationship of art making to verbal interaction, and the other is about enabling factors in groups. We have suggested that theoretical issues are clearer in groups such as the ones we briefly describe, which are outside a mental health institution and are for self-referred members. We also say that we think they have relevance to art therapy groups in other settings with different client groups. We will now look at the significance of these theoretical issues for different client groups described in the chapters in this book. First a summary of the issues, the first three of which are framed as questions: the first is, does the use of art effect the working through of dependency and authority issues in the group? The second is, does the symbolic/metaphorical meaning of the image take precedence over the working through of feelings through a visual, aesthetic medium? The third is, does verbal interaction tend to predominate over art making? The next two issues we have called enabling factors, the first is that one or more images come to symbolise the group process, and the second, that the group use art making and their relationship to the art room, space and materials to enact and communicate feelings.

It appears to us that the dilemmas we have described are far less significant in the groups described in the other chapters, than they are in our own groups. It appears that the less able clients are, to make cognitive links between action, feeling and thought, the greater the significance of the enabling factors. Many of the client groups described would not be regarded as suitable for psychodynamic therapy in verbal groups, chiefly because the group could not be held with words alone. Art in the group allows for an emphasis on the non-verbal, and that may not be the making of images, but can include an interaction with any of the physical matter in the room. The physical boundary of the art therapy room contains the process. This allows meaning to be both given and understood to everything the client does or does not do in the room.

Thus we will begin the discussion of the chapters by looking at the enabling factor described last in our chapter, that of enactment. The group of forensic patients described by Nick Sarra present a good example of the relationship between acting out and enactment. The contained space of the art therapy group, and the art materials allow for a certain amount of regression, which appears from the examples given by Sarra, to progress from acting out to enactment. The role of the therapist, as Sarra describes it, is to contain the client's unbearable feelings, communicated in their acting out, by surviving the internalised projection. Group members, seeing the therapist cope with those feelings, then may be able to engage with them once more. Jane Saotome describes the way patients claimed the new studio as their own by a rare collective decision to put their art work up together on the wall. Angela Byers describes the role of art in her groups with the cognitively impaired elderly as a form of empowerment, whereby people assert their individuality by the marks they make. She describes the holding up of the art work at the end of the group as a form of ritual, which aims to inculcate a sense of relating in the group. Rituals, an important aspect of all art therapy groups, are described in other chapters, such as Frances Prokofiev's one on children. She describes the importance of providing a ritual such as counting down from ten to show the children that the art therapy space is a different one to the classroom. The ritual of putting the art work into the centre of the group is described by Dudley, Gilroy and Skaife in the chapter on introductory experiential groups, as a purposeful act of containment, which is illustrated to students learning about art therapy, as well as acting as containment for themselves in a situation which can be quite anxiety-provoking.

The other enabling factor that we discuss is the group image, and this also seems to be significant for all the client groups. It clearly emerges in Neil Springham's chapter in the 'Magpie's Eye'. There is also an example of it in Frances Prokofiev's chapter in the image of the *Titanic*. The degree to which it is important for this to be verbalised differs with each group.

Do any of the dilemmas we describe in our chapter appear to be significant in other groups? First, the question of whether the use of art effects the working through of group transference. It appears that in institutional settings where clients are already in a dependent situation in relation to authority figures, without much chance of this ever changing (the elderly, the chronically psychotic, the forensic patients), or changing in the near future (children), the question asked has a different meaning. It seems that the therapeutic purpose in these situations may not be the same as for a group of adults, usually somewhere between the ages of twenty and sixty, and 'psychologically minded' (Coltart, 1993), whose struggle is to become released from inhibitive patterns laid down in childhood. The group of elderly patients are coping with cognitive impairment, and the fear of further loss of control and dying. The group of institutionalised mental health patients have to come to terms with a major change in their lives in terms of the loss of their home, the hospital. However, despite these differences in therapeutic purpose, a dynamic group development is described in all the case descriptions. But, contrary to our experience in groups where members are able to make cognitive links, the use of art in the group, instead of inhibiting the development of transference and its working through, is actually the chief factor through which empowerment and thus a lessening of dependence is seen to occur, though this is not appreciated at a cognitive level. Thus, Byers describes a process in her group of elderly cognitively impaired clients whereby the group members became more able to express and communicate their feelings, some of which she felt were in relation to her leadership. Interestingly, it is the inability to allow an experience of feeling dependent on anyone, that is at the heart of Neil Springham's chapter on art therapy with substance abusers. Here, it is the art work, by allowing an individual space in the group, that enables clients to engage with the therapist and each other at a meaningful level. Again it seems that it is the non-verbal aspect of art therapy that enables a therapeutic process to take place, even where there is little cognitive appreciation of this.

Our second dilemma is, does the symbolic/metaphorical aspect of art take precedence over the working through of feelings in a visual, aesthetic medium? It seems that this dilemma is less apparent in most of the groups and in some, where enactment is the chief medium of expression (Sarra, Byers, Saotome), it is not really relevant. In the acute ward groups discussed by Sarah Deco it seems that neither aspect of art would take precedence, and she argues for a return to the old studio-based approach, within delineated boundaries, which allows for more flexibility in art making, given time constraints, however. Frances

Prokofiev describes the therapeutic importance of a shared aesthetic experience and again this dilemma seems less relevant in this setting where children themselves do not experience such a distinction. In Springham's chapter, art as symbol or metaphor is clearly primary. However, this does not seem to pose a dilemma: as Springham points out, the whole point of using art in this context, is that it allows for metaphors about difficulties in relationships, to emerge; the central feature being the importance for this client group of the individual space provided in the group by the art making.

The third dilemma is: does verbal interaction threaten to predominate over art making? This does not seem to be the case with any of the other client groups. In the groups which struggle with any art making (Sarra, Byers) there is also a struggle with verbal interaction.

It appears that we can conclude that art making allows for a group, psychodynamic therapeutic process to take place with clients that would have great difficulty in using a verbal psychotherapy group. And, that this process happens through the metaphor of the group images, but more importantly through a dynamic enactment within the art therapy space, using not only the art materials but also the physical environs of the art therapy room. However, with clients who could make use of a verbal analytic therapy group, dilemmas arise between the use of verbal interaction as the therapeutic medium and art making.

Finally, there are two important features to mention about the book. The first is that one of the chief characteristics that emerges from the chapters is the overwhelming nature of art therapy groups. Most of the authors discuss dealing with strong countertransference responses, and containment of the group process seems to be largely a matter of the conductors' ability to cope with this. The potency of these groups seems to relate to the regressive nature of using art materials, and to the primitive feelings that clients can get in touch with, which can threaten to spill out. There is a wealth of material in the actual number of art works that can be produced as well as the verbal material; the conductor can feel overwhelmed by the amount of material there is to process. (Not forgetting though, that the other side of this is, as Frances Prokofiev says, 'the heady atmosphere of creativity and inventiveness'.) The second and related point is that authors have allowed for their personal process as therapists to be visible in their discussion of case work, and allowed their uncertainties to be exposed. This we feel makes the case material valuable as a tool for understanding the therapeutic process and helpful for other art therapists, in thinking about their own work.

## BIBLIOGRAPHY

Agazarian, Y. and Peter, R. (1989) *The Visible and Invisible Group: Two Perspectives on Group Therapy and Group Process*, London: Tavistock and Routledge.

Aveline, M. and Dryden, W. (1988) *Group Therapy in Britain*, Milton Keynes: Open University.

Bion, W.R. (1962) *Learning From Experience*, London: Heinemann.

Bloch, S. and Crouch, E. (1985) *Therapeutic Factors in Group Psychotherapy*, Oxford: Oxford University Press.

Campbell, J. (1993) *Creative Art in Group Work*, Winslow.

Case, C. and Dalley, T. (1992) *The Handbook of Art Therapy*, London and New York: Tavistock and Routledge.

Coltart, N. (1993) *How to Survive As a Psychotherapist*, London: Sheldon Press.

Foulkes, S.H. (1964) *Therapeutic Group Analysis*, reprinted 1984, London: Karnac Books.

Greenwood, H. and Layton, G. (1987) 'An Out-patient Art Therapy Group', *Inscape Journal of Art Therapy*, Summer: 12–19.

Greenwood, H. and Layton, G. (1991) 'Taking The Piss', *Inscape Journal of Art Therapy*, Winter: 7–14.

Huet, V. (1997) 'Ageing Another Tyranny: Art Therapy with Older Women' in S. Hogan (ed.) *Feminist Approaches to Art Therapy*, London and New York: Routledge.

Klein, J. (1995) *Doubts and Certainties in the Practice of Psychotherapy*, London: Karnac Books.

Liebmann, M.F. (1982) *Art Games and Structures for Groups*, Bristol: Bristol Art Therapy Group.

Liebmann, M.F. (1986) *Art Therapy for Groups: a Handbook of Themes, Games and Exercises*, London: Croom Helm.

McNeilly, G. (1983) 'Directive and Non-Directive Approaches to Art Therapy', *The Arts in Psychotherapy*, vol. 10: 211–19.

McNeilly, G. (1987) 'Further Contributions to Group Analytic Art Therapy', *Inscape Journal of Art Therapy*, Summer: 8–11.

McNeilly, G. (1990) 'Group Analysis and Art Therapy: a Personal Perspective', *Group Analysis*, vol. 23: 215–24.

Molloy, T. (1988) 'Letter' to *Inscape Journal of Art Therapy*, Spring: 27–8.

Ratigan, B. and Aveline, M. (1988) 'Interpersonal Group Therapy' in M. Aveline and W. Dryden (eds) *Group Therapy in Britain*.

Skaife, S. (1990) 'Self-determination in Group Analytic Art Therapy', *Group Analysis*, vol. 23: 237–44.

Skaife, S. (1997) 'The Pregnant Art Therapist in an Art Therapy Group' in S. Hogan (ed.) *Feminist Approaches to Art Therapy*, London and New York: Routledge.

Skailes, C. (1990) 'The Revolving Door: the Day Hospital and Beyond' in M. Liebmann (ed.) *Art Therapy in Practice*, London, Bristol and Pennsylvania: Jessica Kingsley.

Strand, S. (1990) 'Counteracting Isolation: Group Art Therapy for People with Learning Difficulties', *Group Analysis*, vol. 23: 255–63.

Thornton, R. (1985) 'Review of Gerry McNeilly's Article: Directive and

Non-Directive Approaches in Art Therapy', *Inscape Journal of Art Therapy*, Summer: 23–4.

Waller, D. (1990) 'Group Analysis and the Arts Therapies', *Group Analysis*, vol. 23: 211–13.

Waller, D. (1991) *Becoming a Profession: the History of Art Therapy in Britain, 1940–1982*, London and New York: Routledge.

Waller, D. (1993) *Group Interactive Art Therapy: Its Uses in Training and Treatment*, London and New York: Routledge.

Yalom, I.D. (1975) *The Theory and Practice of Group Psychotherapy*, New York: Basic Books.

Yalom, I.D. (1983) 'In-Patient Group Psychotherapy', New York: Basic Books.

# Chapter 2

# Dissonance and harmony
## Theoretical issues in art psychotherapy groups

*Sally Skaife and Val Huet*

## INTRODUCTION

In this chapter, we examine some theoretical issues that arise in art psychotherapy groups. To do this we look at processes in a particular type of group, one that stands outside of a clinical setting, is for self-referred members and is usually the sole therapy in which members are involved. These groups attract a clientele most similar to the membership of groups which have been used by theoreticians to develop models of group psychotherapy. Because of these factors, theoretical issues particular to these groups being art therapy groups are perhaps more easily identifiable within them. However, we believe that these issues also have relevance to groups in other settings.

Theoretical issues arise in the combining of art-making as a creative healing process, and verbal interaction, the material of group psychodynamic practice. Basically, we identify a central problem and that is, *that there is too much material*. In our groups we attempt to work with all of it, but have become aware that this results in some difficult tensions and dilemmas which we will address here. Our intention is not to provide answers but to frame the questions and to allow an exploration of areas of uncertainty in our practice.

It is possible, as is discussed in an earlier paper (Skaife, 1995), that the tensions involved in combining these two distinct processes, verbal interactive therapy and art-making, could have therapeutic potential in themselves. However, here we separate the dilemmas and tensions that we see arising from structure and those that are part of a creative process of therapy. Despite the dilemmas our groups have been running, we feel successfully, for over eight years, and many people have passed through them and have found them of great value. Because of their time span we have been able to identify the art therapy processes within the groups which seem to function well, and we also describe these here.

We begin with a review of the relevant art therapy group literature, and then go on to give a short description of the groups. The transition between the different activities in the art psychotherapy group is where tensions mostly occur. We therefore focus on the phases in a single session of the group and highlight the principal dilemmas that arise between each phase of the group. Finally, we identify and describe two phenomena particular to art therapy groups: the group image and the use of art work in the enactment of group process. We call these 'enabling factors' since we feel that they play a part in facilitating the process of the art therapy groups.

## THE LITERATURE

Within the sparse literature on art therapy groups, conflicts about combining art therapy and group psychotherapy are mentioned, but only briefly. Wadeson (1980) discusses the problem of excessive amounts of material, and Waller (1993) says that interactive art therapy groups can accelerate and intensify the group process, requiring the art therapist to use the skills of a psychodramatist to slow the process down when necessary or to change the type of enactment of the material (Waller, 1993: 40).

Maclagen talks about art therapy as representing 'a potentially dangerous encounter with the irrational and uncontainable' (1985: 7), and discusses the difficulties of using words in relation to images and the dangers of literalism. Skaife (1990) introduces some conflicts in combining art and verbal interaction, such as the ambiguities that arise with the therapist's role, the tendency for words to take precedence over art-making, and the difficulties of dealing with the wealth of material. These will be discussed in more depth in this chapter.

McNeilly (1990) discusses the relationship of words and images and acknowledges a tension between the two processes, but prefers not to make too much distinction between them considering language a form of word painting. He talks about his role as group leader as being a conductor of electricity between different aspects of the group's activities. He states: 'Much of the interpretive and containing work is a process of harnessing one minute and freeing the next. A central feature in my work hinges upon such powers as "opposing forces" or the attraction or pushing away of opposites' (McNeilly, 1990: 224). McNeilly says that his approach has been criticised for placing too little importance on image-making, which he however feels is not true. He thinks this is said because he does 'not chase after the meaning of individual images' (1987: 9).

Case and Dalley (1992) refer to the inherent tension in groups between the individual and the group, and point out that in art therapy groups the difference is enacted in having an individual art making space in the group. Case and Dalley (1992) discuss group painting; that is, the group working together on one piece of art work. They say that the group may do this to avoid facing individual difference, but that it might also be a way in which the group can work with shared feelings at both a conscious and unconscious level, about a theme such as sexuality.

Having looked at what is said in the literature about inherent conflicts in art therapy groups, we will now look at what is said about group-enabling solutions. Instead of 'chasing after individual images' (1987: 9), McNeilly develops the concept of 'resonance' (1983, 1987, 1990) in art therapy groups. By this he is describing a similarity in the visual appearance of the imagery in the art therapy group, and is drawing on a concept originally coined by Foulkes (1964). Foulkes used the word 'resonance' to describe the way in which people link up with one another at an unconscious level. In an art therapy group Roberts refers to its manifestation as 'some form of simultaneous expression of shared unconscious material' (Roberts, 1984: 19). Roberts suggests several reasons for its presence: themes given by the therapist or the group, discussion by members, conscious or unconscious copying and shared experience. McNeilly (1990) later comments on how colleagues express surprise that so much resonance and cohesion can come out of images done individually within the group and that they had been expecting a reverse effect, with individual fragmentation of the group.

Whitaker (1982) also discusses resonance in verbal therapy groups. Using French's work on *The Integration of Personality* she writes on 'A nuclear conflict and group focal conflict model for integrating individual and group-level phenomena'. The 'nuclear' conflict, which stems from a person's past experiences, becomes focal when a situation resonates strongly with its roots. In groups, certain themes echo strongly with all members and highlight a 'group focal conflict'. The group reacts by developing enabling or restrictive solutions:

> A distinction is made between enabling solutions, which allow for the relief of fears and expression of the shared wish, and restrictive solutions, which allow for the relief of fear but not for the recognition or expression of the shared wish.
>
> (Whitaker, 1982: 326)

Whitaker comments that if the group begin to apply enabling solutions when dealing with uncomfortable themes, the resulting exploration resonates strongly with its individual members. This increases the potential for personal growth.

The literature reviewed here highlights areas of tension within the practice of art therapy and verbal therapy groups. Within art therapy groups, these stem partly from combining art with verbal interaction and also from conflicts between individual and group space, made prominent in art therapy groups by the individual art work. Restrictive and enabling solutions to conflicts in verbal groups are discussed since they are relevant to the dilemmas found in art therapy groups. Such tensions and dilemmas create a degree of uncertainty within our practice. McNeilly (1990) acknowledges uncertainty when trying to define 'What is at the heart of group analytic art therapy?' and when conducting verbal or art groups (McNeilly, 1990: 223). He sees the conductor's ability to tolerate uncertainty as an important part of the process.

Although he does not focus on group work, Edwards (1992) discusses uncertainty in art therapy practice and finds value in this familiar but uncomfortable feeling. He sees the art therapist's tolerance of his own confusion as helpful to staying open to the material of therapy, an unpredictable process. We hope this is so here and that our uncertainty is useful in helping us frame the questions found in the next section.

## THE GROUPS

These groups are within a university department, which runs both art psychotherapy and group psychotherapy courses. They run weekly for two hours. The groups which each have between five and eight members are long term, slow open groups, which people come to because they seek a different form of therapy other than the purely verbal, or have heard about the groups from others, or because they have a professional interest in art therapy or have simply seen the groups described in one of the college publications. Sound assessment for the groups is crucial as we do not have the back-up of a mental health institution. We emphasise personal responsibility for the therapy to prospective clients. The average stay in the groups is between two and three years.

## SONATA-FORM

### Phases of the Session

We have found that musical structure provides a useful way to think about the process in time of a single art therapy group session. Musical analogies for group processes have been used before (Foulkes, 1964; Powell, 1982, 1983, 1990; Strich, 1983). Strich describes music as an 'attempt to understand the patterns of human relationships by organising them in symbolic form' (Strich, 1983: 20). Powell (1983) has used the musical structure sonata-form, as an analogy for the group process over time. He points out that sonata-form must have something profoundly satisfying about it to non-discursive symbolism because 'once established, it continued to underpin musical structure, through symphonic form and concertos, opera and chamber music for the next 200 years' (Powell, 1983: 15).

We are using sonata-form here as a way of thinking about the three distinct processes in a single art therapy group session; spontaneous verbal interaction, art-making, and analysis of these two. We are paralleling these to the three phases in sonata-form, the exposition, the development and the recapitulation.

In our experience, when we allow the group to develop their own culture for art-making each session usually, though not always, follows a similar pattern. The group usually starts with spontaneous verbal interaction, followed by art making, followed by analysis and relating of the first two. This pattern, similar to that discussed in groups where the therapist has set the structure (Strand, 1990; Liebmann, 1986; Greenwood and Layton, 1987), though usual is certainly not rigid; on occasion discussion of images made the previous week starts the session, or the group may start with making art work. There are probably many reasons to explain why this format is the most popular, but we think that the fact that the groups are the primary therapy for the members is significant. There is a strong need in the group for members to establish themselves as a group at the start. Also, verbal expression of thoughts and feelings seems to be an essential part of the therapy.

In the first phase of the group, like the 'exposition' in sonata-form, the main themes are expressed. In this phase what takes place is very similar to what would happen in a verbal therapy group. That is, group members will converse about things that have happened to them during the week, and about current issues between them. The chief difference is that in the matrix there are many images like leitmotifs, musical references, that have been made and have often become powerful symbols for the group, developing and changing their meaning over time. Some of these may be visible around the room: sculptures and pieces of construction. There may also be images made at the end of the preceding week which have not been talked about. In sonata-form the first theme is linked to a second theme (usually in the dominant key), by a bridge passage. Events outside the group may be related to events inside the group or to the art work by an interpretation about parallel material.

We have observed that at a certain point it seems as though the group moves down from a peak of emotional intensity into a plateau, there is often a silent pause, and then someone suggests art work. This next phase in the session is like the 'development' in the musical analogy. The group work individually through their art work and it is as if the unconscious is being allowed free reign over the material that has so far come into the group; it is developed, digested and extended in individual ways by each person in the group, as the themes in the musical structure are developed through various keys.

The last phase of the group, the 'recapitulation', is, in both sonata-form and the art therapy group, a reworking of the first phase, through a discussion of the art work that has been made in the group, and in music through a return to the home key.

We have observed that the 'push pull' dynamic between art therapy and group interactive therapy is at its most intense at the times of transition between the phases. Breaking away from the group, the circle of chairs and from the familiarity of words to the physicality of working with materials on one's own is not easy. Finding the right time to stop making art may be artificial, and finding a way to talk about art work can be difficult. The therapist must facilitate movement from one process to another and must make sure her interventions are appropriate to the specific phase that the group are in, for example making an analytic comment at a time when the group are moving into an 'acting' phase can stop the group and keep it stuck in the interactional phase.

## Dilemmas and tensions

It can be difficult to distinguish which of these tensions are connected to the structuring of the group, and which are part of a creative tension present in all groups and here enacted through the combining of art and verbal interaction, potentially with a therapeutic outcome. In this section we will describe those which we consider might be connected to group structure, and in the next session we will address those we feel to be unproblematic.

It appears to us that there are particular tensions specific to each phase in the group outlined above. In the initial talking phase, tensions revolve around how, when, and if the group will do any art work (and what are the implications to the therapeutic process in the art therapist's attitude to this). In the art making phase, the dilemma is whether there is enough time to work through something in the art work. In the last phase, the talking about the images, the issue is whether there is enough time to do all the work justice.

*Exposition: The Initial Talking Phase*

Should the therapist guide the group into art-making or should it be left up to the group? What are the implications for the working through of dependency and authority issues?

In an earlier paper Skaife (1990) discusses the therapeutic possibilities arising from the conductor allowing the group to decide on the time and length of the painting period. Feelings and attitudes towards creativity, towards being alone, towards responsibility come to the fore for discussion in the group. However this mode of working does have implications for the resolution of the transference.

The use of art materials gives the group a resemblance to one that aims to complete a task and therefore needs to make itself into an efficient machine needing a leader to give it direction. When the art therapist does not take up this role the transference to the conductor can be affected. She is in a different position to the conductor in a verbal group, and the initial transference may be one similar to that of a teacher. To examine the implications of this it is useful to look at what is said in the literature on analytic groups about leadership.

Foulkes (1964) describes one of the goals of analytic group therapy as being the correction of infantile dependence on authority figures. He describes two levels functioning in the group and with the leader's role. On a manifest level the members talk about their relationships both within and outside the group; the conductor meanwhile stays in the background and does not lead in the usual sense. The members gain strength through having to grapple with socialising forces in the group. In order to get the protection of the group for themselves, they must be willing to give others attention. At the same time they are influential in socialising others by their response to antisocial behaviour. The conductor's role on this manifest level is to facilitate this process by his own role modelling behaviour and by underscoring the positive social behaviour of group members, but he stays largely in the background.

However, at a latent level the conductor is seen by group members as an all-powerful, God-like figure. This is necessary, says Foulkes (1964), not only to give his remarks weight on a manifest level and to give a sense of safety for strong emotions to be exchanged, but also to facilitate the therapeutic process whereby patients lose their infantile dependence on authority figures. The conductor allows the group to experience him as all powerful, so that they can also experience a gradual awareness of his ordinary humaness as they grow in strength. There is thus a crescendo in the power of the group and a decrescendo in the power of the leader. Foulkes points out that this therapeutic process could not happen if the conductor were playing the part of leader (Foulkes, 1964). If he were to lead, then the group members would remain in a dependent position even if this were actually latent, and they would not be able to work through their individual conflicts with authority figures. The conductor in an interpersonal group is more active and less austere than in an analytic group, the idea being that transference occurs whatever the conductor does. As in an analytic group, he does not actively lead the group (Aveline and Dryden, 1988).

So, in a verbal group the conductor's passivity on a manifest level allows the group to engage with issues around dependency and authority. What are the implications, though, of the therapist taking a passive role in a group which has an activity in it, which needs structuring at least in so far as when, and for how long, it takes place? In our experience the difficulties posed for the art therapy group in there being an activity to organise, and the leader's blatant passivity in taking on this role, can frustrate the group to such an extent that the members of the group often end up deliberately excluding the conductor altogether and organising the group themselves. Foulkes's (1964) description of a group when the conductor does not have potency at a latent level may happen in an art therapy group when the therapist does not organise the session.

> Without having this basic authority at the back of him, the conductor might simply lose all prestige by behaving as he does. The group might be bewildered and anxious, succumb to a hopeless feeling of frustration and interpret the conductor's reluctance simply as weakness and incompetence. In its despair it would look for another leader; not necessarily for another therapist, but worse still would elevate somebody sufficiently vociferous out of its own ranks into the position of leader. He, particularly if neurotic, could be expected to abuse this position and certainly not to use it in the ways here described for the benefit of the group.
>
> (Foulkes, 1964: 62)

Either of these situations, the group members organising themselves or an unsuitable leader presenting themselves, can take some time to undo at the start of an art therapy group. A focus is put on the conductor either in the denial of her presence, or in a confrontation with her which happens too early in the group to be therapeutically useful, but serves rather to undermine the safety of the group. We find that it is better then to give just enough help to the group to enable it to work effectively. Over time this role can be handed over more and more to group members until the impetus for art-making is held by the whole group. This position also fits with the therapist's role in helping the group deal with the physicality of the art materials, she may need to give guidance with this task, for example, how to open bottles, how to use a particular material etc.

However, in an on-going group such as our own, we ask whether having an activity that needs some sort of organising affects the group's potential for working out issues of authority and dependency. A further question is, how far does the fact that the clients have a more neutral arena in which their feelings are expressed other than the transference, that is image making, effect the development of a dependent transference and its working through? Skaife (1997) discusses an art therapy group in which the therapist was pregnant and compares it with similar groups discussed in the verbal group therapy literature. One of the findings was that clients appeared less involved in pre-oedipal material in the art therapy group. (The therapist's pregnancy offers a unique situation for transference to be studied, as when the therapist is pregnant she becomes a primary stimulus for group material whereas at other times, transference towards other group members may be equally strong.) The conclusion suggested was that the physical act of painting enabled feelings to be released and expressed in an alternative and more neutral arena than directly in relation to the therapist.

It seems to us that issues about the development and working through of parental and authority issues often become enacted through the group members' 'control' over whether or not they make art, and what sort of art they make. In other words the group makes use of the tensions around the change in activity to play out issues of power and authority throughout its life, though these will have a different nature depending on the phase of group development (Agazarian and Peter, 1989). This can, however, be problematic because of the intrinsic tension between art and verbal exploration. That is, is the art-making and the preparation for it creativity or acting out?

An example of this is the tension that can arise when the group discusses going to paint. There may be a long period of group time spent coming to some kind of consensus about whether it is time to go and make art work. This can create an uncomfortable tension for the art therapist, as during this time she has no clear role. Her usual role as commentator on group process would only serve to extend the talking time, putting her vote as it were, behind the verbal rather than the change to art-making. If she says nothing she becomes an observer, standing outside the group process and watching on. This role is actually extended as the group members establish new positions in the room, moving furniture, etc., as they settle down to art making. Another way in which the group can make a passive resistance is by leaving it up to the conductor to suggest moving into the art-making phase. Very often an unspoken code of dominance amongst group members is enacted; the group will only respond to one member's proposal about making art work and will ignore anyone else's suggestions. Attempts by the conductor to interpret this also seem to invite more time spent in discussion. The conductor can feel uncomfortably silenced.

It is as if the dynamics in a verbal therapy group become exaggeratedly acted out through the physical relationship to the materials and the activity. Although there is therapeutic potential in an analysis of this material, it can threaten to dominate the group time, leaving less for the actual art-making and the reflection about the images. This has implications for the therapist's technique.

We have discussed tensions in this first part of the group around how to move from talking to making art work. As in the 'exposition' in sonata-form the themes that the group are concerned with have been presented. Now, often following a silent pause, the development of these begins in the art making.

*Development: the art-making phase*

Is there enough time to make art?

As mentioned earlier we have found that group members are heavily reliant on verbal interaction and moving away from this to making art can be difficult. Some weeks there is no art made and no mention made to art work from previous sessions. The therapist can feel that she is in a verbal psychotherapy group and that the two hours is too long for this. It appears that group members feel this too. Often, half an hour before the end, the group will start looking at their watches and bemoan the fact that there is not enough time to do any art work and to talk about it.

We have found that our groups have tended to establish a culture for how long they spend making art, which is usually something between twenty and forty minutes. At times this is negotiated, but at other phases in the group's life there may be a gradual stop, with one person beginning to clear up, thus giving a signal to others who may or may not respond by also finishing. The time the group allows for art making is just about enough time for the initial setting out of the visual idea, or for the finding of the visual idea. At the point at which the artist needs to look at what she has done and think about it aesthetically, they stop. This means that the art work is never pushed onto its next stage. It appears that in response to the group process, symbols and metaphors are released through spontaneous art-making which then come to be seen as a reflection of the group process. They can extend the group process helping to focus the group on important issues – as will be described in the next section – but clients do not have the space to fully engage in the creative process of, for example, putting the idea down, pushing it on, losing it and moving into chaos, and then finding it again in a renewed form. A creative process which is a microcosm of life itself, and so useful therapeutic material.

The most commonly cited reason for this is that there is never enough time to look at, and talk about, the art work made. A feeling that we share. In educational settings we have noticed that where there are two-day workshops of four hours in each day, the working through of issues through the art-making is much more prevalent. In the therapy groups discussed here members seem to find it important to have some verbal response from one another in each session, though this does not seem to be a response necessarily to the art work. This, however, determines the time spent on the art work.

Another factor is that the therapist makes only verbal contributions to the group adding to an emphasis on a verbal culture in the group. Arguments as to why the therapist should not make her own art work in this type of group have already been made (Case and Dalley, 1992). The therapist often finds herself with the dilemma that the intervention she makes will direct the group in one way or another, to focusing on art or on verbal interaction. We have found it necessary to counteract the tendency towards the verbal by taking a much more consciously active relationship to the art materials and to other physical aspects of the art therapy room.

We have asked ourselves whether there is enough art in our groups, and does it matter that the value of the art-making appears to lie mainly in its function as symbol or metaphor for the group process? Is the concern entirely our own and not shared by group members? This discussion is an important one as using art in group therapy raises so many dilemmas that art therapists need to be sure that it does not pose more quandaries for the group than is worthwhile.

*Recapitulation: phase three, talking about the images*

How can the group give enough time to both an appreciation of the images, and to the interactive verbal material which may be sparked off by them?

As in the 'recapitulation' in sonata-form, this phase of the group is a reworking of the themes from the first phase of the group, now expanded and developed through the art work. There is now a substantial amount of material in the group. In this section of the group there is a tension between how far the discussion is going to be about each person's inner dialogue as has taken place in this time spent on their own with their art work, and how far a dialogue between members of the group. This is not to say that the individual's art work would not be relevant to other group members. Far from it: as in verbal psychotherapy groups the culture in the group is for all the art work to be seen in relation to its context in the group process. However, one person's contribution to the group process in terms of their image, may spark off a substantial amount of verbal group interactive material. So the dilemma is, will the focus stay with the images, or will the images be used as a spring-board for further interactive work? There never seems to be time enough for both.

A further tension in this phase is about individual space. Is there going to be enough time for everyone in the group to talk about their image or images? Turn-taking may be used as a means of resolving the difficulty, and self-denial – 'I don't mind if I don't talk about my picture.' Very often these dynamics are not talked about sufficiently as yet again this would take away from time spent on discussing the images. The pull away from talking about the images can also be a way that group members resolve their feelings of tension in waiting for their 'turn'. They may say something provocative about another's image to turn the attention onto themselves.

These tensions may encourage the group to behave in a mature manner, and find a socially acceptable way to manage this part of the group; however, in doing so infantile impulses are repressed. The therapist then often holds the tension, worrying about the unexpressed needs of each individual.

In the following episode these dynamics became close to the consciousness of the group. (In the case examples given, the therapist is one of the authors.)

---

The group had decided to start the session by looking at the art work made the week before during which the members had only spoken about one person's work, though this for a considerable length of time. The subject had been life and death aspects of pregnancy; the painting had been made by a woman who was pregnant. This week the group arranged the pictures of the week before in the middle of the floor and silently looked at them. The members decided that they would not speak about them, but move onto making more art after a short observation period. This seemed like a restrictive solution (Whitaker, 1982) to what I thought was a conflict about wanting individual attention for themselves but being afraid of the resulting exposure, yet also not wanting to feel frustrated by talking about someone else's picture. I was considering whether to, and how to, comment on this when one member interrupted the silent contemplation of the pictures. She said her picture, a pole in the sea, was about her fear that after she left the group she would be at sea without anything to hold onto. She thought the pole was something a boat could hitch onto. The atmosphere of the picture was of a sick landscape she said, she worried she was not normal. She explored what she felt was not normal with the help of the group and eventually came round to saying that she feared she was more selfish, unloving and begrudging than other people. Another member said she thought that everyone felt that, and was she not being too harsh on herself. A third member came in angrily and said that she thought the previous speaker was smoothing over things and trying to make them better. The artist agreed with this and said the view was simplistic and what she was talking about was much more complicated than that. I felt that the second speaker had been rebuffed and felt protective of her. I asked her what she felt about what had been said. She said that if she did try to smooth things over and she thought that she probably did, she wanted to know what the group thought she might be smoothing over. Someone asked if she took this smoothing over role in her family. 'Very much so' she said. 'My mother is domineering and critical. I shrink from her criticism and always try to make things better.' This was just the way she had reacted to the person who had snapped at her. She had visibly shrunk. There seemed a lot to work with here.

Then I looked at her picture. It was of roses and other flowers whose stems did not seem to be growing from the ground but just hovering. It seemed like a pretty exterior with no grounding. (A visual example of what was being talked about perhaps.)

I felt unsure whether to take up the transferences or whether to focus the group on the picture. It felt very tempting to do the former as the group was often dividing into aggressors and victims and there seemed a lot to work on here for everyone. But I was aware that in doing that I would be moving the group away from the images. My comment also felt influential in terms of how much value I place on the images and thus how much value I expect the group to place on them.

In retrospect I realise that what I should have said was that the first speaker's feelings of being selfish and begrudging were perhaps shared by the group in that they were experiencing a conflict about not wanting to hear about other people's issues expressed in their paintings, whilst at the same time fearing talking about their own. Instead I decided to risk alienating the rest of the group by referring Mary back to her picture.

What emerged was that the picture was an allegory about the pregnant woman, her own belief that she was pregnant, about envy and about 'being blessed.' It wasn't quite clear because it transpired that she was telling us that she was pregnant. The rest of the group resonated to this news and continued then to happily take turns to talk about their images which interestingly, were all about pregnancy and fertility. The first member to speak then saw her picture as about getting 'hitched' (to the pole) and spoke about her fears of not finding a partner.

———————

The vignette illustrates the tension between individual and group, the difficulties for the group in how to manage this phase of the session, and the therapist's common dilemma as to whether to take up interactive transference or focus the group on the art work. In the end the group actually found a solution to the dilemma of how to get attention, and arrived back in the 'home' key in the sonata-form analogy. That is, the members were able to find a way to work satisfactorily with the material. Enabling solutions will be discussed in the next section. This example is given here to illustrate the tension the conductor feels about the enormous amount of material that is released into an art therapy group and the impossibility of dealing with all of it.

Although in a verbal therapy group the conductor has to choose which material she will pick up on and which leave until another time, according to what has the most therapeutic potential for the moment, in an art therapy group this dilemma feels much more extreme. Often group members will make several pieces of art work in a single session, and invariably in each session at least one person's work will not have been discussed, or all the work will have been discussed superficially. The feeling this can often give us is of wasted material. It is difficult to know exactly how much this affects members negatively.

As mentioned earlier, it feels as though there is always a pull in the group towards the art work being understood as a metaphor for the group process, and not as something in itself which might extend the group and individuals in it. In other words the work made in the group is made to fit what the group needs it to be. It reflects the group process, maybe extending it by creating a helpful metaphor for it, but it follows rather than leads. It may be that the way through this dilemma is to break the taboo of acknowledging aesthetics. The taboo is implanted in the group first by the conductor to prevent members feeling inhibited by making art, and to inculcate a norm that whatever anybody makes is of interest to the group. However, it may be that this works counter to enabling the group to enter into the unknown, to chaos, and to try to work through to meaning within the art work itself. The 'talking about the images' phase then, could be about relating the struggle in the creative process to personal change.

In summary, in an art therapy group there is a constant tension between interactive verbal work and the making and considering of the art work. Thus an important part of the therapist's technique is to know when to address her comments to which process. Although art-making in a therapy group offers the possibility for group members to regress, the organisation around getting down to using the art materials and how to talk about the resulting work, encourages a more mature response. This must have some effect on the type of therapeutic work done in an art therapy group.

## ENABLING FACTORS

Our experience of conducting art psychotherapy groups over several years has shown that the process does work; clients are able to explore sensitive issues, both verbally and visually. They often comment on achieving some resolution of conflicts, inner or with others, and on their perception of positive personal change. Occasionally, the group acknowledges change in one of its members by reminiscing on their progress over a period of time.

In this part, we describe some of the reasons why the process does work. In the midst of tension and conflict we focus on 'enabling solutions' (Whitaker, 1982: 326), which not only hold the clients at times of heightened anxiety and frustration but also promote individual growth through the art psychotherapy group experience.

## The group image

Stock-Whitaker's focal conflict theory was described earlier as a means of understanding the way in which a therapeutic process with the group material as a whole, can have meaning for each individual. We have discussed how, when lacking time to discuss all images in depth, members may resort to turn-taking or self-denial in order to avoid tension and conflict. These solutions may then be seen as restrictive and might indicate an avoidance of disturbing material if they persist in a group over a few sessions. The art therapist may need to comment on the turn-taking process or challenge the denial of need for personal space.

When the group does not resort to turn-taking, it is often the case that some images may not be discussed and are never brought out again in the group. We may question the depth and efficiency of a process which allows for so much material to remain unexplored. However, a strength may be found in an area other than the individual discussion of art work: often one image (or more) is made which embodies a shared unconscious theme in the group. Its exploration by the whole group slowly reveals the previously unacknowledged topic. We call it a 'group image' and feel that it is an important 'enabling' solution to group focal conflicts. The following example illustrates this. As before, the therapist is one of the authors.

---

This is the second session of a women's group. All members are present and during the initial discussion, several themes emerge: hopes are expressed that the group will help changes to happen but fears that damaging conflict might erupt are also present. When the group gathers back after making art, some of these themes are reflected in the art work: one woman has painted foetal shapes (Figure 2.1), picking up on a topic discussed earlier about whether and when to have children. One woman has drawn her house blown apart (Figure 2.2), having referred previously to

*Figure 2.1* Lydia: second session

*Figure 2.2* Maggie: second session

her need to move from a place which holds too much family history. The group is clearly attentive to all images, questions are asked and comments made by members. Although watchful of me, they are not waiting for me to intervene to feel able to talk. Then one member, Sarah, starts discussing her image: she has painted a pack of hungry wolves which have appeared in a dream (Figure 2.3). They stare and howl for feeding, being desperately hungry. Sarah says this is probably about the group and I become aware of a change of atmosphere in the room: each member looks as though she is leaning forward with increased attention. This does not change when Sarah describes the other half of her painting which represents her father with his heart out and little red dots which represent 'lots of tits'. Her father, who does suffer from a heart condition, is often gallivanting with other women whom she associates with the breasts she painted. Sarah states that she feels angry with all these tits because she never received the attention she craved and all she got from him was 'a

*Figure 2.3*  Sarah: second session

*Figure 2.4* Fiona: second session

*Figure 2.5* Lily: second session

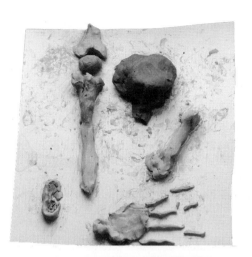

bad heart'. When she stops talking, the group is silent for a while, all eyes on the painting. I am about to make a comment on how her image may reflect preoccupation in the group (too many hungry mouths to feed, too many women to compete with, the disappointment of absent men) when someone remarks there are only ten minutes left and several images to discuss. The end feels rushed and unsatisfactory as though the group is acting out the themes in Sarah's painting of too many needs and not enough to go round. Afterwards, I am aware of feeling helpless, unable to provide enough to meet huge needs.

———

The group's reaction to Sarah's image is significant: all members seem fully absorbed in looking at it and attention is heightened. The group seems very close to acknowledging the fears expressed in the image and the strength of the shared feelings is for a moment very intense. The group then switches quickly to a restrictive solution of taking turns to discuss images superficially and the potentially creative intensity is gone.

As shown here, the group is not always able to work on issues revealed by a group image (in this case, the fact that the group was just beginning certainly affected its ability to take risks and explore it). However, its presence is often denoted by a heightened intensity of attention by the whole group, a 'sitting on the edge of the chair' moment. Its content resonates strongly with all and embodies themes previously not articulated.

McNeilly (1989) discusses five types of images found in group analytic art therapy: the blank page, the written word, the shocking image, the recurring and the copied picture. He finds these five types occur regularly in art therapy groups and discusses the roots of their repeated manifestation and his response to them. Although each type enables the maker to communicate valuable information about their process in the group, frequent recurrence may indicate that issues are not being addressed and resolved. As described earlier McNeilly (1983) also sees a resonance within the collective imagery done in art therapy groups and notes the presence of 'similar shapes, colours and symbols' (McNeilly, 1983: 216). In our experience, pictorial similarity between

———

*Figure 2.6*  Leona: second session
*Figure 2.7*  Fiona: second session
*Figure 2.8*  Irene: second session

images is not the only form in which resonance can occur in art therapy groups. In 'An Analysis of a Single Group Session of an Art Therapy Group with Older Women' (1995), Huet finds few visual connections between images which initially appear to share little content. However, when the pictures are discussed, much common material emerges which stems from their symbolic content. Huet notes that two particular images seem to resonate strongly with all members of the group, bringing out themes previously not articulated. The making of group images is not confined to one group member only. Several clients may regularly produce such pictures, although it is interesting to note that diagrammatic images, described by Schavieren as an '*illustration* of a feeling, rather than an *embodiment* of feeling' (Schavieren, 1987: 78) usually do not resonate strongly with the whole group. Clients who play with the art material and allow some unconscious content to develop seem to frequently connect the group's unconscious material and represent it in the group image.

Gilroy (1995) researches changes in members' perceptions of themselves and others in an art therapy group and uses Lieberman's *et al.*'s (1973) definition of group members with a 'VCIA' role: 'They were individuals who were Influential and Active and whose Values were Congruent with the goals of the group. Such people were found to take risks, were spontaneous, expressed themselves and were helpful to the group through their influence and activity' (Gilroy, 1995: 68). Gilroy finds that an increase in VCIA role in the art therapy group is linked to a decrease in fear towards the unconscious meaning of the image and to an increased capacity to learn about the self and about one's art work (Gilroy, 1995: 75). Further research is needed to establish whether a link exists between the making of group images and an increase in VCIA role although our experience seems to indicate it is a strong possibility.

The group image is not necessarily a weekly feature in an art psychotherapy group: many sessions may go by without it occurring. Sometimes, as in the illustrated case above, it may be present but its exploration may be avoided by the group. A question is raised as to whether a group may unconsciously collude in preventing a group image from being discussed at all, and if some of the undiscussed pictures are put away with a collective wish that disturbing material may also be hidden in a drawer. Schavieren writes on the 'scapegoat transference to the picture' within analytical art therapy (1992: 37) and feels its roots stem from a 'magical-thinking' wish to dispose of the bad feelings by putting them in the picture in order to cast them away. Some similar wishful thinking may be at play with an art psychotherapy group when the group image is avoided. However, in our experience, most groups, working with both images and verbal interaction, eventually acknowledge a wish to avoid or dispose of uncomfortable issues. Whitaker states that 'resonance between group focal conflicts and individual nuclear conflicts as experienced in derived forms *is* transference' (1982: 331). Similarly, we feel that a group image resonates strongly with all members because it embodies a shared, previously unconscious, transference. The group image acts like a mirror to the group. The feelings found in its reflection might be difficult to confront but they are made more bearable by the fact that, although depicted by one (or sometimes more) group members, they resonate with all. If the group allows for an enabling solution to develop through its exploration, the resulting acknowledgement of its resonance leads to a heightened cohesion. This, as Whitaker points out, also increases the potential for individual growth (1982: 330). Group images are often remembered in the group and referred to as a 'visual' account of its history. It is as though the group image bridges in both a concrete and symbolic way the gap between the experience of individual art making and of being in a group.

## The art work and the enactment of the group process

Schaverien (1992: 124) discusses enactment and the image in art therapy. Echoing Khuns' (1983) perception of famous art works as enactments valued and honoured within a culture, she describes 'the picture in analytical art psychotherapy as an enactment within a culture' (Schaverien, 1992: 129). She differentiates enactment from acting out: disturbing feelings may be 'acted out' in a way generally unhelpful to the process of therapy, as is the case with scapegoating or self-harming. The image in art therapy enables the enactment of feelings and 'offers a particular way of mediating the area between patient and therapist' (Schaverien, 1992: 136). We find that this is also the case in art therapy groups where the art work is often used to enact feelings previously not acknowledged, which then become recognised and owned by the group. The following example illustrates this.

———

Over a few weeks, the hut where the group meets has become fuller with three dimensional work made by trainees. At the end of one session, when Martin is trying to find some storage space for his clay work, he exclaims: 'There must be a lot of sculptors working in this place, I can hardly find space for keeping my work!'

The following week, Martin mentions how angry he feels about this: having used a magazine to store his small clay work on, he has written on it: 'This space needed by Martin to keep his work', an angry 'Keep off' sign. Martin says he is angry towards me for not protecting his space. Some discussion follows in the group on who the others are and whether I see them. A link is made with my recent return from maternity leave and whether I can look after them well enough or if I am too preoccupied with other 'babies'. The group expresses relief that these feelings have been acknowledged.

———

Martin's action of angrily claiming space for his work enables the group to question whether I have enough emotional space to hold them and to acknowledge their fear of being crowded out by the new baby. The art work is used to enact these powerful issues. In art therapy groups, the manner in which images are made may enact difficult feelings: for instance, the sound of paper tearing may bring to the group's attention the anger of a previously silent member; a member who screws up and throws away his image may communicate feelings of frustration to the group in a vivid and direct manner. Art work may also be used to enact powerful emotions during significant events in the group, such as when a member leaves.

———

A ritual had developed in the group whereby a person leaving would look through their art work in the presence of the rest of the group. In the session described, the piled up art work took the form of a 'to be opened' present, with all the ambiguities that leaving presents have. The group were waiting for a late member and a dream about a Christmas meal with a dog sitting at the table about to vomit, was described. When the art work was shown, there were great surprises in store for the group. The art work presented a history of the group and revealed group secrets that had been kept from newer members. A split developed whereby it seemed to the leader that half of the group wanted to continue opening 'the present' and the other half were resenting the time and space given to one member. Eventually the ritual opening was abandoned and a fruitful discussion on rivalry in the group took place.

———

Images may also be used in acting out feelings: for instance, a member angry with the group may take his work away or destroy it; a member may drop out of the group and leave his art work and the art therapist has to sort out the effect of things being symbolically and physically dumped on the group. Angry feelings are acted out generally in a destructive manner towards the art work and no resolution is found. In our experience, however, such instances are rare. The images are used to enact feelings and this enactment offers the group a powerful and physical manifestation of its silent preoccupation.

In summary, in this part, we have identified two phenomena that we feel are factors which facilitate the art therapy group process: the group image and the use of the art work in the enactment of feelings. These phenomena do not cancel out the other curative factors found in verbal and art therapy groups (Waller, 1993: 35). They are, however, particular to art therapy groups and give further richness and dimension to the process.

## CONCLUSION

In this chapter, we have looked closely at the phases of an art therapy group session relating this to sonata-form in music. We have highlighted dilemmas and tensions found within each phase and within the transition from one to the next. A central thread emerges; that there never seems enough time to work with all the material in the group. We go on to identify 'enabling factors' found only within art therapy groups, which help express, process and contain their wealth of material. As stated earlier we present the dilemmas without providing answers, and make a deliberate point of separating them from the 'enabling factors' that we describe in the next section. This is because if we were to see the dilemmas and the enabling factors as part of the same creative process, we might ignore important questions. The chief one of these is, how important is the use of art in art psychotherapy groups? Does it substantially increase the potency of the group to merit the difficulties incurred? A further question is, would other forms of art therapy group, such as those that place greater emphasis on art making by structuring the group differently, eliminate many of the difficulties described, and provide a more harmonious form of therapy?

This chapter is underpinned by a shared, on-going questioning of our practice. This sometimes raises great uncertainty. There is a 'pull-push' dynamic here, whereby we feel such questions at times help us pull our understanding into focus, but at others seem to push it away. We often stay for a while with a sense of 'not-knowing' which, although a familiar feeling often found within therapy, may be uncomfortable. We are aware, however, that this parallels the process of the art therapy groups which grapple with a wealth of visual and verbal material and have to tolerate confusion and anxiety before reaching some resolution. It also echoes the artistic process, where the artist allows herself to become unsure and confused during art making, in order for a new creative direction to emerge.

## BIBLIOGRAPHY

Agazarian, Y. and Peter, R. (1989) *The Visible and Invisible Group: Two Perspectives on Group Therapy and Group Process*, London: Tavistock and Routledge.

Aveline, M. and Dryden, W. (1988) *Group Therapy in Britain*, Milton Keynes: Open University Press.

Case, C. and Dalley, T. (1992) *The Handbook of Art Therapy*, London and New York: Tavistock and Routledge.

Coltart, N. (1993) *How to Survive as a Psychotherapist*, London: Sheldon Press.

Edwards, D. (1992) 'Certainty and Uncertainty in Art Therapy Practice', *Inscape Journal of Art Therapy*, Spring: 2–7.

Foulkes, S.H. (1964) *Therapeutic Group Analysis*, reprinted 1984, London: Karnac Books.

Gilroy, A. (1995) 'Changes in Art Therapy Groups' in A. Gilroy and C. Lee (eds) *Art and Music Therapy and Research*, London and New York: Routledge.

Greenwood, H. and Layton, G. (1987) 'An Out-Patient Art Therapy Group', *Inscape Journal of Art Therapy*, Summer: 12–19.

Huet, V. (1995) 'An analysis of a Single Group Session of an Art Therapy Group with Older Women', Unpublished MA thesis, University of London: Goldsmiths' College.

Kuhns, R. (1983) *Psychoanalytic Theory of Art*, Columbia, NY: Columbia University Press.

Lieberman, M.A., Yalom, I.D. and Miles, M.B. (1973) *Encounter Groups: First Facts*, New York: Basic Books.

Liebmann, M.F. (1986) *Art Therapy for Groups: a Handbook of Themes, Games and Exercises*, London: Croom Helm.

Maclagan, D. (1985) 'Art Therapy in a Therapeutic Community', *Inscape Journal of Art Therapy*, Winter: 7–9.

McNeilly, G. (1983 ) 'Directive and Non-Directive Approaches to Art Therapy', *The Arts in Psychotherapy*, vol. 10: 211–19.

—— (1987) 'Further Contribution to Group Analytic Art Therapy', *Inscape Journal of Art Therapy*, Summer: 8–11.

—— (1989) 'Group Analytic Art Groups' in A. Gilroy and T. Dalley (eds) *Pictures at an Exhibition. Selected essays on Art and Art Therapy*, London and New York: Tavistock and Routledge.

—— (1990) 'Group Analysis and Art Therapy: a Personal Perspective', *Group Analysis*, vol. 23: 215–24.

Powell, A. (1982) 'Metaphor In Group Analysis', *Group Analysis*, vol. 15(2): 127–35.

—— (1983) 'The Music of the Group', *Group Analysis*, vol. 16(1): 3–19.

—— (1990) 'Words and Music: an Unsung Therapeutic Alliance', *Group Analysis*, vol. 23(3): 225–35.

Roberts, J.P. (1984) 'Resonance in Art Groups', *Group Analysis*, December: 211–20.

Schaverien, J. (1987) 'The Scapegoat and The Talisman: Transference in Art Therapy' in T. Dalley *et al. Images of Art Therapy*, London and New York: Tavistock and Routledge.

—— (1992) *The Revealing Image: Analytical Art Psychotherapy in Theory and Practice*, London and New York: Tavistock and Routledge.

Skaife, S. (1990) 'Self-Determination in Group Analytic Art Therapy', *Group Analysis*, vol. 23: 237–44.

—— (1995) 'The Dialectics of Art Therapy', *Inscape Journal of Art Therapy*, vol. 1: 2–7.

—— (1997) 'The Pregnant Art Therapist in an Art Therapy Group' in S. Hogan (ed.) *Feminist Approaches to Art Therapy*, London and New York: Routledge.

Strand, S. (1990) 'Counteracting Isolation: Group Art Therapy for People with Learning Difficulties', *Group Analysis*, vol. 23: 255–63.

Strich, S.J. (1983) 'Music and the Patterns of Human Interactions', *Group Analysis* 16(1): 20–26.

Wadeson, H. (1980) *Art Psychotherapy*, New York: John Wiley.

Waller, D. (1993) *Group Interactive Art Therapy: Its Uses in Training and Treatment*, London and New York: Routledge.

Whitaker, D.S. (1982) 'A Nuclear and Group Focal Conflict Model for Integrating Individual and Group Level Phenomena in Psychotherapy Groups' in M. Pines and L. Rafaelsen (eds) *The Individual and The Group: Boundaries and Interrelations*, vol. I, Theory, London: Plenum Press: 321–38.

# Chapter 3

# Adapting the art therapy group for children

*Frances Prokoviev*

## INTRODUCTION

As the title of this chapter implies, art therapy groups have evolved for an adult membership and children form an identifiable group with different characteristics. Expectations of how art therapy groups operate acquired in work with adults, are vividly challenged by the way a group of children react to the permissive environment of an art therapy room. The pace of the children's group is often fast, with interactions between the children happening in different parts of the room at once. While clay or liquid paints can promote regression and a healthy letting go, they may also lead to extensive mess in the room and on clothes. The structure common to adult art therapy groups of dividing the session in half with a separate time for sharing and discussing the artwork, is inappropriate for many children's groups and children often resist discussion as well as cleaning up at the end. Most challenging perhaps, is that the permissive atmosphere of a children's therapy group can become a destructive environment in a flash, when feelings are acted out in a physical attack and an apt intervention or interpretation cannot be found or is disregarded. It becomes essential for art therapists working in this field to think on their feet and yet, in moments of confusion when anxiety mounts, it can be very difficult to think at all.

My own introduction to running an art therapy group for children was as an art therapy trainee in a primary school when I ran a group on my own for five 10 and 11 year olds with conduct disorder. The experience was very challenging and left me with many questions. What structures did other art therapists create for their sessions, and how much time, if any, did they set aside for discussion and reflection; what form did this take? What about the composition of the group? Were some members of my group unsuitable candidates for group art therapy and what mix of presenting symptoms would make them most 'therapeutic' for each other? How could endings be managed in a way that would help a group with the transition back to the classroom? I sometimes wondered whether a non-directive art therapy group for children was viable and if it could be dependably therapeutic. This experience made me aware of the need for a clear conceptual framework to sustain me through discouraging moments and to give me guidelines to hold on to when quick decisions were needed.

A review of the literature, followed by a presentation and discussion of art therapy groups in practice in a mainstream primary school, will address these issues.

## LITERATURE REVIEW

### A review of the literature on group psychotherapy for children

Pioneering work in psychotherapy groups for children began in the 1940s. Slavson's *Introduction to Group Psychotherapy* (1943) in which he describes the 'activity groups' he developed in New York, and Axline's chapter on play therapy for small groups of young children (1947), are both texts which continue to be relevant to children's group therapists today. In the 1960s, the contributions of Ginott (1961) in America and Anthony (1965) in Britain, were important additions to theory and practice. Since then, with a few exceptions, little has been written on group psychotherapy for children in Britain until the last two decades. The recent increase in the literature, including a handbook by Dwivedi (1993) and two collections of papers on children's psychotherapy groups in the journal *Group Analysis* (1988 and 1996), reflect new interest in running groups in Britain, especially for the many children referred to clinics who come under the general umbrella of conduct disorder.

Most writers agree that a psychotherapy group for children (before the age of adolescence) cannot be entirely verbal, and that children's need for action makes it unnatural for them to sit still for the whole session. The child psychotherapy group cannot therefore be a straightforward adaptation of an adult format but is a specialised field of its own. The literature indicates that most group psychotherapists working with children offer games, play and art materials (Dwivedi, 1993; Hámori and Hódi, 1996; Lucas, 1988; Woods, 1993, and others) or drama (Barratt and Segal, 1996) as a vehicle for interaction and a more concrete form of communication appropriate to the latency age group and younger. The question then becomes whether and when the group psychotherapist makes interpretations, and if there is to be any time set aside for formal dialogue between the group members.

In the history of psychotherapy groups for children, Slavson and Anthony developed models at opposite ends of the spectrum. In Slavson's 'activity group' model there was to be no interpretation at all from the therapists, internal and behavioural change was expected to arise through the children's experience of interaction in the group itself and the positive regard of the group leaders, as they learnt craft skills, cooked together and went on outings. It was expected that the children's innate 'social hunger' would come into play, leading them to modify their behaviour and impose limits themselves because of their desire to be accepted by the group.

Anthony, who was an important figure in the development of *Group Analysis*, went further than other writers in bringing child group psychotherapy close to an adult model. His most extreme experiment with groups of latency children was the 'small room technique' in which six children and one therapist sat around a table in a confined space and engaged in free-floating conversation for the full (thirty- or forty-minute) session. The therapist made group interpretations and the tension and anxiety intensified through the group's inability to avoid focusing on their feelings in the here and now of the group. For Anthony, verbalisation and dialogue was an essential ingredient of group psychotherapy for children, and his acknowledgement of the activity needs of children did not prevent his view that verbalisation must take the place of acting out strong feelings.

The work of both authors has influenced psychotherapists in the field today, the majority of whom use aspects from the theories of both. But neither model has been closely imitated. Woods (1993) suggests that the anxiety provoked by Anthony's 'small room technique' proved too stressful for therapists and children and there is no evidence of it being followed in the literature. Slavson's uncritical acceptance of the child which included tolerating damage to materials, is far from the attitude of writers today, who stress the importance of setting limits and understand this to be an essential part of the group psychotherapist's role (Lucas, 1988; Woods, 1993; Barratt and Segal, 1996, and others). But Slavson's concept of the experience of the group as curative in itself has some following: Lucas (1988) and Behr (1988, working with adolescents rather than children) both emphasise the primary importance of the children's experience of containment in the group and Lucas writes:

'There is not much interpretation in work with children; the playing or process is itself the therapy' (1988: 141). But modern group psycho-therapists generally seek to promote reflection and Lucas adds: 'a well-placed question or word game frees the way for unconscious and associative thinking' (1988: 141).

Current trends in group psychotherapy for children as seen in the literature are not standardised, apart from the fairly universal adoption of co-therapy as the most appropriate way of working with children's groups (Farrell, 1984; Lucas, 1988; Barratt and Segal, 1996; Hámori and Hódi, 1996; and Westman, 1996). Nor is there much research in the field. However, Dwivedi, who brings theories and practical examples together in his handbook (1993), goes some way towards giving a coherent picture of the current state of play and of the diversity of practice. He presents theories about a wide range of relevant factors to be taken into account by the practitioner. He also includes examples of focused work in group psychotherapy relating to groups for sexually abused children, for example, or for Black children to work on issues of identity, race, language, culture and religion, in order to re-dress the negative images. In the latter sort of group work there is an educational element to the style of running the groups.

Amongst the texts by group analysts currently working and writing in the field of children's psychotherapy groups, Woods (1993 and 1996) has made a significant contribution to the thinking about boundary-testing in groups and the issue of limit-setting. He describes the pressure on the child group psychotherapist when handling aggressive behaviour to act out his counter transference rather than reflecting on it and in his paper, 'Handling violence in child group therapy' (1996), he points out the need for group therapists to be in touch with their own violence when working with children who act violently in the group.

Other themes in recent writing include: offering more structure in the form of directing activities when anxiety becomes acute (Lucas, 1988; Dwivedi, 1993; Barratt and Segal, 1996), or in order to promote cohesion (Woods, 1993); while Garland points out that children with severe ego-impairment cannot take advantage of structures offered them (1992). Other writers present new work with children formerly considered too damaged to be appropriate referrals for group therapy. Brown et al. (1989), Pfeifer (1992), Spinner (1992) and Westman (1996), all describe work with severely deprived children who have none of the innate social hunger that Slavson deemed a necessary qualification for referral to groups. The rationale behind offering group work in these cases is, Westman writes, that 'emotionally deprived children cannot cope with the intensity of individual relationships [so] the group may offer a context in which these relationships are diluted and therefore tolerable' (1996: 56).

## The literature on art therapy groups for children

At the time of my first encounter with children's groups, there was little literature on art therapy groups for children which paid attention to group processes or issues of practical management. Some early art therapy groups bore more relation to school art lessons or were run as art therapy groups in which the clients happened to be children but were treated similarly to adults (e.g., Liebmann, 1986). There has, however, been more writing on art therapy groups for children in the American literature from the 1950s onwards (for a useful summary of this literature, see Rubin, 1978: 172). Chapters by American art therapists such as Rubin (1978) and Landgarten (1981), described the importance of the interaction of group members in children's art therapy groups, but although both of these authors alluded to the challenges of running children's groups and described the models they used, neither offered discussion or insights into the difficulties of practical management and the ways they approached some of the challenges I had met. Since then, some authors have dealt helpfully with these issues, particularly Dalley (1993), who looks at the art therapy group for children in more depth, giving illustrated examples. Waller, in *Group Interactive Art Therapy* (1993), puts the children's art therapy group firmly in the same theoretical framework as adult groups where the potential of art therapy and group therapy are intertwined, and includes clinical material from a short-term, theme-centred group for pre-adolescents. Nevertheless, the theory and practice of children's art therapy groups is very much at a developing stage because of the limited amount and range of case material available in the literature which would enable art therapists to build on each other's experience and incorporate tried and tested methods into their work.

Historically, group work in art therapy with children has been more in evidence in the literature in America than in Britain, and this echoes the situation in psychotherapy groups for children, where Slavson's pioneering work was so influential. The theory that interaction in group therapy offers an important corrective experience in itself seems to be taken for granted in the American art therapy literature more than in Britain where the legacy of the early art therapy groups which were typically groups of unconnected individuals to whom the art therapist related separately (I think of the open studio models of Adamson or Lydiatt) had a firm hold.

Kramer, one of the pioneers of art therapy in America, cannot be described as working with art therapy groups in the same way as Landgarten, Rubin or Wadeson, because her goal was 'good art which cannot be achieved through group action but only through supreme individual effort' (1971: 109); but she has some things to say about the group setting for art therapy which is helpful and relevant. From her experience as an art educator, she writes:

> Everyone who has worked with groups of children knows that nothing inspires children more than the example of another child working well. The presence of even one child who readily responds to art can get a whole group going the way no teacher can. . . . On the other hand, the talented child cannot function as a catalyst for the others unless the teacher sets the stage and supports the process.
>
> (1971: 103)

The American literature gives examples of theme-based groups and unstructured groups for children. Theme-based groups are often used when there is limited time available. Landgarten (1981) suggests that the use of a single theme for the whole group membership facilitates the development of empathy and relatedness, even in a short time-span. She tells us that 'the art therapy approach has proven to be the treatment of choice for latency-age children in outpatient clinical facilities and therapeutic and public school settings' (1981: 106). This, she indicates, derives to a large extent from the fact that children can be active in making art work simultaneously and quieter members will not be over-run by boisterous ones. In running groups like this however, the art therapist abandons the two-way, more equal relationship between adult and children that Anthony insists on in his adaptation of Foulkes's group analytical group psychotherapy for children (1965). In Landgarten's description, the art therapist adopts the more didactic approach of task-setter and instruction-giver and the group is automatically more dependent on the therapist.

Rubin prefers an open-ended structure because of the freedom it gives the children to operate at the most suitable level for themselves, but she occasionally uses themes in a different way from Landgarten. She describes (1978) picking up on a recurring group anxiety, such as fear of the dark, and offering it as the theme for a session. She makes the point that any theme should be flexible enough to be adapted to individual needs.

In Britain, the earliest descriptions of art therapy groups for children in Liebmann (1986) and by Feilden (1990) are of interest, though each presents only one experimental pilot group.

Case and Dalley (1992) describe excerpts from two art therapy groups for 7 year olds and 9–11 year olds, giving more attention to process and the way children interact in a non-directive group than is found in the literature before. There is reference to the art therapist's need to deal with boundary issues and an indication of the physicality of art therapy groups for children when the authors refer to rivalrous attacks in the older group of children.

Dalley (1993) is a major contribution to the literature on art therapy groups for children in Britain. Dalley presents theory and case material from two groups of 5–11 year old children conducted in the child and parent department of a consultation and therapy centre. Her theoretical framework corresponds to the group interactive art therapy model defined by Waller, emphasising the potential of the group setting to provide a corrective emotional experience through its role as a social microcosm. Dalley herself describes her approach as 'the use of art within a psychotherapy group framework' (1993: 140), although the art is more important than this description suggests.

Dalley's text is particularly useful in her honest discussion of the dilemmas and difficulties specific to art therapy groups for children who have poor impulse control. The discussion and descriptions of the art work produced in these groups show extremes of expressive material which it is not surprising to find amongst children who are described as generally having anti-social behaviour, and this demonstrates the need for flexibility and stamina in the art therapists, especially when the children embark on large-scale joint projects. Her discussion of co-therapy including disagreements between the co-therapists is interesting; more entries on this theme can be found in the child group psychotherapy literature (Barrett and Segal, 1996; Lucas, 1988; Woods, 1996).

## THE PRACTICE OF RUNNING ART THERAPY GROUPS FOR CHILDREN

When I was employed to provide an art therapy service in a large mainstream primary school, I found that there were many children for whom group work seemed more appropriate than individual work.

The general aim of art therapy, whether in group or individual art therapy, was to facilitate and stimulate creativity and to help the children to achieve a better state of adjustment to the world around them and enable change in their patterns of behaviour.

The reasons for referring children to groups are much the same as for adults but there are some additional factors which relate specifically to children.

1  The art therapy group, with its promotion of creativity and playfulness can more easily activate inhibited children when they are in the presence of spontaneous and risk-taking others.

2  The imaginative and *purposeful* approach of some children to the use of art materials can act as a model for less integrated children.

3  The opportunity to be part of a group with its own culture, which is dependent on the contribution of all its members, is an important experience and contribution to the emotional growth of children, especially those who have not had good experiences in their family group or class groups. Erikson writes that in order to develop personal identity and self-esteem, children must discover that their own experience is also that of their peers:

> The growing child must, at every step, derive a vitalising sense of actuality from the awareness that his individual way of mastering experience (his ego synthesis) is a successful variant of a group identity and is in accord with its space-time and life plan.
>
> (1950: 212)

The art therapy group with its opportunity to give the group experience and group identity a visual form makes it an especially valuable vehicle. Even a simple joint group experience, such as marvelling together at the chance patterns made in the sand, is an affirmation of the children's individual aesthetic experience.

4  Children who are already disaffected with adults are more open to feed-back from their peers and find the group a more comfortable milieu for therapy.

5  Children who are afraid that their feelings of hostility are unacceptable can find the group a stronger container than the dyadic situation of individual therapy. As Lucas writes 'the very size of the group . . . makes it a safe place. . . . It is big enough to contain the projections of the child's unwanted parts and to hand them back in modified form' (1988: 146).

Cautioned by my experience of running an art therapy group for children as a student, and yet stimulated by the value the children had attached to the experience, I thought carefully about how I could offer new groups a structure that would help contain the children's anxiety and also my own. In this way I hoped to build up more experience both of group processes in action and about the potential that was available in an art therapy group for children.

The material that follows shares the adaptations I made in the way I ran the groups and some experiences that ensued.

## The physical setting for art therapy groups

The setting for the art therapy groups described in this chapter is a large mainstream primary school in an area of socio-economic deprivation. (For a thorough discussion and rationale for the use of art therapy in schools, see Dalley, 1990.) A room, 30 feet by 16 feet, is allocated for art therapy (Figure 3.1) and is in a different corridor from the classrooms, so there is a sense of privacy. The range of art materials is similar to those used in adult art therapy but there are also some play materials including a doll's house and sand and water trays. These play materials can offer a useful structure for children who are anxious about revealing feelings and unconscious material too quickly. Although they may be used as a defence against working, they more often act as a spring board or as an integral part of the whole process. A pile of cushions are used for sitting

*Figure 3.1* The room

on the floor or are often leapt onto or hidden under. The room has floor coverings and furniture which can withstand spills and bumps. In order to help the children prepare for their return to the discipline of the classroom from the art therapy room, the room is consciously divided into two parts: one has the messy materials and water, while the other area is for cleaner work. It is to this end of the room that I direct the groups for the last five to fifteen minutes of their sessions after they have cleaned up, so they can avoid the temptation to re-engage in mess-making.

## Adapting to the setting and the dynamic administration of the group

The setting in which a children's art therapy group takes place demands further adaptations on the part of the therapists. In a volatile children's group, where noise can be heard emanating from the room, and acting out before or after sessions in the corridors may occur, there is an impact on other staff in the building who need to understand the nature and aims of an art therapy group, so that they can be supportive. In order to create such a supportive 'outer container' of the containing group itself, I have run workshops for the staff, as well as sharing written material, giving talks and taking some care to get to know teachers and assistants individually and answer their questions.

The art therapist running groups for children has more networking to do than in adult groups: linking with parents, school staff and any outside agencies involved in the child's family. Parental permission has to be sought for treatment to begin and, in a school setting, the art therapist is required to meet with the parents and teachers for regular reviews as a part of the Code of Practice of Special Educational Needs (the guidance for implementation of support for children with Special Educational Needs, according to the 1993 Education Act).

In addition to the administrative contact with parents, I now co-run a parents' group in the school. Some authors (e.g., Woods, 1993; Barratt and Segal, 1996; Westman, 1996) consider that running parent groups in tandem with their children's groups is an essential component of the work.

## Composition of the group

The literature on groups for children of latency age shows a variety of approaches to their composition. Dalley selects children of different ages and both sexes 'as the age range tends to set up a sibling type of relationship as if in the family' (1993: 141). Anthony (1965) describes psychotherapy groups for both single sex groups and mixed ones, distinguishing between early and late latency age children, whom he puts in separate groups. Woods discusses the advantages of mixed sex groups:

> Girls are usually more able to contain impulses at this age and to take into account their own vulnerability. Communication is therefore enhanced for the group . . . a sub-group of girls can move such boys [i.e., noisy and unwilling to be reflective] on to a more therapeutic level of communication. The girls themselves can benefit from withdrawing some of their projections of badness and aggression on to the boys.
>
> (1993: 73)

The importance of balancing the group in relation to gender and the ethnic background of the membership is crucial, just as it is in adult groups.

It is often only with hindsight that one can observe that a particular combination of children were therapeutic for each other. Anthony warns of the danger of over-stressing compatibility because 'one of the crucial therapeutic functions of the group . . . is to resolve disturbing differences or the disturbances associated with differences' (1965: 186). In the following case example from a group of three boys and two girls, interaction between the two girls was crucial to facilitating change in one of them.

_____

*Case example*

A 7 year old girl, 'Mary', from a family of six young children had witnessed two suicide attempts by her mother by cutting her wrists. Mary was in a frozen state, almost unable to function in school at all and it was difficult for her teacher to communicate with her. A second 7 year old girl, Sarah, was in the same group. Repressed and harshly treated at home, she was not responding to efforts to teach her to read. While Mary felt anxious about beginning in the group and had physical difficulty in pouring out paint into a palette, Sarah was drawn immediately to mixing paint, sand and glue in pots and making as much mess as possible, giggling as she did so. Sarah's regressive activity was a model for

Mary, who linked up with her for several sessions, getting her hands messy and visibly relaxing. Mary went on to make a series of paper cut-outs of her hands which seemed to relate directly to her mother's suicide attempts. These cut-outs were taken up and adopted as a theme by other members of the group who made pictures of their own hands, thus giving value to Mary's contribution in the group, welcoming her and establishing her as part of it.

## Structuring the groups

The groups have a maximum of six children and are closed, fixed-term groups with hour-long sessions. The usual ground rules of respecting each other and the room and its materials, as well as the boundaries of time and confidentiality, are introduced to the children in the first session. Like Feilden (1990), I emphasise the importance of confidentiality because of the fact that the children are all attending the same school and may meet between sessions. Dalley (1993) includes a rule about not bringing anything into, or out of, the room, to ensure that all the artwork is kept together until termination of therapy and describes it as the most tested boundary issue. I have no easy solution, however, to the child who secretly brings in a collection of cards or whatever is fashionable in the playground and sets up a challenge to the known ethos of the work group; it has seemed wiser to show interest in their culture rather than dismissing it outright.

The children usually begin to work or play as they arrive in the room or, if the tension is not too high, we may sit in a circle to hear children's news. It quite often happens that a group member's news resonates with others in the group, encouraging links and cohesion. They then individually or together collect materials and start working. The group is warned when there are ten minutes left so that the activities can be brought to an end under their own control. Five minutes cleaning up at this point are followed by sitting around the drawing table for the final five or ten minutes at the cleaner end of the room to re-form as a group and share work or thoughts about the session. The pencils and paper on the table are often used to doodle with as the children sit together: the drawing activity helps to contain anxiety and tension and keep the children sitting down together. I think of this ending time not simply as a truncated version of the discussion part of an adult art therapy group, but as a preparation for the ending of the session which is so often resisted by the children, who need space to express the feelings of separation, loss and sometimes rejection which are aroused. With sufficient time given to the ending it may be possible to name the feelings rather than leave them to be acted out outside the session as they leave. Of course there are some important reflections about the group made by the children and the therapists at these times and when pictures are collected together it is more possible to observe aloud the resonances between them and for the children to notice links themselves.

For children to have the optimum benefit of an art therapy group, a period of not less than one academic year (from September to July) has worked best, even though reviews of the individual child's progress occur at least once a term, and some children may need to continue in therapy of some kind after that time.

## CLINICAL MATERIAL

I would like now to share a summary of case material from two children's groups run in the school setting I have described, to illustrate what working in art therapy groups with children can involve. I will then describe a session from a third group in more detail. As this third group was one of an experimental series of short-term groups run with a teacher as my co-therapist, it is unique in other ways and illustrates further adaptations to the art therapy group framework.

### A group of two boys and four girls between 7 and 10 years with low self-esteem

From the first session, the children in this group took enormous pleasure in the opportunity to play and make art work that had meaning for themselves rather than made to order in the classroom. While they seemed to experience the initial weeks as a sort of paradise where they had the freedom to do anything they liked, sibling rivalry soon showed its face and resentments previously hidden under the surface began to emerge in snappish exchanges which made the children anxious and look to me to intervene. I encouraged them to use their own resources to resolve things by appealing to other group members to suggest ways forward, encouraging them to develop autonomy rather than stay in a dependent state. Although the group initially kept within the limits of mess-making that would be typical in a classroom art lesson, they gradually took more risks and by the third session, one 7-year old became so excited by the possibilities of messy play that he became quite out of control and I had to restrain him physically and tell him firmly to calm down. His over-excitement presented the group with the issue of limit-setting: the need to keep the group safe but not to lose its creativity in over-control. As the other group members expressed their irritation with him, I realised that he was in danger of becoming a scapegoat and carrying the split off feelings of aggression for the rest of the group. This child had an on-going project which was a model of the *Titanic* (Figure 3.2), from which bits fell off or hung precariously. It was a suitable symbol for the disaster the rest of the group then felt this boy to be, and their irritation with him made it clear that they wished he would sink out of sight on some occasions as he gaily dashed around the room, threatening the safety of their own work. The model was also a symbol of the uncohesive state of the group itself at that point. But this boy offered a humorous element to the group which I felt the other group members were in danger of losing in their desire to keep things in order. The fierce snowman (Figure 3.3) was made by the three oldest members of the group and stands as a rather sinister male authority figure who was immediately bombarded with 'snowballs' by the younger boy who wanted to enjoy regression and the opportunity to be free of an authoritarian environment.

*Figure 3.2* The *Titanic*

*Figure 3.3*  The snowman

I had decided to run this group on my own, expecting it to be a quiet and orderly experience! However, the group worked well through its difficulties and by the second term the group members had reached a stage of mutual awareness, and three of them had developed a good understanding and concern for each other. The group had become a place where children could share personal issues and worries openly, trusting in the confidentiality of the group. It was common to hear them linking with each other, sometimes over simple things like comparing favourite colours. Figure 3.4 is a drawing of the group made shyly by a 10-year old boy at the point when he began to identify himself very strongly with the group: I am the small figure and the three larger, more important figures are the children (three girls were absent on a school trip on the

*Figure 3.4* Group

day of this session). The presence of some children who were more mature than the others and more able to think in a reflective way was helpful to the development of the group as a whole. Discussion might happen during the sessions as well as at the end. One group member, who was academically very behind in his year group was quite advanced in the art therapy group in terms of his observation of others and the speed at which he picked up on individual children's behaviour patterns; his feedback was often astute and helped the self-awareness of the group. Destructive behaviour sometimes flared up which it might not be possible to discuss until the following week, particularly when it happened near the end of the session (although a comment about how some of them found ending hard was often an appropriate interpretation). I had an on-going challenge to make certain group members take responsibility for clearing away at least some of the mess created by their art work, and to prevent others from cleaning up for everybody! Individually, every child made art work which was pertinent to their own preoccupation, often resonating to a spontaneous shared theme such as negative feelings towards adults, on one occasion.

## A group of 8–10 year olds

The second group was for five children of 8, 9 and 10 years old who found it hard to express strong feelings without acting them out in an anti-social way. I ran this group with a trainee art therapist as my co-therapist. There were three boys and two girls. In the first weeks, we gave particular attention to stating the boundaries and limiting behaviour that might easily spiral and get out of hand, but the children were generally able to take responsibility for setting their own limits quite soon, being well motivated in attending and wanting to be accepted by their peers. Two of the children seemed interested only in the interaction with their peers and with the materials, and it was clear in the transference that they were not initially expecting to find that the adults would be of any use to them and rejected them; on the other hand, some individuals liked to sit very close to my co-therapist or myself as they worked at the table. There was a tendency towards physical contact in this group: fighting could be a way of achieving closeness sometimes but it was also a symptom of sibling rivalry shown in competitiveness for the best materials and our favour. At the right moment it helped the group when the therapists shared their observation and brought the issue of rivalry, and what lay behind it, to the children's consciousness. The children conveyed a sense of neediness that was emphasised by their art work, which often took the form of food made from clay, sand and paint, and a large number of decorated boxes and other containers which they stored away week after week, like squirrels hoarding for the winter when nourishment would not be so easy to find (Figures 3.5 and 3.6). This group filled a very large cupboard with all its creations, then needed more space; parallel to this, we experienced the group as wanting to have a large space in our minds for us to think about them. When my co-therapist was unexpectedly absent for three sessions, the first session of her absence was marked by the children abruptly running out of any creative ideas half-way through the session and feeling empty and stuck, as though one therapist was only enough for half of the time. My counter transference was to experience myself as being inadequate and that the materials in the art therapy room, formerly quite stimulating, looked as though they were running low and seemed boring. My interpretation of this, linking the feelings in the room with the absence of the co-therapist was understood and accepted by the children and the following week they were able to verbalise their sadness at her absence; this time they had no need to act out their feelings of abandonment and rejection (as well as feelings of responsibility for and guilt at her absence). It was significant that all of the children had experienced their fathers leaving the family home.

*Figure 3.5* Bottles/containers

*Figure 3.6* Bottles/containers

## A detailed description from a group of 5-year old boys

Five boys from the same class were selected by their class teacher and myself as a group which we would run together as co-therapists. They were chosen because of their pressing emotional needs which made the teacher feel that she needed to understand them better. One of the boys, 'Matthew', was neglected at home and was withdrawn and had hardly spoken in the classroom; two others, 'Ryan' and 'Misha', were challenging and attention-seeking; a fourth, 'Jack', was puzzling and not achieving, although gifted artistically; and the fifth, 'Carlos', regularly displayed violent behaviour and was barely containable within mainstream education. He was being assessed for special provision in school but no extra help or intervention was yet in place. Although it is doubtful if he would have been placed in a group for art therapy treatment, we decided to include Carlos in this group because he was such a central figure in the classroom dynamics and the teacher wanted the opportunity to think about him and find some strategies for managing him.

The group ran for one hour followed by forty-five minutes for discussion between myself and the teacher. Because of the young age of the children it was important to make the difference between the ethos in the classroom and art therapy workshop very clear to the group. We decided to begin and end the sessions by counting to ten with everyone sitting in a circle, thus marking the session time as distinct and separate from the rest of school time. In the first session some attention was given to explaining the difference of our 'special time' to the children and this was successful enough for the teacher to find she was able to reassert control in her usual manner in the classroom, although there was initially some boundary-testing on the group's return, which the teacher dealt with briefly before leaving the class with a supply teacher and returning for our discussion period.

Because we were limited to six sessions, I wanted the children to understand the time scale of what was being offered and we began preparing for the end from the beginning, reminding ourselves of how many sessions had already passed and how many were to come, in the opening moments of each session. We offered the children a drink and a biscuit in the sharing time which formed the last fifteen minutes. This was not just nurturing in the style of Slavson's activity groups, although we did feel that the children would benefit from having their energy restored, but a method which I hoped would keep these young children seated close to each other in one place for long enough to communicate with each other.

We decided that the teacher would join in the art activity if she wished but that I would be an 'engaged observer' with responsibility for the professional running of the group.

*An account of the second session of the group*

The children arrived holding hands and walking quietly with their teacher; they looked excited. They sat down on the circle of cushions and counting began. The opening circle time was less than five minutes and included this exchange:

Carlos:  It's boring here; there aren't enough toys.
Art therapist:  It sounds as though you're worried there won't be enough to do here today.
(The teacher began to protest that there were so many things to do).

I suggested that they try using clay this week, but they could use any of the other materials if they preferred. The children immediately jumped up to collect aprons.

At this point we felt rather like parents, as the teacher and I helped to tie on aprons and hand out clay, making sure that everyone had the space they needed (some of the children managed such practical tasks themselves as the sessions progressed). All of the children except Matthew gathered around the small clay table with their teacher, making and painting food, little heart shapes and faeces-like lumps, some of which were given to their teacher. It became a reciprocal exchange as she also made pieces for them. This little scene seemed to me in my observing position to be an activity that was fostering a closer attachment between the children and their teacher. It was a subtle change in the habitual relationship between a teacher and children which is usually one-way: the teacher giving instructions and advice. It was a giving and receiving of gifts between children and teacher like a non-verbal conversation. Carlos enjoyed a moment when his teacher tried to make something that imitated what he had made, affirming his inventiveness.

After this group activity the children worked on individual projects but near each other. Jack made a nest out of clay coils, which stimulated Ryan to make a bowl. Jack's finished object was a nest full of worms with a 'mother bird' made of cardboard which stood behind the nest with a dinosaur-like head and very sharp teeth (Figure 3.7). He described his art work as a 'mother bird with her dear little worms' in a voice that made it sound like a charming domestic scene, but it was hard to

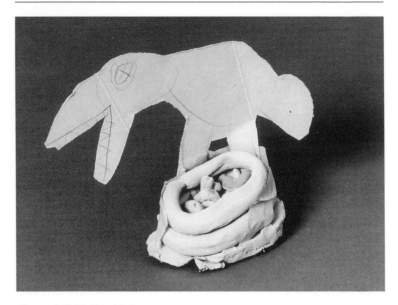

*Figure 3.7* Mother bird

conceive of this image as anything other than an attacking monster about to eat the contents of her nest. The adults conveyed how scary this image seemed at the sharing time at the end. This very potent, archetypal image of a devouring mother – of attack where nurture should be – seemed to have a significance for the whole group as well as for Jack.

Meanwhile, Matthew asked for a large sheet of paper and paints and sat at a table by himself. He enjoyed the sensual and aesthetic experience of losing himself in painting. I watched from a distance, showing my interest in what appeared.

Carlos, still sitting next to his teacher, engraved a dinosaur in his clay, similar to Jack's mother bird, and then started to attack it with a knife, gouging holes in it with such affect that his teacher later told me it made her feel threatened and anxious. He then began to bang the clay so hard with a rolling pin that he finally hurt his hand. The teacher comforted Carlos but this demanded all of her imagination as he felt unprotected and attacked himself, and he struggled against her.

We now announced that there were five minutes left to end their activities before coming to the table for the last fifteen minutes together. Ryan and Misha had begun to play with the sand and were reluctant to stop, but succumbed when they remembered the biscuits. Carlos was now desperate to take over where they had left off and protested furiously at having to leave his play. I firmly insisted and guided him to the table at the other end of the room. The rest of the group watched anxiously as he shouted and tried to kick me.

When it was time to count to ten and end the session, Carlos was so unable to contain his feelings that he flailed about, kicking another child in the process. I leapt to hold him and finally sat him next to me in the circle, keeping his legs still with one hand. I said that he seemed to be showing us how difficult it was to bear the special time coming to an end. On this occasion I helped to escort the children back to the classroom because it did not seem safe to leave the teacher alone.

*Commentary*

This excerpt from the life of a short-term group is both characteristic of other groups for children and unique because of its aims and unusual composition. The young age and immaturity of the children meant that the group was more structured than would be necessary for more mature children: the younger the children or the less mature their inner structures (impulse control, super-ego), the greater the need for a clear external structure in the group to provide adequate containment. It is evident that if the group had been a long-term venture, the structure could have been a very useful framework for supporting the emotional development of these emotionally needy children. As it was, even this short experience did support some changes within the classroom. The children's increased trust in their teacher helped to make the classroom become a more secure base for them. Matthew, who had previously kept silent in the classroom, began to contribute to class news and mix with other children. His teacher felt this stemmed from the third session of the group when she sat by Matthew, who was painting freely on large paper, and listened as he spontaneously poured out his experience of dangerous violence between his parents at home. The privacy and intimacy of the sessions helped to un-block Matthew, but the process of painting itself and its unrestrained quality, was an enabling factor.

The material shows how, if children are looking for nurture, then it will be one of the therapeutic factors that can be found in the art therapy group. Carlos needed to find that his rage could be borne and contained, and although this was difficult, it was possible because there were two adults running the group. One of the things which the experience of running the group made very clear was how physically dangerous it was to have Carlos in a classroom with only one teacher, and how impossible it was for her to be able to think coherently about him with no colleague present to help contain her anxiety. Carlos's protests at having to stop play at the end of the session, his intolerance of having no control of the situation and his experience of having something good taken away, were an exaggeration of the feelings that endings can provoke in many children coming for art therapy. By the end of the six weeks, he was able to process his feelings a little better rather than acting them out so strongly because we had had time to make links between his behaviour and his feelings and could anticipate them.

The central importance of the children's relationship to their teacher as the provider of a secure base, was very clear in the way that they related to her at the clay table in the beginning. It seemed that they needed to be near her first to achieve security and could subsequently branch out and follow their individual interests in the rest of the room. Matthew, who had had so little basic nurturing at home, seemed not even to consider looking for it in either adult, but took his place alone at a table with paper and paints, finding some security (or escape) in his own creativity.

## CONCLUSION

In discussing art therapy groups for children it is clear that there is not one type of group but many, and that art therapists need to exercise flexibility in their approach, taking age and stage of emotional devel-opment into account. Many children are referred to art therapy groups because of unmanageable behaviour, which means that setting consistent limits and standing firm when children test them is often one of the most important tasks for the art therapist running groups for children. This part of the role, so remote from the art therapist's more characteristic task of thinking about images and the process of making them, demands qualities such as sang-froid, quick decision-making and a capacity to anticipate difficulties. Because children have weaker defences than adults and regress more quickly, the art therapist (like the psycho-therapist) has to be more active when running groups for children and provide more structure. This does not necessarily imply providing themes but rather a shape or pattern within which framework the children can feel secure.

If regression and the spiralling of strong feelings can spread through a children's group and take it over quickly, the other side of the same coin is that a heady atmosphere of inventiveness and creativity can quickly infect group members too. As an adult, I often feel some envy of the children's ease in influencing each other freely and their ability on occasion suddenly to conduct a drama or joint art work that sums up a theme that they all resonate to so nicely, it is as if they had planned it for weeks.

Just as art therapy groups for children have a range of ways of operating, so art therapists running children's groups have a range of roles. They may: set limits; provide materials and a facilitating environment which is both safe and invites creative activity; act variously as nurturers, as audience (responding or giving feedback as appropriate) and sometimes as willing participants in play at an appropriate level when called upon. They must also help the group to find space to reflect.

This chapter is the result of my own struggles to find ways of working with groups of children in art therapy which would enable therapeutic change. Because children as a group are so challenging and often raise the anxiety of the therapist, the therapist's own limits of endurance and stamina come into the equation and affect the style of running these groups; there is therefore an inevitable stamp of my own personality in the work described.

## BIBLIOGRAPHY

Anthony, E.J. (1965, 2nd edition) 'Group analytic psychotherapy with children and adolescents', in Foulkes, S.H. and Anthony, E.J. (eds) *Group Psychotherapy: The Psychoanalytic Approach*, London: Maresfield Library, pp. 186–232.

Axline, V. (1947) *Play Therapy*, New York: Ballantine Books.

Barratt, G. and Segal, B. (1996) 'Rivalry, competition and transference', *Group Analysis* 29(1): 23–35.

Behr, H. (1988) 'Group analysis with early adolescents: some clinical issues', *Group Analysis* 21(2): 119–33.

Brown, R., Domingo-Perez, L. and Murphy, D. (1989) 'Treating impossible children: a therapeutic group on a children's ward', *Group Analysis* 22(3): 283–98.

Case, C. and Dalley, T. (eds) (1992) *The Handbook of Art Therapy*, London: Routledge.

Dalley, T. (1990) 'Images and integration: art therapy in a multi-cultural school', in Case, C. and Dalley, T. (eds) (1990) *Working with Children in Art Therapy*, London: Tavistock/Routledge, pp. 161–98.

—— (1993) 'Art Psychotherapy Groups', in Dwivedi, K.N. (ed.) *Group Work with Children and Adolescents. A Handbook*, pp. 136–58.

Dwivedi, K.N. (ed.) (1993) *Group Therapy with Children and Adolescents. A Handbook*, London: Jessica Kingsley Publishers.

Erikson, E.H. (1950) *Childhood and Society*, New York: W.W. Norton.

Farrell, M. (1984) 'Group work with children: the significance of setting a context', *Group Analysis* 17(2): 146–55.

Feilden, T. (1990) 'Art as part of the world of dyslexic children', in Liebmann, M. (ed.) *Art Therapy in Practice*, London: Jessica Kingsley Publishers.

Garland, J. (1992) 'The establishment of individual and collective competency in children's groups as a prelude to entry into intimacy, disclosure, and bonding', *International Journal of Group Psychotherapy* 42(3): 395–405.

Ginott, H.J. (1961) *Group Psychotherapy with Children*. New York: McGraw-Hill.

Hámori, E. and Hódi, A. (1996) 'Reflection of family transference in group psychotherapy for preadolescents', *Group Analysis* 29(1): 43–54.

Kramer, E. (1971) *Art as Therapy with Children*, New York: Schocken Books.

Landgarten, H. (1981) *Clinical Art Therapy. A Comprehensive Guide*, New York: Brunner/Mazel.

Liebmann, M. (1986) *Art Therapy for Groups*, London: Croom Helm.

Lucas, T. (1988) 'Holding and holding-on: using Winnicott's ideas in group psychotherapy with 12- to 13-year-olds', *Group Analysis* 21(2): 135–51.

Pfeifer, G. (1992) 'Complementary cultures in children's psychotherapy groups: conflict, coexistence and convergence in group development', *International Journal of Group Psychotherapy* 42(3): 357–68.

Rubin, J. (1978) *Child Art Therapy*, New York: Van Nostrand Rheinhold.

Slavson, S.R. (1943) *Introduction to Group Psychotherapy*, New York: Int. Univ. Press.

Spinner, D. (1992) 'The evolution of culture and cohesion in the group treatment of ego impaired children', *International Journal of Group Psychotherapy* 42(3): 369–81.

Wadeson, H. (1980) *Art Psychotherapy*, New York: John Wiley and Sons.

—— (1987) *The Dynamics of Art Psychotherapy*, New York: John Wiley and Sons.

Waller, D. (1993) *Group Interactive Art Therapy*, London: Routledge.

Westman, A. (1996) 'Cotherapy and re-parenting in a group for disturbed children', *Group Analysis* 29(1): 55–68.

Woods, J. (1993) 'Limits and structure in child group psychotherapy', *Journal of Child Psychotherapy* 19(1): 63–78.

—— (1996) 'Handling violence in child group therapy', *Group Analysis* 29(1): 81–98.

Chapter 4

# Connection and disconnection in the art therapy group
## Working with forensic patients in acute states on a locked ward

*Nicholas Sarra*

## INTRODUCTION

'Faster than ever river ran towards the sea,
it flashes, darkens, and rolls away'
Charles Dickens, *David Copperfield*
(1850), p. 692

There are times when an art therapy group seems an almost impossible undertaking; when everything seems set against the development of the therapeutic space and we as therapists are filled with feelings of inadequacy and hopelessness. This chapter examines some dilemmas posed by a group that I find particularly problematic. What follows is an attempt to understand the struggle towards meaning in an art therapy group. This struggle also includes the attempted integration of uncomfortable feelings which occurs as a parallel process in the institution so that everyone there, both staff and patients, are involved. In this chapter, I use the term 'disconnection' to mean an avoidance of the painfulness of understanding. This often includes a defensive stance of splitting off unwanted feelings as a means of coping with them. By the term connection, I mean those processes which support the work towards meaning and integration.

After discussing the patients and their institutional context I will explore a particular style of expression common in this group, which I will call the 'autistic image'. In relation to three clinical vignettes, I describe the journey of the image from a state of being disconnected or withheld (autistic) to that of connection or communication. This journey frequently takes more than a single session and so I describe how the process of moving from disconnection to connection occurs over a series of groups. I argue for the importance of seeing the group in the context of a longitudinal time frame as opposed to single sessions unrelated to each other. First I will review the relevant literature.

## ART THERAPY LITERATURE

Art therapists have traditionally worked with psychotic patients, advocating the containing power of the image as a means of developing the therapeutic relationship, e.g., Wood (1991, 1997). Art therapists within the National Health Service have frequently provided a valuable means of psychotherapeutic engagement with such patients. The literature has not been extensive, yet it is slowly growing. The contributors to *Art Psychotherapy and Psychosis* (eds Killick and Schaverien, 1997) articulate the current state of clinical practice and its historical context. Killick (1991) stresses the importance of the containing therapeutic relationship, advocating a therapeutic style which avoids prematurely focusing upon the meaning of images but concentrates instead on what the patient does with the image. Schaverien (1997) explores the image as a transactional object; a fetish which can be magically invested, whilst Foster (1997) links the fragmentation of the schizophrenic body image to certain types of three-dimensional productions. These ideas are relevant to much of the content of this chapter, particularly the section entitled 'an indirect attack'.

Greenwood and Layton (1991) highlight the use of humour in psychotic patients as an adaptive mechanism in a process which they call 'taking the piss' (TTP). They believe that 'TTP' allows the group to defuse and deflate otherwise unbearable interpersonal tensions. They suggest, as does Killick, that the psychotic patient has difficulty in dealing with the symbolic and is prone to using the therapist as a container for projective identification (Greenwood and Layton, 1991). I believe that much of the clinical material that I describe supports the views of Killick and Greenwood and Layton.

Like the above therapists, I emphasise the significance of biding one's time when confronted with problems of splitting, hostility or destructive acting out and therefore find there is a need to work within a longitudinal time frame rather than the single session format espoused by Yalom (1983) for groups with a changing population. I also argue that this way of working allows for the institutional context to be more fully understood and used in relation to the group because they both affect each other. This process is often only apparent over a period of time.

## PSYCHOANALYTIC LITERATURE

Bion's ideas (1959) on attacks on linking have much in common with the subject matter of this chapter. He proposed that an important dynamic in the psychogenesis of psychosis was the violent severing and disruption of relational links both internal and external. He saw in this a defensive strategy; an attempt to fend off unbearable reality. In the same paper ('Attacks on linking', 1959) he also developed Klein's concept of projective identification (1946), expanding the idea to include normal and pathological varieties. I have used Ogden's tripartite model (projection, identification, reinternalisation) of projective identification (1979), which is derived from Bion, as a means of making sense of some of the groups I describe, particularly as regards countertransference issues.

The work of Winnicott, particularly his paper 'The use of an object' (1969), was helpful in exploring the importance of surviving the patients' anger as were writers such as Grinberg (1968) and Horney (1936) who describe 'acting out behaviour' and the negative therapeutic reaction.

Menzies Lyth (1988) puts forward the idea of social defences in institutions by which staff teams cope with anxiety in a variety of avoidant ways. She does not, however, attend to the cultural and gender issues of the workplace, an area which needs further exploration. This has been taken up by Blackwell (1994) who looks at institutions from a number of systemic perspectives.

## GROUP PROCESS LITERATURE

Yalom (1983) suggested that in-patient groups should be convened on a single session format, that is, that no sequel or opportunities for working through could be assumed due to the changing nature of the population. I have disagreed with him in this respect and have argued for a different way of working which has more in common with the ideas of Foulkes (1968, 1986), who put forward the idea of the 'Group Matrix'; a conceptual web in which the history and communications of the group are held and continue to develop. Nitsun's concept of the 'anti-group' (1985) in which he clarifies the potentially destructive dynamics of groups was helpful, as were Sandison's ideas (1994) on working with schizophrenic patients in which he explores their attachment to their illness.

## THE PATIENTS AND THEIR INSTITUTIONAL CONTEXT

I have used clinical material from a group on a locked ward on a five bedded 'difficult and offender patient unit' in a small psychiatric hospital. The group I will describe takes place once a week and is open to all the patients. It has been running for about three years and has become an established part of the ward culture.

The patients have generally presented with psychotic problems, often exacerbated by personality disorders. Manic depressive psychosis, schizo-affective disorder and schizophrenia are common diagnoses. They frequently have forensic histories or have provoked a management crisis elsewhere such as on an open ward or in the community and are invariably detained under sections of the mental health act. The average stay on the ward is about a month but may be for far longer.

I have observed that patients often seem to regard the ward as a sort of womb where they can both regress and be reborn. However, this may be accompanied by a great deal of rage at the humiliation of exposed dependency needs and the perceived insult of being deprived of liberty with a label of mental illness. Staff may easily become the objects of family transferences so that difficulties in the community or at home can get acted out in microcosm upon the ward with staff getting pulled in to play the dramatis personae of important others.

On the staff side the proximity to madness is frequently an uncomfortable experience. I believe staff often find ways, perhaps unconsciously, of separating and distinguishing themselves from patients, affirming the accepted power relationships and hierarchies, as a means of coping with the anxiety of breaking down. Thus the prominence of bunches of keys, stylised dress codes and identification labels may, besides their stated pragmatic purposes, provide a means of differentiating and distancing oneself from the uncomfortable mental states of the patients.

As with the above, a subtle process of disconnection can occur institutionally within the staff team, which may emerge as a failure of empathy or an avoidance of facing psychological pain and anger. This may be especially so when, as is inevitable, events on the ward stir up difficult countertransference reactions, e.g., hostility towards those in one's care or sexual feelings.

This process of disconnection, that every one can get caught up in as a means of coping with anxiety, often has its counterpart in a patient's divided internal world. Menzies Lyth (1988) describes social defences, whereby those in organisations develop particular tasks and rituals as a means of coping with anxiety. Thus it frequently seems that an exacerbating or even precipitating factor behind a psychotic breakdown may lie in a conflict with a split off and unacceptable part of the self. This situation is well described by Laing (1960).

The point I wish to emphasise here is that divided internal mental states get enacted in their social environments and vice versa. The type of divided mental state or disconnection which I am discussing is expressed in the art therapy group. It is sometimes observable in the image-making process and may reflect parallel events elsewhere upon the ward. Therefore, the art therapy group should not be viewed in isolation but within its systemic context.

I believe that this process of defensive disconnection, which also appears as splitting, scapegoating and other manoeuvres that project out unwanted aspects of self; has as one of its aims the spurious accomplishment of a sense of wholeness and integrity. It is spurious because the person does not have to bear the ambivalence of experiencing different, opposing feelings within, and the bonding that results, is not based on the reconciliation of difference, but upon denial. These factors contribute to the dynamics of conflict at every level from the personal to the international, for example, propaganda during warfare.

Within the art therapy group it is the image that provides the potential means of connection that may help to counter the destructive splitting processes I describe above. The image, however, also expresses the current quality of communication. This may be autistic in the sense that connections and relationships with others are severed. I now go on to discuss such images and their relevance.

## THE AUTISTIC IMAGE

Foulkes and Anthony (1968) spoke of the symptom as autistic, mumbling secretly to itself, hoping to be overheard and in line with this I use the term 'autistic image' to denote not only phenomenon such as the blank piece of paper which McNeilly (1989) comprehensively describes, but also events such as the secret or withheld picture, the crumpled-up or torn piece of paper hastily tossed away and other expressions that achieve the end effect of a tangible presence but somehow removed from or not exposed to the gaze of the group. None the less, something is of course being communicated and it is usually the work of the therapist to help articulate this, if not to an individual or group, then within him or herself as a means of processing, understanding and containing. It is within the context of autistic images that art therapists frequently experience problems, and events can take a difficult turn. The image struggles to communicate, to exist; but is hated and rejected by the maker for its propensity for integration and change; perhaps because it challenges the spurious type of integration previously discussed, which is carried out by projection. In the group, the decoding and conscious recognition of the image can threaten to expose a raw and shameful secret world which is controlled omnipotently; omnipotently as long as others have no access to it and therefore no influence, control or capacity for modification. In line with this, the autistic image excludes others and may be accompanied by expressions of anger as if attack is the best means of defence.

However, despite the frustrating aspects of the autistic image, it contains also the seeds of hope for it may be 'overheard' and become a bridge to the interpersonal. A powerful *raison d'être* for using art therapy with patients in psychotic states is the nature of the image whose mode of communication can encompass both the rational and the irrational and find an acceptance interpersonally that need not threaten the integrity of the maker. In the world of the image, both the sane and the insane can potentially find common ground.

Sandison (1994) has remarked on the importance of the theme of loss in psychosis and of how patients may become attached to their madness, experiencing the process of 'getting well' as one of mourning and as a threat to identity. In the above context an autistic image perhaps expresses this fear of what might have to be given up in the process of relating to others in an attempt to maintain a sense of selfhood and identity by splitting off and denying the world of relationships.

The attitude of the art therapist is all important and should, in my view, extend to accepting and encompassing autistic images as bona fide works, albeit ones which have not reached their communicative potential. Let us take the following example from the art therapy group which I introduced earlier. There are three men present and myself. I have entitled the example 'An indirect attack' in order to convey the quality of how it felt as the therapist.

## 'AN INDIRECT ATTACK'

I enter the room at the start of the group and find that the table employed for painting is covered with hundreds of small jigsaw pieces. James, one of the members, is engaged in studying them. Derek sits in the corner silently smoking and looking vaguely hostile whilst Cecil paces the room with a wild smile demanding my direct attention. The immediate problem is the jigsaw, which is preventing any possibility of painting.

James is somewhat disdainful of my attempts to negotiate the removal of the pieces but agrees on the basis that he will put them carefully away himself. The pieces are noticeably unconnected. Painstakingly, and for me infuriatingly, he takes twenty minutes to pick up each piece, carefully examine it and place it in the box. The others are apparently unconcerned, however, I find myself becoming increasingly anxious. At the same time, James informs me that he will not paint since he has been 'medically retired' and no longer has to work. He announces this as if it were a medal of recognition. Perhaps, he ruminates, he might eventually learn how to paint, if he watched others do it for long enough, but this would take an extremely long time.

I feel at this point despondent and hopeless about the prospect of anything fruitful arising from this session. The room had, in addition, developed an unbreathable atmosphere of thick tobacco smoke. Yet, something is happening; all are choosing to remain and there is a sense of expectation, possibly that I will lead them out of this quagmire and in some magical way gratify their unconditional and hated dependency needs. It looks as though nothing much is happening in terms of art therapy. A patient has seized control of the means of production and brought the group to a standstill; or has he?

In the above type of situation it is often difficult to think, and one gets paralysed by the complexity of what is occurring, particularly when the group mobilises aggression in the service of not understanding, or when there is a severe testing of the containing function, and denigration of the therapist's tools. In the session I found myself in this state of mind. Frequently it is only some time after the session that one can make sense of things and connect what has been so assiduously unconnected by the group. This paralysis of thought is possibly what Bion (1959) refers to in his paper 'Attacks on linking' and one might assume that one is in the presence of powerful projective identification.

If the above is the case, the solution to such dilemmas is to wait and survive. To wait is to tolerate and contain without defensively inter-preting or performing actions that would, in effect, be felt as a rejection of what one is being asked to look after or experience. To survive means not to retaliate or fall apart when on the receiving end of powerful affect so that one can, as Winnicott states, survive the patient's hatred and become a real and usable object rather than just 'a bundle of projections' (Winnicott, 1969, p. 713).

Whilst this process of waiting and surviving is going on it may be possible to try to locate the image. In this example, whilst reproving myself for not ensuring the room was in a state to be used, I began to realise the relevance of the jigsaw. The careful placing in the box of the disconnected pieces was a representation of what the group was placing in me. My sense of paralysis, accompanied by feelings of frustration, anger, inadequacy and disempowerment was an accurate mirror of the group members' collective dilemmas. The fragmentation of mental illness, and confinement on a locked ward with all its attendant power issues, was being expressed by the group in a condensed form, and located in the image of the jigsaw. I am here using Foulkes's (1986) concept of location in the group in terms of one member or a particular interaction signifying a wider group issue. Certainly the other two members of the group, Derek and Cecil, were supporting James in his activities voicing no objections and now glancing approvingly in his direction. At the same time they made their own discreet bids for my individual attention whilst also keeping me at a distance. Derek's attitude of enigmatic aloofness was designed to draw me in and exclude others, whilst Cecil, still with unnerving smile, would occasionally paw at me whilst making the sign of the cross and attempting some kind of exorcism. I was left with the impression that all three were asking me to sort things out for them whilst they remained at a convenient distance and yet, at this distance, they attached themselves and demanded a kind of unconditional love. Ogden (1979) usefully articulates three aspects of projective identification that make up a single psychological unit.

He describes how first there is a fantasy of projecting a part of one's self into another person and controlling that person from within. Then there is a subtle pressure to manipulate the recipient of the projection to behave in a congruent manner with what has been projected. Finally these projected feelings, having been worked on by the recipient can be taken back by the projector.

I am assuming in the jigsaw example that some kind of projective identification was in operation and valid at a group level but communicated in a member's image and image-making activity. I was under pressure from the group to take up a role, that is, to reject their needs for waiting and holding and reacting to persecutory feelings of powerlessness and fragmentation, to become punitive and retaliating, perhaps sweeping up the pieces off the table and acting out an oppressive and split off superego in line with their relationship with the locked ward. However there is always some longing behind projective identification, a longing that the recipient will in fact be able to bear and render bearable the dreadful experience on offer.

For the art therapist, the image plays a crucial part in all this. It occurs in the group space and can be tangibly witnessed and responded to. It is transitional in Winnicott's sense (Winnicott, 1951) in that it stands between self and other and perhaps can be controlled. At least its fate is in the hands of its maker. It can be hated and it will survive. This is beginning to sound like the attitude towards the therapist and indeed there is a similarity. What I am saying is that the image also has a function akin to projective identification. An attempt is made to get it to adopt a form (which carries, usually unconsciously, a resonance with the internal world) and something may potentially be taken back, re-introjected and used. In other words, what is unconscious in us, seeks an opportunity to find form and become usable. The image in art therapy is therefore, like the therapist, a container, but everyone can reflect upon it potentially in an 'out there' reality-based way, which may be more tangible than the shifting internal world of the therapist or other group members.

However, resistance to this process may ensue. We do not always wish to be aware. The sight of our self, like Medusa, threatens to turn us into stone. Perseus required a mirror to confront the gorgon and in the same way the image serves this mediating and connecting function between inner and outer worlds. The mirror, however, needs to be a tool; something that can be used in the service of exploration. Hopefully this is achieved by the mutual efforts of the group members, although first it may be necessary to establish the containing function, to wait and survive before anyone can bear to use the mirror.

The autistic image is somehow struggling for articulation; it requires a container and processing before the gorgon can be faced. This whole process is a potential one and is frequently not achievable. The art therapist must bide his or her time and await the opportune moment.

Let us return to the group. James has finally cleared the jigsaw pieces; Cecil is now drawing and Derek is taking an interest in Cecil's developing image. I have been attempting to affirm some sense of relationship in the room and wondering aloud about how people are being affected. I have drawn attention to the image of the jigsaw. The group's attitude towards me seems to be one of interested yet attached disdain and towards each other, one of an increasing forbearance. Cecil is being encouraged to draw by James. Somehow the focus is shifting to a more interpersonal basis rather than purely directed at me. Cecil's image appears to denote the interaction of the group, a diagram of circles connected by directional arrows. I am depicted as a sort of deformed organ pierced by an arrow and dagger.

James suddenly announces, and it feels like a dagger going in, that he 'Does not want to be assessed by some little art teacher who won't be here next week'.

The hostility in the group is now clearly emerging and I suggest that we get around to talk. Interestingly, they resist my suggestion of a circle and we end up sitting in a line with Cecil's image and the box of jigsaw pieces in front of us. Derek confronts James about his fantasy that I will have disappeared next week and confirms my weekly attendance. James now speaks movingly about how no one is ever there long enough to be of any use and how he's always being left. He acknowledges his controlling behaviour using the image of the jigsaw and in a sensitive and protective way he tells Cecil how his actions drive him away. Cecil listens intently and is no longer smiling, although he still touches me and has started calling me 'Father'.

I believe my survival in terms of not retaliating was paramount in the above group. Probably I needed to do little else, yet bringing the attention of the group to the images seemed helpful. Winnicott (1969) has remarked on how patients desperately affirm the existence and durability of others through the use of hatred and the constructive aspect of this emotion in the therapeutic relationship. This does not make for an easy or pleasant experience for the therapist but can amount to a powerful affirmation of self for all concerned. James returned to the following session to draw what he called 'My first picture'. This significant event was made possible by the difficult struggles of the previous group.

The use of images in the above session made, I believe, some sort of work possible. They provided tangible references, points of contemplation and an area in which a process akin to projective identification could occur. It is within what Ogden (1979) referred to as the third stage of projective identification; i.e., the reinternalisation of feelings by the projector; that the process moves on from one of disconnection to that of potential understanding and growth. The image can facilitate this process. Art therapists frequently find that they are able to work with seriously disturbed patients, often in situations where verbal psychotherapy would prove impossible. This may be due to the containing and reflexive quality of image making which provides a transitional point to the tensions of the directly interpersonal.

The image allows, as I have described, a common ground for communication which need not necessarily threaten the integrity of the communicator. Therefore the image may help to affirm a sense of self. This becomes crucially important in an institution where personal boundaries can easily be eradicated. Withholding and withdrawal become an understandable defence against merger with the all-powerful and invasive institution. Hummelen (1994) has written on this conflict between fusion-anxiety and fusion-need, the need on one hand to maintain autonomy by withdrawal from contact and on the other to fuse completely and obliterate difference.

I now wish to discuss another example in the group whereby an autistic image is employed as a direct attack. However, as in the previous example, a sense of meaning and connection gradually emerges.

Nitsun's (1985) concept of the anti-group is useful here. He describes the destructive forces in groups, qualifying the optimism of Foulkes. He talks of the anti-group as a phenomena inherent in most groups, an undermining of the therapeutic work in a variety of forms. Behind this, he thinks, is sometimes a profound envy of the group and a longing for the one-to-one relationship which others at an early stage impinged upon.

## A 'DIRECT ATTACK'

I have described in the group of the jigsaw puzzle, the initial attacking behaviour on the part of the group members and their separate ploys for my undivided attention. You will recall that Cecil, James and Derek had finally come to talk to each other and that the images had played a significant part in this process. Jake has now joined the group. James, Derek and Cecil are all painting, which feels significant and constructive after the previous week's group. Jake is busy distracting other members from their painting or cutting across conversations so that his is the only voice I can hear and it is directed at me. To my surprise, he suddenly leaps upon the table and stands there exhibiting his penis to the group which looks up from below. The scene has an aura of primitive male rivalry as Jake seeks to establish his status in the group with others looking up to his manhood. There is much laughter. Cecil is encouraging him.

I ask him to get down and stop exposing himself. He does so but announces that he wants to urinate in the sink. Here I make the mistake of suggesting that using the paints, he might symbolically urinate on the paper. Of course he immediately equates the symbolic and concrete and proceeds to urinate on his blank piece of paper. I tell him to stop. He tells me nonchalantly that he has not yet finished. The rest of the group rapidly leave the room.

It is difficult to know what to do in such situations and as I have mentioned previously, difficult to think. Here I am, sitting at a table with a patient, both of us regarding his 'picture': a blank piece of paper sodden with urine and the puddle dripping onto the floor. I feel alarmed and powerless, yet fascinated by what might follow.

Outside the alarm bells are ringing, staff have been alerted to the situation within the group and are summoning extra help. Feelings of alarm coupled with issues of power and control, prevalent in the group a few moments earlier, are being enacted in the wider institutional sphere. Through the small glass window in the door I can see a rapidly gathering mêlée of worried staff faces looking at the offensive puddle. I manage to prevent them from coming into the room.

I insist that Jake clean up the mess which, with some direction from myself, he is able to do. His manner changes, he is no longer defiant and provocative, but childlike and compliant. From his hands and knees on the floor (clearing up the mess) he looks up at me like an infant. The task of cleaning up completed, I invite him to continue painting which he now does sitting beside me.

He has, in effect, annihilated the rest of the group and has me to himself. His image, the blank paper sodden in urine, perhaps represents a sadistic and envious attack on the group with territorial aims and with a quality of regression. An extremely self deprecatory attack, he has symbolically urinated upon himself as well as the group, and tested me out in an extreme manner. He is surprised and extremely moved that I am still there. But what of the rest of the group? They return individually for a few moments to check on what is happening and seem curious but the session has been abandoned. There seems a tacit acknowledgement that Jake has needed me to himself and this is to be talked about in the next session. It has been my experience that on occasions, members of a group will keep away in order that a particularly needy individual can sort something out with the therapist or at least that is the hope, i.e., that what is most difficult to integrate can be done at a comfortable distance. Sometimes this particular group will give a member some 'individual time' but return to confront him or her later or in the next session. For example, Cecil, perhaps inspired by Jake, splashes paint around in a later session to the extent that everyone leaves. However, they return the following week and insist to Cecil that he should 'have sorted it out by now' and should only use dry materials.

Let us return to Jake. He has driven away the rest of the group, cleaned up the mess and is now sitting beside me drawing. What starts to emerge, via the drawing, is a confused tale of events leading up to his admission. He draws Tower Bridge and speaks of his search for the hospital where he was born. He writes on his picture 'I love my mother!' and 'married to mum'. As he draws, it emerges that his father died prior to his birth and that he became for his mother a surrogate husband.

This session proved helpful for Jake since it allowed his experience to be validated, via my remaining, and via the image being witnessed and reflected upon. He has referred back to this session on a number of occasions, but in particular to the picture, which has become for him a sort of icon representing feelings that he had not previously been able to articulate. The process included a period of disconnection where the image could be described as autistic. My survival of the situation (perhaps his projective identification) enabled him to eventually forge connections that were hitherto destructively acted out.

This image was helpful to the wider team as well. It became another kind of bridge in helping staff to understand and manage Jake's frequently difficult behaviour. In this sense, the wider staff team acts as the vehicle for projective identification. The unit operates more humanely and professionally when understanding is valued. The converse of this situation is the premature evacuation of identifications by staff leading to low morale all round. Such is the situation Bion (1959) has pointed out as occurring between mother and baby. By this I mean that staff are continually being invited by patients (and vice versa) to play a role that corresponds to their internal drama; Father or Mother are typical ones. Thoughtful attention and understanding of this process is a prerequisite for good patient care as opposed to a reactive stance that discounts the inherent symbolic meaning of the staff–patient relationship.

We have seen in the previous two examples the emergence of the image from a state of autism into one of interpersonal communication. I shall now describe how this process can occur over a period of time and is to some extent trans-personal, i.e., themes develop and get worked through despite the changing patient population. An awareness of this process can be extremely helpful for the art therapist; reducing the pressure to compromise the containing function and interpret prematurely due to lack of time.

## THE LONGITUDINAL TIME FRAME

Sometimes it is not possible to think in a group or to do anything apart from survive the experience. However, it is just this 'being there' and sitting it out that may confirm to the patients the resilience and potential of the therapeutic space, hatred of that space, as previously described, often being a necessary phase. I believe that using the concept of a longitudinal timeframe helps considerably with difficult in-patient groups, for example, it may allow for thinking between sessions to occur. The material from the group may enter into a reciprocal relationship with other systems, such as ward rounds and community meetings, and may return in a modified form.

I doubt, therefore, that Yalom's often quoted concept of 'The single session timeframe' (Yalom, 1983), for in-patient groups, is always applicable. Yalom (ibid., p. 106) suggests that in-patient group therapists cannot use a longitudinal time frame but must treat the group as only lasting for a single session. He explains that the rapid turnover of in-patient groups allows no time for building groups and no time for letting things develop, that such groups are one-off events and to be treated as such.

I do not believe that the above view takes into consideration the developing matrix of the group which despite the changing population is communicated to new staff and patients not only at a conscious level but also subliminally. Foulkes (1986) differentiates between the Foundation Matrix and the Dynamic Matrix. The former constitutes the cumulative biological and cultural background which the patients have brought to the group. The latter represents the development of the group itself, 'The theatre of operation of ongoing change' (ibid., p. 132). The first art therapy group, for example, on an in-patient ward, will be quite different from those that take place some time later once a culture has been established. A culture develops within an institution and is transmitted despite the changes. Everyone involved is responding to numerous communicational cues, established or developed by those who have come before. Group culture is built and continues to develop regardless of changing personnel. Because of this, it becomes possible to use a longitudinal time frame. Frequently issues are raised by one set of people and continue to be worked through by another. I use the word 'people' deliberately here in order to emphasise that it is not only the patients that do the work. All staff in the unit are continually being worked upon through the process of projective identification. It is this quality of putting into, holding and understanding, and then giving back in a modified form that would appear to be an important dynamic in the development of group culture; a process reflected in and facilitated by the use of art objects. This process does not occur, as Yalom implies, in an insular way, as if each group were a distinct and unrelated entity, entire unto its self, but is trans-personal and trans-group. Let us look at an example which illustrates the above, along with the process of the image from a state of autism to that of communication.

**First session**

In the art therapy group, Simon starts to talk of his father's death by cancer, scribbling angrily as he does so. Pete who has also lost his father, does not want to hear about this. He draws a football slogan and picks a row.

**Second session**

Simon has now left and Susan has joined. Pete complains about the previous group and teams up with Susan to attack any meaning the group might hold. They are both vociferous about the pointlessness of talking about their fathers, although I have said nothing about the subject. They vicariously use the session to displace their anger onto me and then complain to staff that I have raised inappropriate topics and demand medication to calm them down. Actually, they have shouted enthusiastically about their own losses for an hour but with no insight. There are no images produced, and the issue of bereavement is now a live one in the staff group.

**Third session**

Brian and Tracy have now joined. Uncharacteristically a staff member tries to deliver a tray of orange juice in the middle of the group (a comforter) and also attempts to remove a patient because 'a visitor has arrived'. Another member of staff has arranged for social workers to interview a patient during the time of the group. Staff are feeling ambivalent about the material arising from the group, that is, sensitive issues around bereavement and mourning that are possibly touching on their own experiences. At times like these the therapist often experiences boundary testing from outside as well as from within, and there may be an unconscious collusion by staff and patients to maintain a disconnection in order to avoid an uncomfortable experience. Such collusions are frequently effected under the guise of patient management.

Meanwhile in the group, Tracy has spontaneously started speaking about the death of her 'surrogate father' of a heart attack. Brian has drawn a heart with 'No one knows me' written upon it. He tears it up. Pete has stayed away.

**Fourth session**

Susan and Tracy have left. David and John have joined. David has drawn a Buddha and to my surprise starts talking about his father's heart attack and cries. John has drawn 'Jah and a woman', he associates this with his father and talks of how he has never known him. David joins in the conversation and speaks of his abusive stepfather. Brian, who will in a future session speak of his own difficulties with his father, cannot bear the conversation and walks out. Pete makes a friendly appearance late in the group and is now interested in, and more able to bear, the current topic of exploration.

One can see from the above a clear thematic development and also a process of a struggle with difficult material. The group composition has almost entirely changed, yet from week to week the theme develops and gets increasingly talked about. It continued in this way for some months with the group increasingly able to contain the feelings aroused by the material. It was noticeable that the image always initiated such material and appeared to be being used as a store house for cultural information and as a prompter and transmitter just as it does in society at large.

Of course the above sequence could be explained largely in terms of transference, and no doubt this is a factor, but it does not account for the development of the theme over a number of groups. Perhaps group culture shifts in order to accommodate and adjust to new environmental stimuli. The group struggles to either integrate (connect) or exclude (disconnect) these events, with the therapist usually facilitating the former. The art object as a concrete artefact has an important role as an integrator. It can be contemplated and talked about. Its fate is in the hands of its maker so that it can remain autistic, i.e., disconnected from relationships with others. This process happens within a longitudinal time frame and may often extend beyond the boundaries of a single session. It is trans-personal, i.e., one person may raise the issue and leave the group but another (via resonance) continues it. The therapist is the most consistent culture carrier since he or she is always there but patients and staff group also carry this function. A continuous process of unconscious communication about the group occurs (and on a locked ward this is both in and out of the group) which may build upon and redefine the culture. The development of a theme over a number of sessions and its capacity to be taken up by patients, despite member changes, is in its relationship to the therapist. It is the therapist's capacity for containing and processing the material within him- or herself that makes for a sensitivity to, and facilitation of, the opportunities presented.

For the art therapist, the image plays a crucial part. Not only may it represent a condensation of group or individual issues but it also has a unique power via these qualities, to engage with us and be held and contemplated; a type of aesthetic imperative. In this respect there is something similar to the mother and baby relationship and, as I have outlined earlier, it introduces a third and facilitative area into the process of projective identification, i.e., the image itself acts as a type of alchemical container.

## CONCLUSION

In conclusion I wish to summarise the points made in this chapter; those that pertain to certain difficulties which may be faced by art therapists on locked units and indeed in other environments.

I have discussed two parallel processes within the institution: one is towards connection, the acceptance of difference and a move towards integration; the other, its opposite, has a tendency to split off and isolate what cannot be assimilated. In the art therapy group, this latter process may be expressed via phenomena which I term 'autistic images', i.e., expressions that have the effect of cutting or attacking interpersonal relations. I have suggested that this is liable to cause the therapist problems with thinking. I have also drawn attention to the importance of the therapist being able to tolerate a period of apparent impotence. In this respect I draw attention to the importance of projective identification and the need to bear with and just survive what can be an unpleasant and hostile experience. I suggest that patients within the group some-times have the capacity to move images from an autistic to a more fully communicative state and that this process has its parallels elsewhere in the institution. Very often, the above process only makes sense or becomes apparent over a period of time and thus I emphasise the importance of a longitudinal time frame; a conception of which may help the art therapist to cope with the periods of bleakness and despair that may constitute a session.

I also suggest that 'anti-group' (Nitsun, 1985) phenomena are prevalent on locked units, not surprisingly since those within them are at least temporarily excluded from the wider social group. The longed-for intimacy of the one-to-one relationship frequently underpins hatred of, and attacks against, the group, as put forward by Nitsun (1985). Image making in this context may sometimes contain and transform destructive elements, enabling them to be of some use.

I have found Bion's images of container and contained to be extremely helpful, but when talking about the quality of experience in such an art therapy group, they can at times be misleading. The impression can be one of something with impermeable walls holding another something inside as if *in utero*. The experience of containing I have explored here is something more akin to the river that Dickens describes. This experience leaves its impression on the senses and at times threatens to bear one away on the current as if into madness. Yet somehow we learn as art therapists to bear this experience, to allow something to flow through us; to be permeable as 'it flashes, darkens, and rolls away', connecting with the sea.

## BIBLIOGRAPHY

Bion, W. (1959) 'Attacks on linking', *Int. J. Psycho-Analysis*, 40, pp. 308–15.
—— (1961) *Experiences in Groups*, London: Tavistock/Routledge.
Blackwell, D. (1987) 'Alienation, projective identification communication and meaning', *Group Analysis*, vol. 20(3), p. 172.
—— (1994) 'The psyche in the system' in *The Psyche in the Social World*, eds Brown and Zinkin, London: Routledge.
Foster, F. (1997) 'Fear of three dimentionality: clay and plasticine as experimental bodies', in *Art Psychotherapy and Psychosis*, eds Killick and Schaverien, London: Routledge.
Foulkes, S.H. and Anthony, E.J. (1968) *Group Psychotherapy, the Psycho-Analytic approach*, London: Penguin, p. 259.
Foulkes, S.H. (1986) *Group Analytic Psychotherapy*, London: Karnac, pp. 131–2. (First published 1975.)
Greenwood, H. (1994) 'Crackpots: art therapy and psychosis', *Inscape*, vol. 1 (1994), pp. 11–14.
Greenwood, H. and Layton, G. (1991) 'Taking the piss', *Inscape*, Winter (1991), pp. 7–14.
Grinberg, L. (1968) 'On acting out and its role in the psychoanalytic process', *Institute of Psycho-Analysis*, 49, pp. 171–8.
Hinshelwood, R. (1985) 'Projective identification, alienation and society', *Group Analysis*, vol. 18(3), pp. 241–51.
Horney, K. (1936) 'The problem of the negative therapeutic reaction', *Psychoanalytic Quarterly*, 5, pp. 29–44.
Hummelen, J. (1994) 'Psychotic decompensation during group psychotherapy: early recognition and treatment', *Group Analysis*, 27, pp. 433–9.
Killick, K. (1991) 'The practice of Art Therapy with patients in acute psychotic states', *Inscape*, Winter 1991, pp. 2–6.
—— (1997) 'Unintegration and containment in acute psychosis', in *Art Psychotherapy and Psychosis*, eds Killick and Schaverien, London: Routledge.
Klein, M. (1946) 'Notes on some schizoid mechanisms', in *The Writings of Melanie Klein*, vol. 3, London: Hogarth Press, pp. 1–24.
Laing, R.D. (1960) *The Divided Self*, London: Tavistock.
McNeilly, G. (1989) 'Group analytic art groups', in *Pictures at an exhibition*, eds Gilroy and Dalley, London: Tavistock/Routledge, pp. 151–8.
Menzies Lyth, I. (1988) *Containing Anxieties in Institutions*, London: Free Association Books.
—— (1989) *Dynamics of the Social*, London: Free Association Books.
Nitsun, M. (1985) 'Destructive forces in the group', *Group Analysis*, vol. 18, pp. 7–20.
Ogden, T. (1979) 'On Projective Identification', *Int. J. Psycho-Analysis*, 60, p. 358.
—— (1983) 'The concept of internal object relations', *Int. J. Psycho-Analysis*, 64, pp. 227–40.
Sandison, R. (1994) 'Working with Schizophrenics individually and in groups: understanding the Psychotic process', *Group Analysis*, vol. 27, pp. 393–406.

Schaverien, J. (1997) 'Transference and Transactional Objects in the treatment of Psychosis', in *Art Psychotherapy and Psychosis*, eds Killick and Schaverien, London: Routledge.

Van Der Kleij, G. (1985) 'The group and its matrix', *Group Analysis*, vol. 18, p. 102.

Winnicott, D.W. (1951) 'Transitional objects and transitional phenomena', *Int. J. Psycho-Analysis*, 34, pp. 89–101.

—— (1969) 'The use of an object and relating through identifications', *Int. J. Psycho-Analysis*, pp. 711–16.

Wood, C. (1991) 'A personal view on Laing and his influence on Art Therapy', *Inscape*, Winter 1991, pp. 15–18.

—— (1997) 'The history of Art Therapy Psychosis 1938–95', London and New York: Routledge.

Yalom, I.D. (1983) *Inpatient Group Psychotherapy*, New York: Basic Books, p. 106.

Zinkin, L. (1989) 'The group as container and contained', *Group Analysis*, vol. 22, pp. 227–34.

—— (1992) 'Borderline distortions of mirroring', *Group Analysis*, vol. 25, p. 27.

# Chapter 5

# Return to the open studio group
## Art therapy groups in acute psychiatry

*Sarah Deco*

## INTRODUCTION

The care in the community policy and the closure of the larger psychiatric institutions has had many implications for the practice of art therapy in the in-patient setting. The large studio rooms that often housed art therapy departments are fast disappearing. The ambience created in these studio rooms allowed the art therapy space to be an asylum from the asylum, a place in which the impersonal anonymity of the institution could be moderated by the creative ethos and culture of art therapy.

New environments – day hospitals, drop-in centres – call for new ways of working. The studio space often no longer exists and therefore cannot be the primary focus for attachment and therapeutic change. There has been a change in emphasis from the setting being the primary object of attachment to relationships carrying the main focus for therapeutic work. The role of the images has also gained a new emphasis, often being utilised to support and deepen communication between group members or between therapist and patient.

The art therapist working in in-patient acute psychiatric services may encounter patients who are quickly discharged as soon as they become stabilised on medication and may therefore find themselves working with patients for very short periods of time. Shortages of staff on wards and underfunding in general, compromises the containment possible within the institution and creates an atmosphere which is often sterile and depersonalising.

As our profession has grown over the last twenty to thirty years, we have become more knowledgeable and sophisticated in our application of psychoanalytic and other theoretical models and we have developed many diverse methods of approaching image-making in therapeutic groups. Various models and styles of art therapy groups have found favour and then waned in popularity. I remember during my own training most of the experiential groups were theme-based with a structure designed by the art therapist/tutor which created a particular focus. This method of working in groups with art therapy appears to be now less popular and widespread and has given way to a more free-associative or 'non-directive' style of working influenced by analytic or interactive group psychotherapy. The additional skills that have been introduced into the practice of art therapy as practitioners explore and are trained in, various models of psychodynamic therapy, all enrich and extend our therapeutic effectiveness.

I, like many other art therapists, have been keen to develop groups which use methods and skills relating to further training in group psychotherapy. I would not want, however, to abandon the open studio and theme-based groups. I have found myself particularly re-appraising the advantages of the open studio groups in working with more disturbed patients in in-patient and day care settings.

In this chapter I wish to return to the open studio group and see how to apply this technique, making use of the increased knowledge and skill that our profession has gained. I begin initially by defining what is meant by the types of patient and the nature of the setting referred to here. I then go on to discuss some of the difficulties facing the art therapist working in this context, my own experience of working in acute psychiatry and strategies I applied to deal with some of the difficulties described. I then look at how the Open Studio Group may provide an appropriate group structure for the acute psychiatric setting.

## ACUTE PSYCHIATRY

### Classification

Acute psychiatry is a term which may be applied to those patients suffering from disorders with a recent onset and expectation of recovery in the short term. Often, however, it applies to patients suffering from an acute exacerbation of a chronic disorder. Many problems such as anxiety, depression, alcohol abuse and adjustment disorders are dealt with (or suffered) without recourse to the medical profession. People who do get as far as consulting their general practitioner can find that sufficient help is usually offered to prevent them ever having to come into contact with the psychiatric services. It is therefore only patients with an extreme or intractable degree of disturbance and distress who are likely to come into the care of the acute psychiatric services. These patients may be in danger of harming themselves or other people, or may be behaving in ways which prevent them from continuing to co-exist with others in the community. This may often be because of an exacerbation of a chronic problem and many patients repeatedly return to the acute services, are discharged and in a few weeks or months return again. This has become much more obvious over the past few years as the larger institutions have closed and community resources have failed to adequately meet the needs of the chronically mentally ill.

The full range of psychiatric disorders may be represented within the population of a general in-patient psychiatric service. This will include individuals with neurotic disorders, mood disorders, schizophrenia and paranoid syndromes, cognitive disorders and drug and alcohol abuse.

Specialised provision for adolescents or offenders or young people with schizophrenia may offer more focused and long term work for those with acute psychiatric difficulties.

**The care in the community policy**

The care in the community philosophy coupled with a general shortage of beds in acute psychiatry has resulted in patients being offered a shorter period of in-patient treatment and after discharge, continued treatment at a day hospital, outpatient clinic or drop-in centre. There have been a number of controlled studies comparing hospital treatment for acute psychiatric disorder with intensive community treatment: Stein and Test (1980), Hoult et al. (1983), Merson et al. (1992), Dean and Gadd (1990). Intensive community treatment involves assessment and treatment at home by a multi-disciplinary team. Outcomes relating to symptoms, social functioning and patient satisfaction were found to be better in the community treatment sample. It was also more cost-effective and reduced the need for hospital beds. Unfortunately the implementation of the care in the community policy in Britain has generally been a rather half-hearted affair which is often approached as a means of reducing expenditure on mental health rather than as a method of improving the service. There are rarely enough community psychiatric staff to adequately monitor the more disturbed patients, who may relapse without this coming to the attention of the medical team. Many patients continue to be treated as in-patients long after they need to be so, as accommodation for them may be extremely difficult to find. Shortage of beds is a considerable problem for many acute in-patient services.

## PSYCHODYNAMIC TREATMENT IN ACUTE PSYCHIATRY

Acute psychiatry is characterised generally by brief contacts with patients. The admission may sometimes extend into several months but is generally between 3–8 weeks. These patients may be in crisis and will often exhibit psychotic symptoms and be fragile and withdrawn. The prognosis for recovery is likely to vary enormously, as will the therapeutic needs. For some patients this may be a first admission, for many others it will be one of many return visits. The greatest challenge to the art therapist in acute psychiatry is providing a psychodynamic therapeutic service for these hugely varied and highly demanding difficulties.

Yalom (1985) poses important questions regarding the provision of group therapy for this particular population.

Many clinicians question whether group therapy is a viable form of treatment in the contemporary acute in-patient unit. They point to two troublesome clinical facts of life on the acute ward: the brief hospital stay and the wide range of psycho-pathology (from mild neurotic disturbance to florid psychotic decompensation). How, these clinicians ask, can therapy groups be effective under such conditions? After all, membership stability and homogeneity of ego strength have always been prerequisites for the development of the cohesiveness and the therapeutic climate so essential for effective group functioning.

(Yalom, 1985: 25)

These criticisms undeniably have substance and should persuade us to look carefully at the style of conducting groups. As I mentioned above the emphasis of art therapy training has moved towards the group analytic or group interactive approach. This, however, may not give us a very helpful model for approaching work in acute psychiatry. Yalom goes on.

Researchers have reported that in-patient group therapy led in traditional psychoanalytic style (that is with an inactive non-directive, insight-oriented leader) is ineffective in the in-patient setting. It is an error, these studies indicate, to apply a clinical approach developed in one setting (long term outpatient work) to another setting in which it is inappropriate.

(1983: 29)

A wide range of difficulties are represented in the population of the average in-patient unit. I will focus on two broad categories widely represented in the patients referred to art therapists:

- Borderline and personality disorders
- Psychosis and schizophrenia

## Borderline and personality disorders

Borderline patients often demonstrate great fluctuations and swings in mood, along with a tenuous hold on reality. Other persons are not related to as separate and autonomous, but as 'need satisfying objects'. An extreme degree of primitive rage is often expressed during the course of therapy and projected onto and into others. There is an attempt to manipulate others by means of projective identification to become suitable recipients for sadism and destructiveness.

> It is with the more disturbed borderline patients that the profoundest levels of primitive rage and destructiveness are encountered. Once the defences against exposing this rage are weakened or removed, patients become terrified by the intensity of the savagery, become frightened of the fantasied destructiveness and often appalled by the overwhelming sense of evil and destructiveness that they now experience as originating within the self. Desperate attempts to remove this threat by projection then ensue.
>
> (Pines, 1994: 139)

K.W. Fried (1979) describing groups composed predominantly of borderline patients points to the importance of the establishment and maintenance of a 'real relationship' and working alliance. He believes that the therapist needs to modify her approach and be more active and involved than may be the case in a classical group analytic therapy.

By acting as a 'real person' the therapist tends to diminish survival anxiety and facilitate the emergent expression of the 'true self' (Winnicott, 1960). If the therapist and the group can withstand the rage and destructiveness that accompany the emergence of the 'true' expression of the personality then it is possible to move on to a more integrated mode of functioning. The therapist and group represent the maternal function that receives the infant's terror and rage and contain, transform and reflect it back in a manageable and articulated form.

In art therapy groups with a predominantly profoundly disturbed population it may not be possible to enlist the help of the group in this way. The images, however, and the regularity and indestructability of the setting can provide an equivalent holding experience. Borderline patients may, however, do very well in interactive groups. Care has to be taken to consider the effect they may have on other group members. The capacity of borderline patients to project their own sadism may be very damaging for vulnerable people with an unformed sense of their own boundaries.

## Psychosis and schizophrenia

I will present here two varying views about working with schizophrenic patients. Skolnik (1994) in his work with therapeutic communities for psychotic and borderline patients puts forward a view that treatment systems fail to function adequately as 'containers for emotional pain'. He believes that with an adequate and appropriate holding experience patients can be encouraged to 'un-freeze' from a 'fortress like state of non-being' and engage with others in meaningful interaction.

Yalom, however, describes a 'consensus in the research literature that psychotic patients are most successfully treated in supportive, reality-focused, structured group therapy *and require a sealing over rather than an opening up*' (1985: 32). I have found this to be the view held by most members of the medical profession and it is therefore not hard to see why there is often great resistance to appreciating the appropriateness of art therapy groups for these kinds of patients.

I have found Killick's (1987) work in developing a specialised therapeutic method in art therapy for these patients helpful in integrating these two opposing views. She proposes that schizophrenic patients may only be able to relate to and use the group on a very concrete level, and therapists' attempts to communicate through symbolic language are inappropriate.

> The language employed by patients with schizophrenia has rules which do not permit the degree of abstraction from context which is necessary for the use of symbols in communication. . . . Words are experienced as part of an object or situation, not representative of them.
>
> (Killick, 1987: 17)

Killick supports a therapeutic approach which assumes that this concretisation and avoidance of abstraction is defensive and arises to protect the self from overwhelming anxiety. This notion is broadly in agreement with Skolnick's. However she also proposes that social interaction increases anxiety to unbearable proportions, particularly where there is an expectation that symbolic communication will be part of the exchange. An approach that manages relationships purely through the concrete negotiations regarding space, materials, etc., and allows an interaction to develop slowly between the patient and his images is more conducive to containment and possible change. Yalom (1985) also holds the view that psychotic patients do less well in groups where they disclose a great deal about themselves and that group therapy which aims at insight and derepression is contra-indicated. He does not acknowledge that a containing environment as described by Skolnik or the containment afforded by images can effect a thawing and a reconnection to the world of shared experience.

Skolnik acknowledges that once the unfreezing has begun there may be a great deal of primitive affect projected into the group. This may be containable within a specialised and integrated community situation; within the average in-patient or day care facility however, it could be disastrous and result in the patient being offered increased medication and a greater sense of isolation as a result. His attempt to emerge from a frozen state may result in a much deeper degree of freezing. There needs to be institutional support for work of this kind, for it to have a successful outcome.

## ART THERAPY IN ACUTE PSYCHIATRY

Art therapy in Britain developed primarily within adult in-patient psychiatric institutions. One could see art therapy therefore as one of the only forms of psychotherapeutic treatment that has been designed to cater for the needs of more disturbed patients in the in-patient setting. The majority of patients referred to art therapy departments in adult psychiatry are fragmented to a degree which renders them unable to use the possibilities afforded by a group in which interpersonal interaction is the main focus. Nevertheless, it seems as though much of the art therapy offered within acute psychiatry is within some kind of group context. Art therapy is unique in that image-making can provide a bridge which makes it possible to engage severely disturbed people in psycho-dynamic therapy. It still however needs a coherent boundary structure with an assessment, referral and selection system.

### The institutional context

The institutional context is as important a focus for the therapist's attention as are individual patients. The context within which any art therapy group is placed will profoundly influence its efficacy and general outcome. 'The in-patient group is not "free-standing" but is always part of a larger therapeutic system' (Yalom, 1983: 459).

Feelings of impotence and confusion are engendered by an institutional context in which the art therapist has very little control over the boundary framework of her own work. Referrals may for example be blanket referrals from the O.T. Dept in which unsuitable patients are sent along to art therapy as a matter of course in the same way as they are sent to cookery classes or quiz groups. The art therapist may have to rely on O.T.s to represent her at ward rounds and may never have any direct contact with the consultant psychiatrist who makes the decisions about when the patient will be discharged and what kind of treatment is prescribed. The art therapist may be expected to conform to a general group programme which does not allow any autonomy or control over the duration or frequency of the group, the kind of patients referred or the period of time for which patients are able to attend. Other staff may be ill informed about the nature of art therapy or indeed hostile to it and may misrepresent it to the patients with whom they come into contact.

In her well-known paper 'Social Systems as a Defence Against Anxiety' (1960) Isabel Menzies Lyth describes the ways in which a nursing service organises itself so as to unconsciously avoid awareness of the anxieties associated with caring for the sick and dying. There are equally difficult factors to deal with in involvement with people who may behave and communicate in disturbing ways and who do not respond to social interaction predictably. The hopeless situations that many people with mental health problems find themselves in may also prove difficult for staff to acknowledge.

The changes which have taken place over the last few years in government policy and funding for the health service have added to an already very difficult working environment. Under-funding, the introduction of the internal market and decisions made with accounting rather than clinical effectiveness as a priority have all put an enormous strain on an already beleaguered psychiatric service. In many institutions the art therapist may provide the only stable point of continuity for patients in an environment where staff morale is low and turn-over high. Wards are therefore often staffed by a high proportion of agency nurses who do not have the time or the motivation to develop relationships with patients or provide a containing atmosphere. Shortage of beds has meant that levels of disturbance on the wards and for day patients is higher and the capacity of staff to successfully monitor patients and reach an accurate diagnosis is extremely difficult. These problems put a great deal of strain on professionals, such as art therapists, trying to create a space for therapeutic work in the institution. Added to this is the additional burden of the new administrative and managerial systems which require art therapists to put resources into developing business plans, operational policy statements and so on.

Whatever we may think however about the ethics of the internal market it does offer us a challenge to improve our communication with other professionals and to 'market' ourselves effectively. It is probably the only way we can survive in this more competitive climate.

A situation in which lines of responsibility are unclear or excessively bureaucratised creates a virtually unworkable situation for the art therapist. This is unfortunately often the case within psychiatric services. Often there is little that can be done by the art therapist or art therapy department to change this. But there may sometimes unconsciously be a collusion with this state of affairs. Art therapists are generally used to, and may feel happier with, working quietly in an out of the way corner of a large institution. They may feel uncomfortable standing up amongst other potentially hostile professionals and promoting art therapy. There may be links with other professionals who are known to be sympathetic to art therapy, but sometimes it appears difficult to take on the task of raising the profile of art therapy and informing other staff of what it has to offer. The high turnover of staff may lead art therapists to feel that informing and educating staff is a rather hopeless task and a futile use of time which already feels over-committed. As soon as nurses, occupational therapists and other staff begin to understand more about the role of art therapy they often seem to move on to new establishments, leaving the art therapist to liaise again with a new and inexperienced team.

## The art therapist's role

One of the most important and often the most difficult tasks for an art therapist, particularly a single-handed art therapist, working in acute psychiatry is to achieve some control over the external parameters governing the structure of the group. She needs to be in a position to consider the composition of the group and have enough flexibility and control over the referral system to be able to choose only those patients which she deems suitable. She also needs to feel involved in the decisions about discharge. This is often not easy to achieve and depends a great deal on the philosophy and working practice employed in the hospital. Some institutions are highly autocratic while others employ a truly multi-disciplinary team approach. Whatever the situation, however, the consultant who holds responsibility for the patients' care needs to be aware of the art therapist's input and for it to be considered as part of the whole treatment programme. The art therapist's level of control and her relationship to the institution and role within it will greatly affect her capacity to provide and maintain an appropriate boundary structure.

## Attitudes to art within the institution

Another important factor is the unconscious attitude held by staff in the institution to both art and art therapy. Artists are often perceived as 'special' people who see things differently to others. There is often a link made between being artistically creative and being eccentric or even mad. I perceive two major stereotypical images of art and artists within psychiatric institutions. The first is an image of art as a genteel, benign and harmless activity which is worthy, relaxing and undemanding. The second sees art as marginal, subversive, unintelligible and disturbing. Both of these stereotypes are deeply destructive to the use of art as a therapeutic medium and disempower art therapists in their attempts to create workable structures within which to form a creative space.

Art therapists may also be affected by these stereotypes, particularly the second, and may marginalise themselves and become identified with the patients in ways which affect their capacity to offer patients a neutral and containing space to work in. In some circumstances the perception of art as mysterious and powerful may further the development of art therapy, albeit on a somewhat insecure basis.

## The experience of working in acute psychiatry

Experiences of working in acute psychiatry are often dominated by a sense of helplessness as patients are admitted, referred and discharged without any consultation, leaving the art therapist to deal with abortive relationships with clients who are discharged before there can be any real therapeutic engagement. The aroused and vulnerable state of many patients, however, can create an intensity of contact with patients which makes the premature and sudden ending feel even more catastrophic and leaves the therapist with feelings of confusion, helplessness and loss.

The rapid turnover of patients can be very difficult to deal with. Constantly having to make new beginnings with patients who may possibly be seen only for one or two sessions takes a toll on the therapist's ability to approach each new contact with a fresh and open attitude. Unconscious defences may come into play to protect against the pain of loss and the feelings of impotence which premature and uncontrollable endings engender. Art therapists may experience feelings not unlike those experienced by their patients who feel unable to control or influence what is going on around them. A response to this may be one of resignation or detachment. Balanced against this, however, the art therapist may often be one of the longest-serving members of staff within an acute psychiatric unit. This means that he or she may hold a great deal of historical information about patients who have been re-admitted over several years. This gives the art therapist a very important role within the team to provide continuity for both patients and staff.

## STRATEGIES FOR ADDRESSING THE INSTITUTIONAL CONTEXT

On starting work in an acute psychiatric unit attached to a general hospital, I found a situation in which the art therapy room was customarily open for two long periods each day. During that time a number of people came in and out of the room. I had no idea who any of these people were. There was no formal referral procedure and therefore no list of who was expected. I had no way of knowing even if any of these people using the studio were patients or not. Initially I asked the occupational therapists for a list of names of who was expected to come to art therapy. Although they were co-operative and helpful, the list provided bore little resemblance to the patients who actually arrived. I realised that they were equally in the dark about who was expected to come and what the cause might be of their lack of attendance.

This situation made it impossible for me to develop the kind of containing environment I felt was necessary. At the same time I felt rather hopeless about tackling what seemed to be an institutional problem. Shortly after I arrived I was joined by a new colleague and the joint support we provided for each other aided our motivation in instituting some important changes.

I felt that it was important to make contact with the consultant psychiatrists who were ultimately responsible for the patients' care and was initially disappointed by what seemed to be complete commitment to pharmacological treatment and a scepticism about the effectiveness of any psychodynamic approaches. We decided, however, to make a presentation to the medical staff's weekly training seminar. This felt like a risky enterprise and we were not expecting a sympathetic response.

There were a number of critical and rather hostile comments, but this event also contributed to a change in perception about art therapy. There was some very positive feedback from doctors who realised that we had substantial training and skill that they could call on. They had previously been unaware that art therapists had a post-graduate level training, and there were a number of other misconceptions about art therapy. We set about addressing these in two ways. First, we developed a programme of regular staff workshops and contributions to training seminars and second, we sent a questionnaire to all members of clinical and managerial staff within the unit. The questionnaire posed questions designed to make people think about the purpose and nature of art therapy within the institution. Its aim was to make people aware of the shortcomings in their understanding of what we offered. We hoped this would encourage staff to attend one of our workshops or seminars, or contact us to find out more. The questionnaire was distributed to many members of staff with whom we had little contact before and therefore raised awareness of our department and brought us new referrals.

We instituted a system which required referrers to fill in a form asking for information about family history, medication and the circumstances surrounding the referral. It asked the reason for referral and we were clear that this must be appropriate: we expected other professionals to think about the reasons why art therapy may be useful, rather than use the department as a dumping ground. We added closed groups and individual work to the already existing programme of open groups.

All patients were required to meet with us before attending art therapy for the first time and were formally assessed. We followed up each new referral and kept the referrer informed by attending ward rounds or by writing regular reports. In this way we were able to achieve much more continuity. Consultants became aware of importance of the consistency provided by the contact with art therapy and then began to request that this be continued when patients were discharged. These developments required considerable persistence and the process at times was slow, laborious and demoralising. It also took a lot of time away from clinical contact. It was, however, crucial in creating a workable framework for the department and laying the foundations for a clear and professional relationship between the art therapy department and the rest of the institution. There was substantial resistance from O.T.s and medical staff to our new system, which they felt was rigid, bureaucratic and involved them in more work. Patients also had mixed feelings about these developments. They were no longer free to drift in and out of the room without being noticed, but they soon began to use the room in a new way. The images became invested with greater importance and attendance became more consistent and regular, and gradually a new attitude to art therapy emerged. There was the experience of being known and recognised and therefore contained and held. In time the resistance diminished and art therapy became understood and appreciated as a resource that was consistent, effective and therapeutically potent.

There are many persuasive reasons which dissuade art therapists from gaining more control over their position and role within the institution. Some of these may stem from resistance on the part of art therapists themselves. It is often easier to accept the *status quo* than to risk coming into open conflict with other staff. There may be a sense of hopelessness about the wider context and possibility of change for the patients. There may be an unconscious decision to avoid gaining more power and responsibility because it requires facing the pain of having to make painful decisions regarding a patient's future and fully acknowledging the reality of a poor prognosis. Brief and unsatisfactory contact with patients may be tolerated because it avoids the necessity of making relationships of any depth with patients who are either frightening and/or unsatisfying to relate to, or who will shortly be discharged and with whom there is no possibility of prolonged contact.

## A NEW LOOK AT THE OPEN STUDIO GROUP

### The open studio group method

The studio is laid out in such a way that individuals may find a space to work away from others in the room or in close proximity to them if they choose. The position of the tables, easels, etc., is always the same. The studio is open at regular times and patients are free to make their own choice of which materials to use. The art therapist makes an initial contact with each patient and then leaves them to work without interruption unless it seems that some help is needed. This is largely influenced by the art therapist's ability to pick up non-verbal cues and behave as a kind of midwife to the creative process, allowing the process to proceed naturally unless some extra help in 'giving birth' appears to be necessary. At the end of the session the art therapist approaches each group member and acknowledges the patient's experience of the session and the image produced (if appropriate). The art therapist may comment on the work or how the patient has seemed during the session in a way that takes account of the level of integration and anxiety of each patient.

It may be possible to make links, ask questions and even with some patients make transference interpretations. It may also be possible to facilitate communication between patients in the group. This may be approached in an unstructured way within the group or there may be a time within the session when patients come together to talk together about their work. This will depend on the constitution of the group. With some patients this may be completely inappropriate, whereas with others it may be highly beneficial.

## Theoretical objectives

In this way of working the group acts as a backdrop to the individual's involvement with his images. This backdrop, however, has very particular characteristics and a very important role. The integrity of the boundary structure or 'frame' of the group is vitally important and determines whether the group space can develop as a regular and reliable entity to which group members can make a reliable attachment. In individuals who are extremely fragile, fragmented and have little reliable sense of their own 'Self', the 'reliable entity' that the group comes to represent can provide a kind of life raft to which it is possible to cling while the ego and personality strengthen. The group under these circumstances forms a representation of 'mother' at a very primitive level. This is mother as container, mother as a consistent, regular, reliable presence. *The challenge here is to provide this framework without also creating an unduly demanding relational environment.* The aim is to create a group environment where there is the opportunity for interaction, but also for withdrawal.

Skolnick describes the particular quality of containment required:

> The adherence to something outside the self may be for some patients analogous to the new-born's adherence to the mother when she was more of a surface than a person, providing a boundedness to counteract the anxiety of draining into infinite space inherent in the process of adjustment to life outside the womb.
>
> (1994: 250)

This can be provided by the physical constancy of the environment. For patients in a 'closed fortress-like state of non-experience':

> The rhythmicity and regularity of meetings stopping and starting on time, the presence of bodies, the places to sit with bodies (aloneness in the presence of the other), a reliable temperature range. . . .

comfortable furniture, respect for personal space, and protection from being coerced or intruded upon before one is ready – these are some of the characteristics that patients who present in a walled off defensive state of non-experience seem to require for initial engagement.

(Skolnick, 1994: 250)

The holding described here relates to the experience of living within a 'community'. The open studio group is able to provide in many respects an equivalent setting.

Yalom describes the need for psychotic patients to be provided with 'opportunities for social interaction that are undemanding, broken into brief time segments, and interspersed with periods of solo activity' (Yalom, 1985: 281). This need is fulfilled by the situation within an open studio art therapy group. Patients may withdraw into the solitary world of image-making or emerge to interact with others in the room as they wish. The use of a theme or a structure may also be considered here as a way of providing containment, but this may also contain the risk of seeming coercive. The open studio group allows individuals to follow their own rhythm of working while still feeling attached to and involved with a group of other people.

The 'adhesive attachment' described by Skolnick (1994) as a 'first step beyond an autistic capsule towards relatedness' (p. 250) may itself lead the way to a form of attachment in which the 'other' is perceived enough as a whole object for a sense of the 'space between' to develop. Here the group can become a manifestation of what Winnicott calls the third area – the area in which play and make believe flourish along with all the forms of creativity which constitute what we call culture.

In the verbal psychotherapy group attachment produces as its consequence the arousal of unresolved conflicts relating to parental figures, siblings and early peer group relationships. In an art therapy group set up along similar lines, i.e., with a circle of chairs, free-floating discussion, etc., this is also the case and the focus of therapeutic intervention will relate to these conflicts. There is a conflict here between the kinds of interactions which commonly take place in groups and the needs of the more fragmented individuals. Intimacy and connection with individual group members is not what is required. Along with conflict and confrontation it threatens the security of the primitive and wordless attachment to the-group-as-a-whole and makes impossible demands on individuals who are not able to relate to themselves as whole objects, let alone to others. The open studio group allows each individual to make use of the group according to their own needs. The setting of the group, the room where it takes place, the regular weekly time, may have as much significance as the individual group members. It may be possible for fragmented individuals to make an attachment to the room, objects in the room and materials before even apparently recognising the presence and reality of the people in the room.

## Group composition and selection

In an analytic or interactive group there are many advantages to having a heterogeneous rather than homogenous group membership. Patients with varying difficulties and personality structures will be able to create between them richer and more varied possibilities for communication and interaction. A group may find it difficult to deal with more than one borderline member because of the degree of destructive rage that the group may have to contain. In the acute in-patient environment however, it is not usually possible to have much control over group composition. The open studio group accommodates a population of patients not considered suitable in a classically composed group.

## Levels of communication in the open studio group

Communication in groups according to Foulkes (Foulkes and Anthony, 1957), leads from the surface to hidden aspects through four levels. The current or social level; the transference level; the projective level and the primordial or archaic level. Images expand the possibilities for expression at each of the four levels and each image contains elements of all of them. I find this a helpful structure in understanding the particular role of images in the open group.

At the *current level* the descriptive or diagrammatic aspect of the images is emphasised. They are perceived as illustrations accompanying verbal descriptions of events, dreams or relationship issues outside the group. This is in contrast to 'embodied images' described by Schaverien (1992), which become containers for projections of primary process material.

The *transference level* may be brought to the fore more quickly by the process of image making, which encourages regression. The association of art activity with play can encourage a reliving of the experience of playing in the presence of parental figures. The images become significant in the exchange with the conductor perceived as parent figure, and the need for approval and validation may be greatly emphasised.

In the 'embodied images' mentioned above, the part objects of the *projective level* are contained. The relationship with the image becomes intense and involving as it is felt to become 'alive'. The artist feels intensely identified with his creation, the physical activity of painting and the sensual qualities of the paint emphasise bodily experience. In the open studio group projective mechanisms are guided towards the images rather than towards other members of the group.

The *primordial level*, if it is to be articulated at all, expresses itself in archaic language. 'Singing, like the head of Orpheus in death and from afar' (Jung and Kerenyi, 1951: 5). At this level the group can function as a 'paradigm of coherence for the system' (Killick, 1987: 33) This is an experience which exists in a realm of pre-verbal knowing and corresponds to the archetypal realm described by Jung.

The art therapist's response to the images may be addressed to one or more of the levels of experience and communication described above.

## On being alone in the group

In group therapy individuals repeatedly lose themselves in the group identity and then find themselves as unique individuals. Painting, however, is essentially an individual activity. When the group stop talking and begin to paint, energy becomes focused away from others and on to the self.

(Skaife, 1990: 243)

Is painting essentially an insular activity, or is it that energy becomes focused on an internal dialogue in which the inner object representation of the group is intensely present? Winnicott identifies the capacity to be alone as one of the most important signs of emotional maturity. By this he does not mean merely being on one's own but rather, 'the experience of being alone while someone else is present' (Winnicott, 1958). An example is the young child or infant who plays with the mother nearby. The aloneness is in the presence of the other and is given its special quality by her presence. Winnicott suggests that paradoxically it is the 'infant's awareness of a reliable mother' that enables him to develop the capacity to be alone.

The reliability of the group in terms of its regularity and growing integration, which comes about through increased familiarity and development of trust, can allow the group members to experience what Winnicott calls this 'ego relatedness'. The group may then paradoxically become an environment where its members feel truly able to 'be alone' and to engage in an internal dialogue through the process of painting.

When the group reaches this stage of 'ego-relatedness' the atmosphere is qualitatively different. Marion Milner recognised when working with children 'a particular kind of absorption in what they are doing, which gives the impression that something of great importance is going on' (1952: 30). This is the 'aesthetic moment' described by Bollas, 'rapt intransitive attention, a spell which holds self and others in symmetry and solitude. Time seems suspended' (1987: 30). I have recognised this kind of concentration, as an art therapist, where a hush descends upon the room and one has a sense of deep and satisfying involvement.

## The role of the art therapist in the open studio group

The open studio art therapy group exists in a variety of settings and institutions and the art therapist's approach may differ in each one. I want to propose an approach in which sensitivity to unconscious processes and psychoanalytic method exists alongside an awareness of the demands made by the creative process. Where a respect for the idiosyncratic unfolding of the creative in each particular individual is held alongside an awareness of the group-as-a-whole. This requires the capacity to hold in mind many disparate elements simultaneously and to recognise the effect that an action in response to one element will have on the other elements. This is by no means an easy task. It may often look as if an art therapist in an open group is doing very little, however the task of holding the various elements may involve a great deal of internal work and few obvious external signs of intervention.

Although there may be no direct interaction between the group members in the open group, they all have an awareness of each other and are influenced in some way by the presence of the others. Patients are also acutely aware of the art therapist's communications with other patients in the room. It is therefore necessary to remember that something said to one patient is a statement to the whole group. Even if it can barely be heard, the tone of voice and general tenor of the communication has an influence on those around.

The role of the art therapist then, is to be a kind of weather predictor who can gauge the temperature of the group and the various elements that it contains, maintain the climate within a temperate range and the currents within it moving freely. All this, while attending to the development and needs of each individual. A clinical example may help to illustrate this.

A woman, I will call her Sue, with a long history of manic-depressive illness came regularly to the open group when she was an in-patient. She had a keen and developed interest in image-making and set about it with great enthusiasm. Her images had a quality of spontaneity and freedom which often rubbed off on other patients in the group and encouraged them, through observing her, to experiment with new techniques and styles of painting and drawing. As her mood changed, however, and she began to become 'high' she generated an excited atmosphere in the room which for some patients was enlivening and freeing, for others anxiety provoking. As her mood became more extreme the excitement and freedom threatened to turn into dangerous chaos and Sue needed to be excluded from the group as her chaotic and intrusive behaviour threatened to overwhelm its boundaries. I was aware that my response to Sue would give a message to other patients in the group about what I approved or disapproved of, what was tolerable and what intolerable. I needed to make the group safe by limiting Sue's out-of-control behaviour, while avoiding giving the message that freedom and spontaneity were dangerous. I needed to attend to different group members' varying responses to Sue's exclusion.

## CONCLUSION

Acute psychiatry may be said to be the natural home of art therapy, particularly of the open studio group. This method of working has fallen out of favour as analytic and interactive models have come to the fore. I propose that it be re-appraised as a model which provides the flexibility and containment necessary to work with the diversity of often highly disturbed patients that are found within the acute psychiatric setting and to accommodate short-term contact. In order to function effectively however it must exist within an integrated boundary structure in which the art therapist can control the referral, assessment and selection procedure for the group. This may involve challenging the established mode of operation in which confused boundaries act as an unconscious defence against the uncomfortable and frightening feelings associated with proximity to profound disturbance. There may be resistance both within the system and within the art therapist herself to clarifying boundaries and challenging stereotypes.

The open group provides a setting to which an attachment may develop which allows for the introjection of a coherent structure. The non-interactional nature of this group allows patients who are unable to communicate symbolically and who find interaction threatening to make use of the concrete features of the group to establish a relationship to it. The group as an embodiment of Winnicott's third area gives even patients who have short term contact the experience of an environment in which play can develop. The experience of the group-as-a-whole as a holding environment can offer a point of focus or 'paradigm of coherence' within the maelstrom of acute breakdown. The images provide a bridge which facilitates the transition from autistic withdrawal to symbolic communication, from walled-off non-existence to interactive creativity.

## BIBLIOGRAPHY

Bollas, C. (1987) *The Shadow of the Object: Psychoanalysis of the Unthought Known*, London: Free Association Books.

Dean, C. and Gadd, E.M. (1990) 'Home Treatment for Acute Psychiatric Patients', *British Medical Journal* 310: 1021–3.

Fried, K.W. (1979) 'Within and Without: The Exploration of a Ubiquitous Resistance in Group Therapy' in Wolberg, L. and Aronson, M. (eds), *Group Therapy*, New York: Stratton.

Foulkes, S.H. and Anthony, E.J. (1957) *Group Psychotherapy*, London, Penguin.

Hoult, J. *et al.* (1983) 'Psychiatric Hospital Versus Community Treatment: the Results of a Randomised Trial', *Australia and New Zealand Journal of Psychiatry* 17: 160–7.

Jung, C.G. and Kerenyi, C. (1951) *Introduction to a Science of Mythology*, London: Routledge and Kegan Paul.

Killick, K. (1987) MA Thesis, Hertfordshire College of Art and Design, St Albans.

Menzies Lyth, I. (1960) 'Social Systems as a Defence Against Anxiety: An empirical study of the nursing service of a general hospital', reprinted in *The Social Engagement of Social Science Volume 1: The Socio-Psychological Perspective*, eds Trist, E. and Murray, H., London: Free Association Books.

Merson, S., Tyrer, P., Onyett, S. *et al.* (1992) 'Early intervention in Psychiatric Emergencies: a controlled clinical trial', *Lancet* 339: 1311–14.

Milner, M. (1952) 'Aspects of Symbolism in Comprehension of the Not-Self', *International Journal of Psychoanalysis* 33: 181–95.

—— (1955) 'The role of Illusion in Symbol Formation', in (eds) Klein, Heimann and Money-Kyrle, *New Directions in Psychoanalysis*, London: Tavistock and Maresfield Reprint.

Pines, M. (1994) 'Borderline Phenomena in Analytic Groups' in *Ring of Fire* (eds) Schermer, V.L. and Pines, M., London: Routledge.

Schaverien, J. (1992) *The Revealing Image*, London: Routledge.

Skaife, S. (1990) 'Self Determination in Group analytic Art Therapy', *Group Analysis* 23: 237–44.

Skolnik, M.R. (1994) 'Intensive Group and Social Systems Treatment of Psychotic and Borderline Patients' in *Ring of Fire* (eds) Schermer, V.L. and Pines, M., London: Routledge.

Stein, L.J. and Test, M.A. (1980) 'Alternative to Mental Hospital Treatment. 1 Conceptual model, treatment program and clinical evaluation', *Archives of General Psychiatry* 37: 392–7.

Winnicott, D.W. (1951) 'Transitional Objects and Transitional Phenomena', in *Collected Papers: Through Paediatrics to Psycho-Analysis*, London: Tavistock.

—— (1958) 'The Capacity to be Alone', in *The Maturational Processes and the Facilitating Environment*, London: Hogarth.

—— (1960) 'Ego distortions in Terms of True and False Self' in *The Maturational Processes and the Facilitating Environment*, New York: International Universities Press.

Yalom, I.D. (1983) *The Theory and Practice of Group Psychotherapy*, New York: Basic Books,

—— (1985) *Inpatient Group Psychotherapy*, New York: Basic Books.

# Chapter 6

# Candles slowly burning

*Angela Byers*

## INTRODUCTION

This is the story of life, death, hope and despair. It is about the development of an art therapy group for cognitively impaired elderly people, which I ran for six years.

I chose to work with these patients because few non-medical workers did. I discovered that this reluctance was caused by the feelings of helplessness and despair which the work generates. Over time I was able to understand the power of countertransference, which enabled me to change my approach, and gave me new hope about working in this area.

The patients were approaching their deaths, the ward where they lived was due to be closed, and thus death was both in and outside of the group. One of the members wrote 'candles slowly burning' into an image she was making, and I have used it for my title because it describes the group well.

I start this chapter by referring to the literature about art therapy with elderly people and some of the more recent publications about groups and psychotherapy with them. The literature shows how theory has developed.

For a background to working with this age group I refer to ideas about death, and I describe the theories of holding and containing that explain the value of the art therapy group.

Then I describe the patients, their environment and the process of closing their ward. Finally, I describe the development of the group.

## A REVIEW OF THE LITERATURE

The literature shows an historical development in the practice of art therapy with elderly people.

At first Dewdney (1973), Weber (1981) and Wald (1983) aim to encourage a stronger sense of identity in their elderly patients, and improve self esteem and socialisation. Simon (1985) adds that 'imaginative life can continue to develop' (p. 9) through 'free painting'.

Review of past life is a natural process for elderly people, but Zeiger (1976) aims to release repressed memories so that her patients can enjoy the present more fully. She acknowledges that it can be a stressful experience. Wald (1983) describes how art therapy can release the 'pent-up emotions' (p. 59) of patients with Alzheimer's disease.

Death is a taboo subject in Western societies and therefore hard to talk about. Weiss (1984) describes how thoughts and feelings about death can be expressed through the whole art process, whilst Miller (1984) focuses on the use of symbols for the same purpose.

Crosson (1976) and Forrest (1991) address the lack of spontaneity amongst elderly people and their reluctance to engage in art. We (Wilks and Byers, 1992) acknowledge this as frustrating for the therapist.

From the late 1980s the literature identifies transference and counter-transference. Shore (1989) emphasises the strength of countertransference in work with elderly people. Johnson, Lahey and Shore (1992) add that it resembles 'those feelings experienced by patients' (p. 275), and can thus serve to increase the therapist's empathy. We (Wilks and Byers, 1992) say that sometimes 'the therapist is seen as a son or daughter or even a grandchild', when the child has often become 'the carer' instead of 'the one who is cared for' (p. 94).

The literature shows differing concerns about the art. Wald (1983 and 1984) uses images to diagnose regression caused by Alzheimer's disease; Miller (1984) writes about the symbolic meaning of images; and Simon (1985) uses a method of classifying the style of the images to understand her patients better.

The interest then turns to the art of cognitively impaired patients. Osler (1988) and Shore (1989) show that associations prompted by abstract painting can give people with Alzheimer's disease more to communicate. They describe the calming effect of making marks, which is also observed by Maiorana (1989) in her work with a man with Parkinson's disease. We (Wilks and Byers, 1992) and Johnson, Lahey and Shore (1992) observe that the physical quality of art can make fleeting experiences permanent.

Psychodynamic group processes are rarely mentioned. Increased socialisation is said to be a major benefit of group work (Weber, 1981; Wald, 1983), and also universality (Drucker, 1990). We (Wilks and Byers, 1992) consider that 'an overall group dynamic' (p. 99) is not possible with cognitively impaired patients. However, Johnson, Lahey and Shore (1992) find that group cohesion can be achieved when therapists recognise the affective states of the group members in an 'Alzheimer's Unit'.

Altogether art therapy has moved from being a directive and activity-based therapy, where increased self-esteem is the main objective, to one in which strong countertransference is recognised as enabling greater empathy. There is now an interest in the power of the art to hold the attention of those with severe memory loss for longer. Johnson, Lahey and Shore (1992) have also suggested that cohesion is possible in groups of cognitively impaired elderly people.

The literature of the 1980s and 1990s on verbal group work and psychotherapy with elderly people is necessarily about those who can still communicate with words. Nevertheless, comments on group processes and themes specific to this age group provide a useful background to art therapy groups with more severely impaired patients.

Pearlman (1993) says universality and increased self-respect are important benefits of group work with elderly people, reaffirming the self-value that society has taken away. Sadavoy and Robinson (1989) describe how 'old values regain their importance, hunger for social relationships returns, regression is halted and an urge to contribute to group cohesion emerges' (p. 106) in psychodynamic groups for cognitively impaired patients. Bleathman and Morton (1992) find increasing awareness and improved communication at a deep level in validation therapy groups for elderly people with severe memory loss.

Blank (1974) challenges 'the untested belief that older persons cannot develop further psychologically after becoming old' (p. 148). Much later, Culhane and Dobson (1991) and Wood and Seymour (1994) say that it is therapists' attitudes which inhibit psychodynamic group therapy with elderly people, who are quite capable of working effectively in the here-and-now.

Johnson (1985), Treliving (1988) and Culhane and Dobson (1991) point out that elderly people often have much unacknowledged anger. Johnson (1985) attributes this to their dependency on their own children or substitute children.

Some of the writing describes the generation gap, which leads staff to avoid good contact with elderly patients. Poggi and Berland (1985) and Treliving (1988) demonstrate how the different requirements of older and younger adults make it difficult for staff to listen to their elderly patients' disappointment and despair. Treliving adds that the experience of death 'again and again with patients' (1988: 226) is too much for staff at their stage of life.

Many authors describe part of the transference of the elderly patient as of a parent to an adult child. Johnson's (1985) group sometimes resented him, whilst Poggi's and Berland's group infantilised them, leaving them feeling deskilled and angry (Poggi and Berland, 1985). But Johnson's group made a positive shift when he recognised his resistance to their transference (Johnson, 1985).

Knight (1986), Martindale (1989) and Horowitz (1991) draw attention to the similarity between the real issues therapists face with their own elderly parents, and those issues that belong to the therapeutic relationship. This can cause the therapist to feel unusually guilty and anxious. Knight and Martindale add that it can result in the therapist desiring friendship, which leads him to slacken his professional boundaries.

This review of the literature demonstrates that both group art therapy and psychodynamic group psychotherapy are of value for elderly people. Art can engage the patient who has severe memory loss. Both art and group processes are, in essence, non-verbal, promoting cohesion in a group where verbal communication is poor. Beliefs that psychodynamic techniques are unsuitable for older people are found to be a result of ageist assumptions and it is shown that there can be a focus on the here-and-now. However, the feelings resulting from transference and countertransference can be strong and inhibiting.

Central to any psychotherapeutic work with elderly people is the fact that they will soon die. The literature suggests that the subject of death has a different impact on elderly people than on their younger therapists.

## DEATH IN OLD AGE

Gordon describes death as:

> the experience of that particular psychological state, the state of non-being, which might be felt either as a 'dissolution' or as an absorption in a transpersonal union. In either case boundaries are felt as non-existent, and all differentiation, separateness and the tension of opposites seem to have been eliminated. It is, therefore, essentially a non-dualistic state, in which there is no foreground and no background, no subject and no object, no 'I' and no 'you'.
>
> (Gordon, 1978: 16)

Cognitively impaired elderly people are already experiencing mental disintegration through the loss of conscious awareness of reality, although their bodies may be healthy. Benoliel (1991) describes this as 'social death' (p. 146).

The members of the validation therapy group run by Bleathman and Morton (1992) said that they were not afraid of physical death. Benoliel (1991) states that elderly people are more anxious about lack of control over how they die than of death itself.

Death indicates the end of life. In his theory of 'epigenesis', Erikson (1963) says that unresolved components of the psychosocial conflict of each stage are carried into the next stage. His theory suggests that there are unconscious conflicts in old age which are associated with past life. There are also many losses to grieve. Elderly people with severe memory loss often appear to be trying to resolve conflicts of their younger days, and are frequently to be seen searching for lost people and places.

Art therapy groups for elderly people are involved with themes of death, unresolved conflicts and loss. The themes emerge in the artwork, group processes, transference and countertransference.

But art therapy also provides containment, which acknowledges the value of each individual at a profound level. This is important for cognitively impaired elderly people, who are increasingly isolated on account of both the age gap and their disorientation.

## CONTAINMENT

Winnicott (1965) describes the infant's experience of being 'held' within a responsive and mostly predictable environment. By 'environment' Winnicott means the total experience of the infant, at a time when he is unaware of himself as an entity separate from his surroundings. In Erikson's terms, holding is a feature of trust in the stage of trust versus distrust.

Bion's theory of containment also concerns the first stages of the mother–infant relationship. When the infant projects his primitive experiences into the holding environment, of which the mother is part, she thinks about him and what he might be experiencing and tries to make sense of it. Then she gives back to him some meaning for his experiences, through her reactions to his projections.

The therapeutic relationship echoes these early experiences. In art therapy groups each client communicates through her image, the art process, words and behaviour. The therapist and group ponder the communications and give back their understanding both verbally and through their behaviour. The images are permanent and also reflect the experiences of the members.

The experiences of my group members resembled the experiences of infants. They required physical help and most of them were incontinent. Their lack of awareness of time jumbled the past and present. It was consequently hard for them to put experiences recorded through their senses into context, and differentiation was unclear. Containment would have been reassuring to them, as it is to an infant, although many of their conflicts were different.

Many of the group members did not seem to be involved with their images and verbal communication was difficult. In projective identification intolerable feelings are split off from consciousness and projected into another person, so that this person will feel them instead. It is a feature of transference that causes the therapist to experience her patients' feelings in countertransference, and thus understand and respond more fully. It was some time before I realised that the strong feelings I experienced before, during and after each session were affected by my countertransference to powerful feelings in the group.

Sinason (1992) writes that 'the more severely handicapped the child or adult, the greater the need to work more by understanding the countertransference or the nature of the communication the patient has sent to the therapist to be held' (p. 80).

Greenwood and Layton (1987) write about 'outer containers'. The ward is an outer container for the ward-based art therapy group. It is an effective container if the purpose of the group is understood by staff, and if their reactions to group members and therapists are appropriate. Their understanding is facilitated if there is good communication between them and the therapists. Clinical supervision is another form of outer container.

I have now described a theoretical background to art therapy groups for cognitively impaired elderly people; I have shown that certain themes emerge because of their stage of life; and I have suggested that containment is an important feature of the work.

The next section describes my clientele and the environment in which the art therapy group took place. Thus I begin with an evaluation of the environment as an outer container, before I tell the story of the group itself.

## AN UNCONTAINED ENVIRONMENT

My remit was to work with elderly mentally infirm patients in the mental health unit. I decided to work with those who received little input from other non-medical professionals.

The elderly patients in the continuing-care service were both old 'long-stay' patients and those who had been admitted more recently, due to severe memory loss resulting from organic brain deterioration.

The long-stay patients had been admitted many years ago, or had been in and out of hospital and were now there permanently. Most of them had chronic schizophrenia and all were institutionalised; many of them also had memory loss. They had received a variety of treatments over the years.

Many of them still had delusions, some were hard of hearing and some would not, or could not, talk. It was not possible to have a coherent conservation with most of them.

The more recently admitted patients had very poor short-term memories. Spoken and thought words were lost to them within minutes and they were consequently confused and confusing.

The ward in which I ran the art therapy group was situated in a part of the hospital built in 1887. The facilities were poor by modern standards.

Many of the staff had been there for ten or more years. It was a physical job because the patients needed help with everyday tasks and some were doubly incontinent. Some of the staff had found the more direct emotional challenges of an acute psychiatric ward too difficult to cope with.

The literature suggests that there are powerful emotional challenges in working with elderly people. In transference patients devalue staff and provoke powerful feelings in countertransference. Patients may be cautious about expressing their feelings directly because they are dependent on staff, or they may be too confused. Consequently feelings are expressed indirectly, which can be bewildering for staff.

Sinason (1992) describes how countertransference is an important means of communication for handicapped people. But if it is unacknowledged as such, and not thought about in a contained environment, the feelings it engenders in staff can have a profoundly demoralising effect and are all too easily projected or acted out. It is important that the staff themselves have some form of containment for these feelings.

As the ward approached closure staff were faced with redeployment or redundancy. Management was also being reorganised and in my opinion there was not sufficient containment for staff.

On top of this I was not telling them much about the group. Although I was unable to attend ward meetings, at first my co-therapist and I gave feedback after each session. There was not a lot to report on a weekly basis and it was an inconvenient time for staff. They looked relieved when I suggested that we stop. After that I wrote in the group members' files when there was something to report, and I chatted to those staff who were responsive to me, thinking that at least we could get to know each other.

So, by the end of my time with the group, staff were not sufficiently contained and did not fully understand what I was trying to do. It is not surprising that I was not contained by them. As they became increasingly anxious and angry so did I. Kahn, Sturke and Schaeffer (1992) describe how the dynamics on an in-patient ward affect the dynamics of therapeutic groups held there.

## THE FIRST STAGE OF THE ART THERAPY GROUP

I set up the art therapy group in 1989 in a ward which had a room where I thought we would be uninterrupted for an hour. At first we took patients from other wards but eventually all of the group members came only from this ward and one other. For the first two years of the group's life, I worked with a co-therapist. She was an occupational therapy technician who had an art degree.

Since 1986 I had worked non-directively with elderly people and I had found that many of them would not make images. In my opinion a directive approach would foster dependency, which was undesirable with patients who had already lost much independence.

But I was afraid of the empty space which would be there if nothing happened; probably I was afraid of despair and the sense of death itself. We decided, therefore, that we would introduce the group members to art techniques and encourage both the art process and the talking.

The staff were supportive of our proposal to work with these people. They referred patients to us and in these early days we did not attempt assessment interviews. Instead we let the patients assess the group for themselves by attending a session.

Before each session we asked every group member if they wanted to come. If we thought they did not understand us, we brought them to the room and if after a while they showed us that they did not want to be there, we took them back again.

It was difficult to bring everyone to the group in time, and we often had to leave the room to take someone back to the ward. Our inability to keep the boundaries of time and consistent presence added to the confusion of sessions.

In the first five months a group composed of six women was established. Two of them, who came from another ward, could speak intelligibly and wished to be seen as different to the others, whom they saw as 'more ill'. They struggled to make 'good pictures', perhaps in an attempt to demonstrate their good mental health. One of them copied pictures of flowers and birds, whilst the other sought our help to do the same.

There was thus a split between those who could communicate intelligibly and those who could not. Probably they shared a fear of the deterioration, confusion and dependency which they could see in each other.

One of the other four members of the group, Ada, had chronic schizophrenia (Figure 6.1). She painted images of houses, people and flowers. She worked with concentration for the whole session and her work clearly held her wandering thoughts. There was a dreamlike quality about her images where the original intent got lost, but colours, shapes, or lines triggered further associations. If we asked Ada about her work she would talk in a rambling way which was hard to follow.

*Figure 6.1* Painting by Ada

*Figure 6.2* 'Book' by Beattie

Beattie (Figure 6.2) also had chronic schizophrenia and was deaf mute. She used her finger to trace round shapes such as walls and windows. At first we encouraged her to draw around our hands and even our bodies and she would take her slippers off and draw around them or her feet. She also drew shapes and wrote words. Later she made books of folded drawings and would often take them away with her. She was argumentative and would occasionally threaten other people. Sometimes she appeared to be hallucinating and at other times she was watchful of the group. This kept her from concentrating on her drawing.

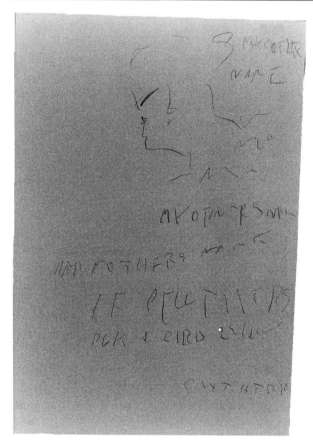

*Figure 6.3* Pencil drawing by Connie

Connie was the third patient with chronic schizophrenia (Figure 6.3). She made the odd stroke of a pencil or brush, whilst at the same time looking around her like a bird. In this way she frequently contrived to draw her mother's face. Doreen had severe memory loss and found it hard to do anything.

Other people with severe memory loss came for a session or two, but did not settle into the artwork or the group. Apart from Ada group members did not concentrate on their images for long. We were unable to hold intelligible conversations with most of them about their work and this left us ignorant of what meaning the images had for them. It felt as though we were being deprived of something.

I was unsure of the value of what we were doing and felt a sense of inadequacy and shame. This was magnified by what seemed like indifference and contempt from various group members. My feelings were surely similar to the feelings of the group: I was a receptacle for their projections.

The two patients who came from another ward expressed dissatisfaction with their images, which I found hard to accept. I wanted to provide the group with hope because I was uncomfortable with their despair.

This was not clear to me at the time, and I did not feel able to discuss my feelings with my co-therapist. She continued to do what she did well; encouraging fun with and without the materials and working at her relationships with individual group members.

In the first year of the group's life they settled into a grumbling rivalry with each other. There seemed to be a pecking order of symptoms, with the member with severe memory loss at the bottom. Each individual seemed to depend on our help and it was hard to see the group-as-a-whole.

Yalom (1975) describes the first stage of a group's life as a stage of orientation, when there is dependency on the conductor. But dependency was a real issue for these people and it took me some time to believe that the group could have its own identity.

However, the core membership remained stable and they continued to make images. A man with Parkinson's disease joined.

## NEW UNDERSTANDING

The next year saw some changes in membership. The most articulate member, and the two members who had severe memory loss and Parkinson's disease, left to live in nursing homes in the community.

Emily (Figure 6.4), who had previously lived alternately at home and in hospital, joined the group. She had a diagnosis of manic depression but seemed to be institutionalised. Once she had settled into the group she drew her house to which she hoped to return, and herself. She drew these same images in every session until the end of the group's life. She laughed about them, but to me they made a statement of personal identity.

Then Fred joined (Figure 6.5). He had been in hospital since he was eight years old and he had no diagnosis of mental illness. He remained the only man in the group until he died. Fred could not talk but he seemed to like being in a group of women and he liked painting.

*Figure 6.4* Crayon drawing of her house and dog by Emily

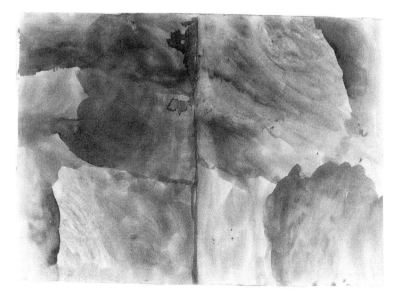

*Figure 6.5* Painting by Fred

He would take paint from the paintbox or palette by dipping a very wet brush into each colour in turn, before applying it to paper. He methodically covered the whole piece of paper with paint whatever size it was, so that the resulting image was in varying hues of grey and brown. He seemed proud of what he did. His paintings communicate something of Gordon's description of death (1978: 16), for shapes are not clearly defined and he has ignored the edge of the paper.

At first we would demonstrate ways of using the materials and ask questions to stimulate a response. Then I became aware that it might be possible not to try to stimulate the group like this. When we accepted their apparent unresponsiveness to us, each other and – in the case of most of them – their images, we could be more aware of how the group was feeling.

Then I realised that we could focus on the group and not just on the individuals within it. I observed that the group members were aware of each other and realised that it was possible to work with the group-as-a-whole.

I talked to my co-therapist about this, suggesting that we should give less attention to individuals and more to the whole group. I was asking her to make a fundamental change to her approach. Soon she found that she was unable to come any more.

My co-therapist was missed, for she had brought much richness and affection. I feared that I was boring by comparison, but persisted in trying to focus more on the whole group.

During the period of her leaving, when sometimes I was running sessions on my own, I was aware of anger in the group. Although members were reacting to the loss of the co-therapist, I realised how angry they must feel in their daily lives.

I also understood that they were making a statement when they stayed for a whole session without making images. It seemed, paradoxically, to be an assertive action, an attempt to be independent.

Most groups would find it hard to tolerate a split between the co-therapists and the resulting separation and loss of one of them. All except one of the members continued to attend. I think they were encouraged by my growing ability to tolerate their negativity. Their images and the processes of making them did not change.

I have shown how I had underestimated this group's ability to communicate. I undervalued them and was left with feelings of inadequacy, shame and frustration. My aims were different to theirs, and as a result I found it hard to empathise with them. The literature describes similar feelings and differences between the goals of elderly people and their younger therapists (Johnson, 1985; Poggi and Berland, 1985; Treliving, 1988; Johnson, Lahey and Shore, 1992; Wood and Seymour, 1994).

Yet the group was continuing to come. Each member's idiosyncratic way of making images tended not to change very much, but the group became more cohesive in the next stage.

## GROUP-AS-A-WHOLE

After the co-therapist left there were squabbles and bad temper amongst group members.

By now we had a routine. The session, which was an hour long, began with a cup of tea which brought the group together. Then I would try to ensure that each member had the materials she wanted. Some would get to work straight away and others would take their time. Ada and Fred could work for a whole session, but the rest of the group would spend only a minute or two at a time making marks, if at all.

I introduced the practice of circulating notes on which I wrote what I was saying in large letters. I hoped that this would combine with speech to enable me to communicate to the whole group. The notes were appreciated, and Beattie sometimes took them with her when she left.

Then I took time at the end of every session to invite each member to show her image to the group. If she was in agreement I would hold it up so that everyone could see it. Some of them looked and perhaps nodded. There was not a lot of interest displayed, but there was a response.

These were physical ways of bringing the group together and it now seemed to be more of an entity than it had been. They watched each other and sometimes argued, although there were times when they were separately dreaming.

Grace, Hattie, Jean and Kitty joined the group, one at a time over the next sixteen months.

Grace had chronic schizophrenia (Figure 6.6). She would draw and paint shapes which resembled windows or mugs which were in front of her, but could not talk about her work. She worked for a short time only, otherwise watching the group or dreaming.

Hattie, Jean and Kitty (Figures 6.7 and 6.8) had severe memory loss. Hattie would write lists of words, it seemed in an effort to keep control of them, although manifestly she thought she was doing a school exercise for me. Kitty also wrote words and painted images which held her wandering thoughts. Jean would sometimes sort material, a common activity of people with severe memory loss (Byers, 1995), and this could

*Figure 6.6* Painting by Grace

hold her concentration for long periods. At other times she seemed dazed or confused.

I was now more able to hold onto my feelings and think about them, because I was becoming aware that they were triggered by my counter-transference. Milner (1969), when describing her work with a regressed patient who did not use words, writes, 'I felt I had to learn to wait and watch and let her know that I was there, watching, and not let myself be seduced into working too hard for her' (p. 42). This was what I was having to learn.

But I was becoming sleepy during sessions. The room was stuffy, the atmosphere was depressing and I was bored. I also felt heavy, tired and depressed after sessions.

Beneath the sleepiness was anger. I was frustrated and ashamed, both with my behaviour and the apparent lack of achievement in the group.

When my eyelids dropped Emily would ask me if I was tired. I discovered that she was afraid that I would leave them because I was bored. My capacity to accept these people as they were was being tested.

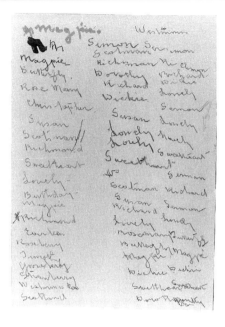

*Figure 6.7* Words by Hattie

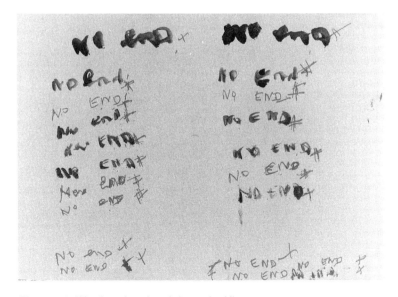

*Figure 6.8* Words painted and drawn by Kitty

It is significant that I did not retaliate by leaving the group. Sinason (1992) describes how the holding of an infant calms him after he has projected what he has found unbearable into the mother and 'then faces those frightening forces in the mother' (p. 187). 'The baby then sees its terrors have been modified' (p. 188). In spite of feelings of pointlessness I continued to come.

I was acting as my patients did when they dozed on the ward. It was like a psychic death, although for me – and perhaps for them – it masked a deep frustration. Through projective identification I was experiencing feelings that the group could have been expected to have.

I was younger than them and yet they were dependent on me. I felt as though they had deskilled me. It was like the countertransference of the adult child described by Poggi and Berland (1985).

Occasionally I told the group what I thought they might be feeling, having observed their activity or lack of it and my countertransference. Once when I suggested they seemed to be 'fed up', two of the members nodded. They were responding to my efforts to understand and acknowledging some containment.

Fred, Connie and another member died at different times. The group reacted, first by being more responsive to each other, then by refusing to come, and lastly with bad temper. I did not feel as strongly about their deaths as I did about their day-to-day lives.

The room where we worked had a door to the outside and this had become the main door for the ward. I used screens to ensure that the group would not be visible to people who came through the door.

This introduced an interesting new dynamic. Members could leave the table to sit behind the screens. They now had another means of communication at their disposal.

I wondered if sitting behind the screens was a way of playing with the concept of absence or death, as well as being assertive. Sometimes two or three members would form an outer sub-group behind the screen, where they would take milk and biscuits from the tea tray, play the piano, or just sit together. I enjoyed this playful assertiveness until the day when all but one of the group left. Then I felt hurt. They had found another way of showing me how their emotional isolation gave them feelings of despair and anger.

By now I was experiencing very strong feelings, and although I acted them out by dozing, I did not stop coming nor trying to understand what was happening. The group was an entity and they must have felt containment in my persistence, each other and their images. But the closure of the ward was drawing near.

## THE LAST STAGE

I had discovered that the other ward, where Emily and Grace lived, was going to close within a month. I wanted the group to function right up to the time when our ward was to close, but management were unable to give me a date. Afraid that it would happen suddenly, as with the other ward, I decided I would end the group before the closure. I could then be sure that I could give the group three month's notice before its termination. Fortunately Emily and Grace were able to continue coming.

I informed them every week for the final ten sessions how many more there would be, using speech and notes. However, I was concerned that Beattie might not understand.

Ada would hover over a blank sheet of paper, sometimes for a whole session, and there was less work done generally. At times they reacted to my communications about the ending by looking pained, or by jolting as though with shock. I felt sad.

In the last session, I did not want to sleep. Beattie gave me more eye contact than she had given me for a long time and on the way out she kissed Grace's hand. I thought she may have understood after all. After the session I felt relieved, guilty, sad and loving.

## DISCUSSION

I am struck by my lack of interest in the art work of this group. At the time most of them seemed to be scantily involved in their work; their images were often similar to, if not the same as previous ones and their body language tended to be flat.

But each member had her own way of approaching her art. Hattie struggled to remember words when she made her lists, and probably the words triggered further thoughts and memories. The physical presence of the lists reminded her of her task.

Kitty wrote words that conveyed emotion as well as meaning and were sometimes woven into her images. The physical presence of her images enabled her to maintain some concentration on them.

Connie would make a mark, look around her and later add another mark, continuing thus for a whole session. She seemed to be uninvolved with her images, but sometimes her marks came together as a representation of a face. At such times she must have had a 'mental image' (Schaverien, 1992) of the face, either before or during the process. When she did not draw anything recognisable, something still moved her to make marks.

Grace would be involved in the art process for a short time and then watch the group, or close her eyes. Emily would draw quickly and then cover her face with her hands. Their images stayed in front of them, statements of their presence. The repetitive nature of Emily's images declared their significance.

Fred and Ada were absorbed in the art process for the whole session. Their images held their concentration.

Schaverien (1992) describes a period of 'identification', in which an image is contemplated after it has been made. I assumed that the group had lost interest in their images at this stage because they did not seem to look at them and probably could not remember them. But perhaps the occasional glance stirred a memory and inspired contemplation.

Only Beattie showed concern about what happened to her images, which she often took away with her. Perhaps she wanted to retain something of the session, or maybe she did not trust me to look after them. Certainly her action demonstrated that she valued her work enough to take charge of its 'disposal' (Schaverien, 1992).

In spite of my negative feelings it can be seen that the images and the art process did have a function in the group. They brought meandering thoughts back to physical focus; they conveyed emotion; they bore witness to the personality and presence of each group member; and it is possible that they inspired contemplation. I can only conclude that my feelings were influenced by countertransference; and this brings me back to my findings from the literature about art therapy and psychotherapy with elderly people.

When I describe the literature, I show how art therapy with elderly people has changed over the last two and a half decades. At first the aims were to encourage elderly patients in groups to engage in art in order to stimulate creativity, and also to use the group to increase their sociability. Lack of motivation was seen as a challenge to the therapist, whose feelings were not recorded. Now it is recognised that countertransference is a powerful aid to understanding and empathy, and that cognitively impaired elderly patients are more responsive when the meaning of their behaviour is recognised. It is said that images can be used by elderly people to express thoughts and feelings about death which are hard to put into words. Images also record and hold the fleeting thoughts and feelings of cognitively impaired elderly people.

The literature about psychotherapy explores transference and countertransference further, suggesting that therapists block their ability to empathise with elderly people because they are at a different stage of life, but that their recognition of this can shift the therapy.

The literature shows that death is less frightening for elderly people than is dying and losing control. However, the nearness of death intensifies unresolved conflicts from past life. I describe containment as a focus of therapy with cognitively impaired elderly people, and projective identification as a powerful means of communication.

I write about the lack of containment for myself and the group on the ward where we worked, due to conflict and anxiety in the face of closure; I then describe the life story of the group, its powerful effect on me, and how I and the group changed during this time.

When I began the group I aimed to encourage artwork and socialisation. During the first year I was strongly affected by the group's apparent lack of interest in their art. I wanted to feel a sense of achievement and instead I was faced with despair. However, I noticed that I could be more empathic if I paid attention to the group's lack of response instead of trying to stimulate them. I noticed that the group members were more aware of each other than I had thought and realised that the group itself was an entity. This provided containment.

When my co-therapist left I became aware of anger and assertiveness in the group, and at the same time I introduced techniques to improve communication and group cohesion.

But I was beset by difficult feelings. I was still afraid of the emptiness and acted out my frustration and despair by almost sleeping in the sessions.

When I began to think about my feelings as being related to countertransference I became more aware of the group's feelings. This brought about further cohesion, presumably because they were better contained.

One of the group members voiced a fear that I might be bored, and later the group shifted away from me. It seemed that they wanted to test my perseverance as well as showing me how they felt.

Finally, I was able to bring the subject of termination of the group into its last sessions, so that we could contain some of the feelings this evoked.

## CONCLUSION

I have shown that there are links between my personal development with this art therapy group and developments in the theory of art therapy group work with cognitively impaired elderly people. The way forward is for therapists to pay constant attention to their own feelings. I could not have done so without clinical supervision and I believe that all who work with elderly people should be given a similar form of containment.

We question the value of art therapy groups with cognitively impaired elderly people all too easily. Such doubts are themselves a result of the devaluing transference of younger people to their elders. It is true that many of these patients do not respond to art materials. But some of them do, and as my patients showed me, art therapy groups can be empowering and containing at a time when body and mind are disintegrating.

## BIBLIOGRAPHY

Benoliel, J. (1991) 'Multiple Meanings of Death in Older Adults', in E. Murrow Baines (ed.) *Perspectives on Gerontological Nursing*, Newbury Park, London, New Delhi: Sage.

Bion, W. (1962) *Learning from Experience*, London: Maresfield Reprints, Karnac.

Blank, M. (1974) 'Raising the Age Barrier to Psychotherapy', *Geriatrics*, Nov. 1974, pp. 141–8.

Bleathman, C. and Morton, I. (1992) 'Validation Therapy: Extracts from 20 Groups with Dementia Sufferers', *Journal of Advanced Nursing*, vol. 17, pp. 658–66.

Byers, A. (1995) 'Beyond Marks', *Inscape: the Journal of the British Association of Art Therapists*, vol. 1, pp. 13–18.

Crosson, C. (1976) 'Geriatric Patients: Problems of Spontaneity', *American Journal of Art Therapy*, vol. 15, pp. 51–6.

Culhane, M. and Dobson, H. (1991) 'Groupwork with Elderly Women', *International Journal of Geriatric Psychiatry*, vol. 6, pp. 415–18.

Dewdney, I. (1973) 'An Art Therapy Program for Geriatric Patients', *American Journal of Art Therapy* 12(4), pp. 249–54.

Drucker, K. (1990) 'Swimming Upstream: Art Therapy with the Psychogeriatric Population in One Health District', in M. Liebmann (ed.) *Art Therapy in Practice*, London: Jessica Kingsley Publishers.

Erikson, E. (1963) *Childhood and Society*, 2nd edn, New York: Norton.

Forrest, K. (1991) 'Applications of Art Therapy with the Elderly', *Canadian Art Therapy Association Journal*, vol. 6, No. 1, pp. 1–17.

Gordon, R. (1978) *Dying and Creating: a Search for Meaning*, London: The Society of Analytical Psychology Ltd.

Greenwood, H. and Layton, G. (1987) 'An Out Patient Art Therapy Group', *Inscape: the Journal of the British Association of Art Therapists*, Summer 1987, pp. 12–19.

Horowitz, M. (1991) 'Transference and Countertransference in the Therapeutic Relationship with the Older Adult', in R. Hartke (ed.) *Psychological Aspects of Geriatric Rehabilitation*, Gaithersberg, MD: Aspen.

Johnson, D. (1985) 'Expressive Group Psychotherapy with the Elderly: a Drama Therapy Approach', *International Journal of Group Psychotherapy*, vol. 35 (1), pp. 109–27.

Johnson, C., Lahey, P. and Shore, A. (1992) 'An Exploration of Creative Arts Therapeutic Work on an Alzheimer's Unit', *The Arts in Psychotherapy*, vol. 19, pp. 269–77.

Kahn, E., Sturke, I. and Schaeffer, J. (1992) 'Inpatient Group Processes Parallel Unit Dynamics', *International Journal of Group Psychotherapy*, 42(3), pp. 407–18.

Knight, B. (1986) *Psychotherapy with Older Adults*, Beverly Hills, Newbury Park, London, New Delhi: Sage.

Maiorana, W. (1989) 'When Art is All There is: Art Therapy in the Treatment of a Man with Parkinson's Disease', *American Journal of Art Therapy*, vol. 28, pp. 51–6.

Martindale, B. (1989) 'Becoming Dependent Again: the Fears of some Elderly Persons and their Younger Therapists', *Psychoanalytic Psychotherapy*, vol. 4, No. 1, pp. 67–75.

Miller, B. (1984) 'Art Therapy with the Elderly and the Terminally Ill', in T. Dalley (ed.) *Art as Therapy*, London and New York: Tavistock.

Milner, M. (1969) *The Hands of the Living God: An Account of an Analytic Treatment*, London and Toronto: Hogarth Press.

Osler, I. (1988) 'Creativity's Influence on a Case of Dementia', *Inscape: the Journal of the British Association of Art Therapists*, vol. 1, pp. 20–2.

Pearlman, I. (1993) 'Group Psychotherapy with the Elderly', *Journal of Psychosocial Nursing*, vol. 31, No. 7, pp. 7–10.

Poggi, R. and Berland, D. (1985) 'The Therapists' Reactions to the Elderly', *The Gerontologist*, vol. 25, No. 5, pp. 508–13.

Sadavoy, J. and Robinson, A. (1989) 'Psychotherapy and the Cognitively Impaired Elderly', in D. Conn, A. Grek and J. Sadavoy (eds) *Psychiatric Consequences of Brain Disease in the Elderly*, New York and London: Plenum Press.

Schaverien, J. (1992) *The Revealing Image – Analytical Art Psychotherapy in Theory and Practice*, London: Routledge.

Shore, A. (1989) 'Themes of Loss in the Pictorial Language of a Nursing Home', *Canadian Art Therapy Association Journal*, vol. 4, No. 1, pp. 16–32.

Simon, R. (1985) 'Graphic Style and Therapeutic Change in Geriatric Patients', *American Journal of Art Therapy*, vol. 24, pp. 3–9.

Sinason, V. (1992) *Mental Handicap and the Human Condition*, London: Free Association Books.

Treliving, L. (1988) 'The Use of Psychodynamics in Understanding Elderly In-Patients', *Psychoanalytic Psychotherapy*, vol. 3, No. 3, pp. 225–33.

Wald, J. (1983) 'Alzheimer's Disease and the Role of Art Therapy in its Treatment', *American Journal of Art Therapy*, vol. 22, pp. 57–64.

—— (1984) 'The Graphic Representation of Regression in an Alzheimer's Disease Patient', *The Arts in Psychotherapy*, vol. 11, No. 3, pp. 165–75.

Weber, B. (1981) 'Folk Art as Therapy with a Group of Old People', *American Journal of Art Therapy*, vol. 20, pp. 47–52.

Weiss, J. (1984) *Expressive Therapies with Elders and the Disabled: Touching the Heart of Life*, New York: Haworth Press.

Wilks, R. and Byers, A. (1992) 'Art Therapy with Elderly People in Statutory Care', in D. Waller and A. Gilroy (eds), *Art Therapy: A Handbook*, Buckingham and Bristol: Open University Press.

Winnicott, D. (1965) *The Maturational Processes and the Facilitating Environment*, London: Karnac.

Wood, A. and Seymour, L. (1994) 'Psychodynamic Group Therapy for Older Adults: the Life Experiences Group', *Journal of Psychosocial Nursing*, vol. 32, No. 7, pp. 19–24.

Yalom, I.D. (1975) *The Theory and Practice of Group Psychotherapy*, New York: Basic Books.

Zeiger, B. (1976) 'Life Review in Art Therapy with the Aged', *American Journal of Art Therapy*, vol. 15, pp. 47–50.

# Chapter 7

# The Magpie's eye
## Patients' resistance to engagement in an art therapy group for drug and alcohol patients

*Neil Springham*

## INTRODUCTION

This paper is concerned with the problems incurred when patients with the same pathology are grouped together for the purposes of treatment. I aim to describe how, in the case of designated drug and alcohol groups, highly narcissistic individuals attempt to only engage in group therapy at a 'false-self' level, which if unchecked, can result in a therapy group where no one is properly the patient. I begin with a case example in which I particularly wish to emphasise the therapist's experience of strong feelings of being repulsed and excluded, which link to the patients' anxieties about the therapist. A group member's image of a 'Magpie's eye' gave this anxiety a concretised form for the group and in so doing demonstrated the particular value of the pictorial images in processing this material. I then discuss the theoretical issues this raises, beginning with how narcissistic pathology manifests in patients unifying, by over-identifying with each other's perceived similarities, against the therapist. This results in the therapeutic resource of individual differences within the group being seen as a threat. I suggest that art therapy is particularly useful in this setting because the use of image-making facilitates an engagement by proxy of those individual differences, otherwise resisted in the group relationships.

When I use the term 'drug and alcohol patient' I mean those patients whose primary problem is substance misuse, and the groups referred to here do not include those patients who have primary mental health problems. My reason for primarily concentrating on how the collective pathology of the patients manifests in the art therapy group, rather than how the working conditions of the group programme effect therapeutic functioning (see Springham 1992 for a discussion of this), is because my aim is to describe my experiences in offering art therapy to drug and alcohol patients, which might most usefully be generalised beyond this specific working environment. I would briefly mention that this case example is taken from a group I have been running for eight years within a N.H.S. drug and alcohol programme. This programme consists of a series of groups ranging in orientation from the cognitive-behavioural through to the psychodynamic. The programme has the capacity for five in-patients and five day-patients to attend for a period of six weeks. All patients enter the programme voluntarily, but once on the programme they sign a contract to attend all groups and remain totally abstainate for the duration of their stay.

## CASE STUDY

The five group members featured in this case all have long-standing alcohol problems and one also has a more recent drug habit. All of the members were male and the age range was from twenty-four to fifty-five years. This was not the first art therapy group for any of these patients.

All of the group members arrived on time and sat down in the circle of chairs. At first they were quite jovial with comments such as 'doesn't it smell like school', or 'now's our chance to make prats of ourselves'. I felt a little uneasy about this atmosphere. Although no one was actually hostile towards me, it seemed that some of these comments were meant as a challenge to my role as a therapist. My image of this situation was that it was as if we were down the pub having a good time and I was like some unwanted moralistic voice ruining the fun. I started the session by introducing the aims of the art therapy, and the group very quickly became quiet and attentive. I said that this was not an art class and we would not be looking at the images in terms of skill. We would be more interested in looking at exploring what might be learned from the pictures in terms of attitudes. People could paint and draw whatever they wished, they did not have to paint about their feelings or about drugs and alcohol issues. There was some consternation at this. One person said 'yeah, yeah, but what should we draw?' and there was a ripple of laughter. To this I replied that it was up to them. This was accepted and the group got up to go and paint at the tables whilst I remained in my chair.

As they went about finding palettes and selecting paper the atmosphere reverted to one of ebullience. Someone squeezed a bottle of paint too hard and it exploded onto the paper. A cheer went up. The individual said 'don't mock, this might be worth millions now in an art gallery!'. I found myself inwardly experiencing a momentary wave of exasperation and I wondered what kind of a group this was going to be. It is useful to consider all comments as being descriptions of how the group is perceiving the here and now. My thoughts about the comment of the image being 'worth millions' was that there may be some anxiety around about how to be worth something in this group. After this incident people began to paint and gradually a hush descended on the group which lasted until the painting time had finished. My feeling of exasperation evaporated during this time and I was struck by the intensity of absorption that the activity of image production had inspired in all of the group members.

When I said to people that it was now time to bring the pictures back into the circle, they were quite reluctant to break from their painting. This is an important juncture point in the session and as is often the case, its crossing was a matter of anxiety for many that day. As the first people sat down they kept their images folded over on their laps. However, one picture had been painted in such a thick and liquid manner that the maker had to put it flat on the ground to avoid the paint running off the page. He then said 'Come on then you lot, if I've got to put mine down then I don't want to be alone.' With a half smile the rest complied and put their pictures down. At this point the group seemed a little relieved and everyone leaned forward attentively to look at the pictures. They did not actually say anything and it seemed for a few moments as though it was hard to start talking again. In response I asked how people had found the image making. Somebody said it was 'fine'. Someone else said that it had been surprisingly enjoyable and he had wanted to continue. After a short silence I noted aloud that not everyone had expressed such a positive opinion and I wondered if it felt hard to say it had been otherwise. My aim in doing this was to communicate as quickly as possible my receptivity to any negative affects. Someone did say that they had found it 'weird' and this was echoed by someone else saying that it had been 'quite hard'. I noted that the group had been able to share mixed feelings about the experience so far.

I then said that this part of the session tended to work best if people made comments about their own or other's pictures or indeed anything else that struck them as being important within the session. Robby then said to Mike that he thought his picture was good: 'yeah, that's really artistic'.

I reacted internally to this comment with some irritation and anxiety. I worried that it was immediately contravening my suggestion not to look at artistic skill in the art therapy and I was concerned not to let this initial comment set any unhelpful criteria for viewing. Mike went on to say how he liked doing art because it was relaxing and this added to my concern. I felt that I needed to say something about this without squashing the fragile communication that was emerging. I asked the whole group if they were still concerned that their pictures needed to be good. Robby said that I should know that many of them had not painted since school. Andrew said that he had always hated art at school, although some of his mates were really good at it. Bob said he thought it was a bit of a waste of time at school but then he quite liked it

*Figure 7.1* Mike's picture

for that. These school analogies seemed to confirm that there was an anxiety about authority being at the very least unhelpful. I said I wondered if people were wondering how the art therapy experience might be helpful for them. 'It's about feelings isn't it' Mike told me flatly and this response being in such absolute terms seemed to somehow stop any further exploration of that issue within the group.

I asked him if his picture was about how he felt now or how he would like to feel. He said 'I feel peaceful now', which I thought was not how he looked. Andrew then quickly stepped in and said 'I'll do my picture now shall I? This is the booze, I'm really sick of it. Here are the bad things it brings into my life: debt, isolation, self hatred and criminal charges. Now I feel more positive because I've given it up and it's out of my system I don't want it any more. I can think about the things I want: work, house and a woman'.

He sat back in his chair and then said 'That's it then'. Other people responded by saying 'Very good' and 'That's very clear'. I was alarmed to hear this because my own reaction was so very different. I felt that this communication was one of 'I've cracked

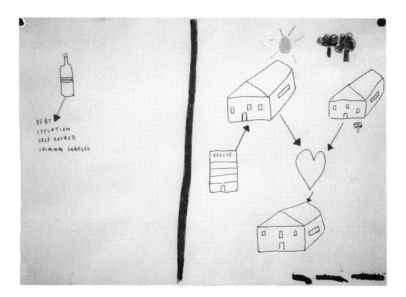

*Figure 7.2* Andrew's picture

it, I've got no problem, I don't need this help, end of conversation'. I felt useless for a moment and I glanced at the clock with an anxious fantasy that the session time could not be filled. After inquiring if there were perhaps other viewpoints on this, and receiving a negative response, I said I felt alone in voicing my concern that it could be so simple and that maybe it was hard to air doubts about giving up and staying off alcohol.

Bob reacted to that by saying in a jovial manner that the staff always wanted a deeper meaning, as if they wanted people to be miserable. 'Funnily enough that is what my picture is about', he said. 'Being on that "psycho" ward is driving me nuts. The staff don't give a toss about us up there'.

Being the staff member present, I was alerted to this being a comment about myself and felt that I ought to draw attention to it. A day patient asked which staff Bob meant and he replied that it was the night nursing staff. He continued: 'First I wanted something to help me sleep, but they said 'no, see your doctor tomorrow'. I thought, great, the night will be gone then so what's the use. Then I said I wanted to watch telly because of not being able to sleep and they wouldn't let me. God, you could be dying up

*Figure 7.3* Bob's picture

there and they would step over you'. Andrew agreed and came up with a similar story. I was struck by how this group was vociferously complaining about the lack of regard being offered from the staff, yet at the same time was rejecting any attention from the member of staff in the room. I said that I wondered if people were asking themselves if this art therapy group was at all helpful, perhaps I was only trying to give them miserable feelings.

'No', was the answer. Mike said he liked art, had liked it at school and found it relaxing. This comment took up only a part of what I was saying as if it were the whole and so diverted the attention from the issue I was raising. The art therapy group involved more than painting as our current discussional activity demonstrated. I noted how hard it had been for anyone to say anything directly negative about this. I found it hard not to express the exasperation I felt with them at this point. I suspected that this feeling was countertransference and that I needed to both tolerate it and somehow facilitate a more direct expression of it from the group. I commented that this group was not only about doing art, but also about talking about feelings and this could be difficult.

There was then a prolonged silence. I saw that a few of the group members now looked at the clock as I had done and I noticed that I no longer felt anxious about filling time since I had identified my previous strong feelings as to do with projections from the group. It felt as though the pressure was rising between myself and a group apparently unified against me. Mike began swinging on his chair and looking out of the window. I noticed that he glanced rather conspiratorially to Bob and they both rolled their eyes as if to say how typically boring this was.

This difficult silence was broken by Bob saying 'What's yours then Robby, a fried egg?'

The tense silence erupted into giggles all round, apart from me. 'Ah well', said Bob 'at least that made something happen and cheered us up a bit'. It seemed to me that this group must do anything to stay cheerful as an anaesthetic against the present concern about the art therapy session. Robby set his position out by saying that he was now two weeks abstinent and that he

*Figure 7.4* Robby's picture

was not thinking about alcohol. He said that he found that not thinking about things was generally most helpful. I thought how this defensive position could only put him in conflict with the thinking function of the art therapy group.

I asked for any thoughts on this. There was a short silence and I thought how hard it must be in this group to break away from consensual 'party line'. I suggested that whilst thinking about problems brought some immediate anxiety, it surely must be needed in the long run. Robby replied rather coolly that this strategy had worked all right for him so far and he didn't want a drink if he didn't think about it. I thought how well what I had been saying had been dismantled and it did not seem possible to argue this point further. I did not feel useless as I had done before because this communication had confirmed my hypothesis that it was hard to think and discuss difficult issues in this group and that all efforts were made to defend against me, as the representative of this function, lest some catastrophe followed.

Vic asked again what the image was of. Robby said 'I don't know what it was, it just sort of happened'. Andrew said 'I like that, I don't know why. It's kind of moody'.

I suspected that Bob had originally referred to Robby's picture not out of interest but as a way of moving away from the discomfort of the silence. But it now did seem that a real interest was being stirred up by this picture and this felt qualitatively rather different.

'It looks like an eye', Vic said. 'Not a very nice eye', said Bob, 'like a Crow'.

'Or a Magpie', said Andrew. 'Like it's looking for something to steal . . . Oh that was deep'. This seemed to be said in a half joking manner but neither he, nor the others, seemed to want to retreat into that defensive laughter again at this point. He added, 'No, actually I like that, it's powerful'.

I also found this image to be powerful and felt the gaze of this eye was penetrating and predatory. I associated the group's material of dark attributes, not being very nice and thieving, with its perception of me. This made some sense of the group's exclusion of me. I attempted to articulate this negative transference, which at the time felt like speaking forbidden and dangerous words. I said that perhaps the interest in this eye and what it might be looking for may be expressing people's thoughts about what I might be looking for. I noted that I was different in that I had no image to put down and disclosed little about myself. I then said 'Like the Magpie's eye, what is this art therapist looking for?'

'Well we don't really know you, do we', replied Robby. Bob said 'We don't know what you want. We were all talking before about what we would draw in art therapy and we were saying we were all worried about it. We had been joking about all doing the same picture to see how you coped but it didn't happen somehow'. My feeling changed dramatically at this point. I was struck by how this image of the magpie's eye had somehow acted as a bridge between the group and myself. The current communication about me was now directed to me. If they had conspired to draw the same image I would have felt very attacked and I felt more able to consider that this would probably reflect their anxieties about what I might do. Moreover, because they were now more able to admit their negative feelings directly to me, the nature of our alliance felt more trusting.

Andrew continued by asking 'Anyway, how can all this tell us about feelings?'

I noted to myself how it now seemed to be safe enough in the group to be directly critical. I said that 'We seem to be learning about a very important feeling that is around right now. That is, how hard it is to discuss the worry about whether I will be a helpful sort of person'.

Vic said 'I suppose none of us tend to let people in'. Others agreed with that, saying that they had been let down so much. To this I noted that I had felt that I had been judged in that way before there was any evidence and I asked if this was what people did generally. This comment seemed to cause a rather more reflective silence.

'Perhaps that links with my picture'. said Vic. 'This is my country cottage. Somewhere to get away from it all, no people, no stress, just nature and animals'.

I said that sounded a bit like Mike's description. The group agreed and added that many of them felt like they wanted that. Someone used the word 'escapist'. At this point I noted how different I felt in the group. It seemed warmer and the conversation seemed greatly eased. 'I do want to escape', said Vic, 'drinking is one big escape'.

*Figure 7.5* Vic's picture

At this point Vic turned to Mike and said 'I wanted to ask you earlier, but somehow it felt too hard to. Have you actually tried living in that sort of place?' Mike replied that he hadn't but thought it would be great. Vic then said 'In fact I've tried going to the countryside and it has been peaceful but only for a while. I get there and I begin to feel bored and that is the most dangerous time for me. In the end I drank there too.'

I was struck by how the initial unified front of the group was now dissolving. At the begining it seemed the way of preserving the group's unity was by only acknowledging the contrasting difference of the therapist to it. But now that the therapist was admitted as a more cooperative element, acknowledging differences between individual patients seemed to become more tolerable. I thought about the topic of boredom now current and linked it with the emptiness of there seeming to be no helpful relationship available.

I then said that it had looked as if some people had felt a bit bored in the group at the points where it had been difficult to talk about anxieties.

Robby said he had felt bored for a while but didn't now. 'It feels more interesting and deep' he concluded. It was now just about the end of the group. There was a short silence and I said that I had been struck by how the group had been anxious about me watching and this had made it difficult for people to use the space to think. The group stopped being anxious and boring, I thought, when people were more direct with me in asking what my role was and admitting to the worry about a stranger.

Vic said that put him in mind of his drinking because of social anxiety and being shy. I reiterated that it seemed that what we had learnt was how strong the effect of this was even though it was based on an untested assumption. I then said it was time to finish. Robby then said 'Thanks, that was good' the sentiment of which others echoed. In my mind I contrasted this ending with the start of the group.

———————

## THEORETICAL ISSUES

The theme from this case example on which I propose to concentrate is the difficulty this group had in admitting the therapist into it. This was evident in the initial unifying of them against me which left me feeling angry and useless. The image of the 'Magpie's eye' gave a safe form to the fantasies about the therapist and allowed the problem to be usefully worked on in the group. In my experience these processes form a particular feature that makes group work with drug and alcohol patients so distinctive. In order to expand upon this, I propose to discuss how an understanding of narcissistic pathology, which is commonly attributed to this patient group (Tahka 1979, Meissner 1980), can be of great help in understanding why therapeutic engagement of the patient is so problematic and how art therapy can offer workable solutions to this.

## FEATURES OF NARCISSISTIC PATHOLOGY

Narcissism as a general term concerns one's attitude to oneself. A certain amount of self interest is a central part of being healthy and good self esteem is helped by having a realistic sense of one's own strengths and weaknesses, gained through self observation. Pathological narcissism refers to self interest in a different service. Here the view of the self is partial, where positive aspects are held onto defensively and negative ones are disowned.

The etiology of narcissistic disturbance can be located in a critical failure of empathy in the early parent–child relationship. The consistency amongst life histories show how commonly this does occur for people with drug and alcohol problems. Pathological narcissism describes the child's defensive structures formed in response to this failure in empathy. Here, interest is withdrawn from the mother and redirected onto the favoured aspects of the ego. As Freud (1913) points out, if one cannot fall in love with the mother one must fall in love with one's self. Being filled with this interest, the ego artificially inflates. The individual develops grandiose fantasies of his importance as a direct compensation for the actual paucity of received empathy. The void left between parent and child easily casts a fearful aspect onto the actual parent and this reinforces the child's attempt at a kind of 'do-it-yourself' parenting strategy. The image of the 'Magpie's eye' is a clear example of the fearfulness of the unconscious parental figure which so inhibits accepting help from others.

This pathogenic situation is one where the child is having to empathise with the parent, rather than the other way around. The child's withdrawal of needs may be connoted as 'being good' by the parent and this reinforces the process. This 'good', 'false self' (as Winnicott [1986] termed it), leaves the 'true-self' unowned and infantile. The salient point here is that the 'false-self' constitutes an over-adaption to the perceived needs of the 'other'. In adult life, narcissistic individuals have little sense of personal identity and in the absence of being able to gain empathy tend to become the same as who they are with. This rather confusing phenomenon occurs because they cannot identify their own needs. Yet this merging with 'the other' is unconsciously a struggle to omnipotently regain archaic levels of intimacy, that is intimacy without reciprocity. Trying to live through other people usually becomes unsatisfying and reinforces pessimism about the potential for relationships as any source of help or enrichment.

The drug and alcohol culture is one that is exclusive and feared, and this adds to a general prejudice against people with these problems. In my experience, few types of patients are so unpopular with general psychiatric care staff as these. They are described by some staff as being deviant, abusive towards others, demanding and unable to self accuse. Their distinction is such that it usually is deemed necessary to separate them from the general psychiatric milieu and create specialist drug and alcohol services for them.

Such negative feedback from others generally reinforces the drive for relief through means other than human relationships, such as with drugs or alcohol, which in giving false feelings of being connected to others becomes part of a compulsive self reliant pattern. This can create a potentially dangerous state of affairs for the individual. Being able to self-medicate against unwanted feelings adds to the fantasy of omnipotence. This makes it hard for the individual to maintain appropriate concern for himself, as is so evident in the life-threatening consequences of substance misuse.

In discussing this pathology I would add that narcissistic disturbance must be considered as existing on a spectrum. It ranges from the merely shy to the frankly psychopathic. Whilst the drug and alcohol patient group may be restricted in the breadth of pathology, it varies greatly in its severity and depth. In considering this Meissner (1980: 300) suggests that the narcissistic individual's preferences for the compensatory effects of particular substances is indicative of important differences in the features of this single core pathology.

Having outlined the pathology in terms of how it affects relationships

I would now like to consider points that the therapist needs to bear in mind when encountering it within the art therapy group.

Therapy for narcissistically disturbed people rests on being able to first help them reclaim their unwanted feelings. If these feelings can be found and tolerated, the need to be rid of them through substance misuse is dramatically lessened. This short description of the aim of the therapy in no way describes how difficult that task is and why there is such resistance to it from narcissistically disordered patients. Miller (1979) rightly points out that any problems with relating generally are particularly heightened in the therapeutic relationship, where the therapist will be seen 'as if' he were the original care giver. Because most of these patients had such poor maternal relationships it will be hard for them to see the therapist as helpful. Not only this, but any admission of needing help from another is at once a puncture in the grandiosity of feeling self sufficient and a cause for envy. Kernberg (1975) suggests that the central tragedy of narcissism is that the patients who have the most need are least able to accept help. This most basic of issues, the contracting of a therapeutic alliance between patient and therapist is immediately a problem, as shown in the case study.

The therapist attempts to create an environment safe enough for patients to allow their anxieties and defences to come to the fore. It is these that I wish to concentrate on next.

## ENGAGING THE GROUP – THE 'THEM AND US' STAND OFF

In group psychotherapy the optimal therapeutic effect rests on the embracing of the heterogeneous aspects of the group's membership, including the therapist (Foulkes, 1975). A mixture of different problems implies then, a mixture of different individual resources. However, difference also creates an inherent tension, which can be a source of anxiety. Groups need to work to accept and use their differences. When this is successfully managed each individual will contribute from their own unique perspective. This all increases the capacity of the group's collective ego and makes it a resource above the individual's. By engaging this collective ego, the individual can eventually internalise new approaches to situations and feelings and so change.

To dedicate an art therapy group, or any psychotherapy group, to a defined and exclusive patient group will therefore have a marked effect on how that group can function therapeutically. It can be argued, however, that certain gains can be made by moving to a homogeneous group format. The initial shame at admitting an inability to control drinking or drug taking is lessened by having the differences between group members de-emphasised. Patients do say that 'all being in the same boat' accelerates their ability to discuss their situations in the group because they feel understood by those who have had similar problems. This principle is employed in addiction support groups such as 'Alcoholics Anonymous'.

Gains made through homogeny in groups nevertheless have a price. Support groups function differently from psychotherapy groups. The speeding up of the patients' initial engagement in the group has been achieved at the cost of reducing the group's therapeutic resources. Any group which builds its safety only on uniformity is liable to become fragile when individual differences begin to appear. To not recognise the distinction between homogeneous and heterogeneous functioning in groups can put the therapist in the difficult situation of potentially becoming locked in this pastiche of individual therapy where the group becomes to all intents an individual patient and the therapist must provide the 'antidote' for a common pathology. This keeps the therapist rather central and may inhibit contributions from other patients. In the extreme, if patients define their unity by being the same as each other and distinct from the therapist they cannot accept or internalise the therapist or his therapy. Indeed it has been suggested that: 'It is a feature of psychotherapy groups with patients sharing the same pathology, that the patients collude together to stop the psychotherapy progressing' (Temple *et al.* 1996: 246).

It is a consideration for the practitioner working in drug and alcohol teams that the very fact of these treatments being exclusively dedicated, acts contextually against heterogeneous functioning within the group. It can only be seen as an efficiency to group together patients who have problems of a similar nature if one assumes that they need a similar remedy. Crudely speaking, this rationale might be seen as an extension of the medical model because it assumes that for any specific condition there is a uniformly matching treatment. This assumption sits well with the behaviourally orientated interventions, because here there is a common 'antidote' of coping skills to be administered. In such cases the group is a forum for teaching and not the central therapeutic resource. Homogeny puts this common group task more sharply in focus because it suggests: 'we are here to look at what is common amongst us, namely our drug and alcohol problems'. But if, as in the case of art therapy, the focus is shifted within this context from being a group-as-forum-for-teaching onto a group-as-central-therapeutic agent, then some potential confusion needs to be pre-empted by the therapist. I find it useful to follow Yalom's (1975) suggestion that the therapist be explicit in introducing the group as focused not on drink and drugs, but on what occurs within the individual as they relate to the group.

Drug and alcohol patients tend to prefer homogeneous styles of groups because they find differences between people so difficult. The 'false-self' defence creates a tendency to over-identify with each other's perceived similarities, resulting in the defensive 'huddling together' evident in the case study. The group's plot to all draw the same image can also be viewed as evidence of this and as an attempt to be rid of any rivalrous feelings in the group. The danger of unifying against the therapist is that this is also a rejection of the therapy process he represents. Being shut out of the group is not always limited to the therapist though. On other occasions, I have found myself trying to support those patients who by exploring personal feelings stray from the uniformity of the group and find themselves treated in a severely cool manner by others. To be seen as siding with the therapist against the group, is quite a deterrent for any patient contemplating moving away from the joint narcissistic defence.

This type of 'them and us' stand off between group and therapist needs careful handling. In writing up the case study earlier I was struck by how I experienced such extremes of feeling in quick succession throughout the session. These feelings need to be linked to the events of the group and are ignored at the therapist's peril. I have observed on numerous occasions how the passive resistance in groups can infuriate staff to the point of either swearing at patients and/or storming out of sessions. Deskilling and infuriating the therapist out of his or her role may be viewed as a form of 'dethroning' the mother as an envious attack on his or her imagined power. It is my opinion that patients would prefer to make the therapist shout at them and retain a feeling of being in control, rather than face a therapist who can maintain their empathetic stance against such countertransference. Donnellan and Toon (1986) link the harshness of some non-psychotherapeutically orientated substance misuse treatments to an acting out of the patients own self destructive projections.

## A GROUP WITH NO PATIENTS

The case example highlights another related defence against engaging the therapist. When Robby was adamant that the best way of staying sober was to not think about drinking, he was attempting to alter the therapeutic alliance so that our two roles become the same. The patient as a person needing help is removed from the therapeutic relationship and is replaced by a person who is apparently an expert on his own problems. This can often be sensed when one has the disquieting feeling that the discourse in the group is between a series of professionals who are all talking about someone else who is the patient. It is particularly a feature of drug and alcohol work because often the patient can quote volumes of minutiae about their chosen substances. This deluge of detail often obscures the fact that the patient's history attests to them being anything but the expert on being abstinent.

In a similar vein I am often told, in rather patronising tones, that I should realise substance misusers all understand each other more than non-substance misusers can understand them. If this notion is pursued fully in the groups it often comes to light that the fantasied other substance misuser with whom so much empathy is expected must have so many identical qualities to the individual that they cannot truly be described as 'other' at all. The communication is that the patients can only relate to a mirror image of themselves and here one is reminded of the mytho-logical Narcissisus forsaking all others in order to gaze lovingly at his own reflection. This can leave the therapist feeling irrelevant and useless, just as the nymph Echo did. It was notable that the imagery at the start of the group was of an idealised place which offered great support. It could be conceived that this is the imagery of the longing to bypass the present therapist in order to reach a more ideal object.

Essentially all the defences I have so far described aim to use the 'false-self' to keep the therapist at a tolerable distance. These anxieties are often prevalent at the early stages of any therapy group but they are particularly emphasised with drug and alcohol patients. It is the level of psychic functioning behind these initial 'false-self' defences which, if accessed, reveal the reason for such defensive manoeuvring. This has been referred to by Rosenfeld (1971: 169) as the hidden transference in narcissistic disorders.

Once patients do begin to engage beyond the 'false-self' level, it becomes apparent how immature the once 'hermetically sealed' ego is. The compulsion to self-reliance is paradoxically a representation of how feared the individual's own unconscious dependency is. Anxiety about not being able to cope with ambivalent feelings towards the care giver is high. If all hope is invested in the therapist there is a fear of a collapse into despair at the loss of the ideal object, should he fail to be perfect. Moreover, any frustration with the therapist may incite the patient to want to destroy him, regardless of losing everything themselves. Early maternal experience has generally taught these patients that they cannot look to their own parents for help in processing such ambivalence. Expressing negative feelings directly to the carers and maintaining any hope of help from them or of care being continued is seen as impossible. Hence ambivalence becomes unconscious and is as Svrakic (1985) suggests replaced by an all-pervasive pessimism as to being able to find any satisfaction from reciprocal relationships. Experiencing the loss of other group members through relapses illuminates this process. On these occasions, it is frightening for the patient to see that the therapist is not omnipotent and cannot guarantee absolute safety from self-destruction for the group members. At moments like this the group may take the confusing step of attempting to appease the therapist and displace the dissatisfaction. When patients bemoan motivation of other patients or, in the case example, the deficient skills of other staff, it is vital that such criticisms are drawn back onto the therapist. It is an enormous relief for the group when, without being punitive, the therapist can be the bad object and voice what feels 'forbidden', e.g., that it is the present staff member that the group may be doubting.

The particular danger then in the treatment of patients with narcissistic disorders is that they will engage convincingly, but only at a 'false-self' level which results in them saying all the right things in therapy, but making no change emotionally. I would now like to look at how art therapy can be of use in managing this considerable resistance to engagement.

## ENGAGEMENT BY PROXY IN ART THERAPY

Although there are considerable difficulties in treating exclusively dedicated drug and alcohol groups, this has not resulted in their being abandoned by group therapists. Knauss and Freund (1985) and Arroyave (1990) have championed the use of modified group psychotherapy for this patient group within the public services.

Art therapy has generated its own body of literature on drug and alcohol work, but little of it relates to groups. However, some of the principles discussed in individual work are applicable to the group setting. Albert-Puleo (1980) suggests that art therapy is particularly useful for engaging narcissistic patients because the presence of the art object in the therapy offers the patient the facility of regulating the distance between themselves and the therapist. It seems to me that this distance regulation has several aspects in group work. The relationship with the therapist can be de-emphasised by the experience of withdrawing into a narcissistic reverie during the image production phase. Paradoxically, the image that is produced can then bring into therapy transference material otherwise not available through the relationships in the group. This material is then reintroduced back into the group during the discussion of the images which offers additional symbolic forms with which the patient can process it. I would now like to expand upon this.

The patient's relationship with their image is of a different nature to their relationship with others in the group because the activity of image production demands a solitary approach. At the start of the group patients were unwilling to separate from their uniformity, thereby denying the potential for relationships. This was in marked contrast to how they related to the image production. Their defensive plan of colluding together to all draw the image can be seen not only as an example of trying to be identical, but moreover as a way of being solitary by denying relationships. The plan was abandoned in favour of solitary relationships with their own individual images. These patients were typical in how, despite initial protests, they settled into a silent reverie with their images. Their preference for entering the image production phase may be understood by the fact that no-one else paints their picture and this tends to support a sense of omnipotence. Whilst there may be frustrations in execution at a technical level, these seem to be less than the anxieties of relating to a therapist, whose 'otherness' threatens the patients' omnipotence more. The patient can be the lord of all they survey in their image, and the image concedes without demanding anything in return. This reduction in reciprocity is attractive to such regressive patients. In life they are unable to negotiate engaging their needs equally in human relationships and so drink because they want something external to make them feel better. For this service they hope to have to give nothing in return. It is clear from an observer's distance that much is asked in return for this service, but in the actual moment of putting alcohol to the lips the fantasy is clearly that this will make all well. Image making may be seen as attractive because some of the process resembles substance consumption. I suggested earlier that these patients often fantasise about the existence somewhere of a relationship with someone who has identical attributes and is totally empathetic. In having such an exclusive relationship with their image, some of this need is gratified. Narcissus is offered the mirror. During image production the patient may turn away from relationships and enter their narcissism. Art therapy uniquely allows such a legitimate degree of departure from directly relating to the therapist to exist within the bounds of the therapy.

In this way the paradoxical notion of a group of narcissists is made possible.

Lachman-Chapin (1983) suggests that this reduction in relationships during the image production in art therapy also reduces potential shame at expressing such archaic longings for merger with an all empathetic object. Inherent in this longing is the dilemma that Winnicott (1970) refers to as wanting to hide and be seen at the same time. I think that the role of images in art therapy can offer some resolution to this. The image invested with personal material can stand in for the maker who is otherwise secreted behind a 'false-self'. When it is seen in therapy, it allows the maker to feel seen indirectly. These archaic longings are often so well hidden that the only other indication of their existence is expressed by the action of abusing substances. Andrew's attitude in the group was an example of this. In the group he claims to hate alcohol, yet only days ago was vigorously pursuing his consuming passion for it, regardless of the consequences to himself and those around him. Because he offered his 'false-self' to the therapy, the needy person never entered treatment, leaving us feeling that we had the wrong patient. Interestingly, the ruthlessness attributed to the Magpie actually describes well this type of patient's passion for drinking.

I would suggest that the production of images in itself is not enough to produce a therapeutic effect. It is true that in art therapy the patient's withdrawal from the therapist into image making does not put them outside the bounds of the greater therapeutic relationship. This is the notion of the art therapy triangular relationship between therapist, image and patient. But the balance of all aspects of the triangle must be maintained. I have explored in a previous paper (Springham 1994) how patients resist links between the discussion material and the art objects within the group. When the patient marginalises the present therapist by relating only to their image and the therapist unconsciously colludes with this by not viewing image in the context of their relationship, the danger is that the image production process stops being therapeutic and becomes part of the very narcissistic defence it sought to engage.

The case study shows how my position is to consider all the images as indirect communications about how the patient is construing the relationships in the therapy session. Therefore, even when the patient is more distant from the therapist during image production, the art serves as a vehicle for processing their present relationships. In this way the art therapist is never fully 'out of the picture'. The images are of great value as representations of this otherwise hidden material which can so easily be lost in the discussion phase of the group.

The permanence of the art object and the disclosure it carries, can later be a source of anxiety for the patient when it comes to the group discussion of the images. Returning to the relationships with the other group members once back in the circle, the patients seem often rather surprised, even disturbed, by how absorbed they had been with their images. There are now anxieties about how the images will be received and what others, primarily the therapist, will see in their work. 'I worry about what I've said without knowing it' one patient once said to me. In the case study this was evident in the initial resistance to taking the images seriously. Patients need to be helped greatly at this juncture because they are anxious that their images will have breached their own 'false-self' defences, thus bringing problems in the continuation of care to ensue. The style of therapy that I use is more active in this sense because I have found that these links need to be forcefully maintained.

Against considerable anxiety from the group, the art therapist has to be firm in their conviction that the revealing in the group of privately made visual communications is helpful. Art making has the value of offering access to an additional set of symbolic visual forms to process this anxiety. That which cannot be spoken may possibly be shown. The image of the 'Magpie's eye' is an example of how the hidden negative transference could be embodied in an image and then reconsidered verbally in this safer form. The group's resonance with this image increased as more members contributed their associations, so that it developed into an image of the shared pathology of the group. Now, instead of an undiscussible sense of dread about the presence of the therapist, the issue could eventually be named. The taboo of having negative feelings towards, and about, the 'mother' could materialise in concrete form only because it was born in a moment of narcissistic reverie whilst making the images. In the patient's fantasy, this ideal mother could more readily see than be told, that her child had negative feelings towards her. Moreover, in reality no punishment ensued.

In the light of day, which is the light of the collective ego of the group, this nightmare mother of the Magpie could be discussed. Whereas previously the therapist was perceived to actually *be* a predatory mother who would steal more than she gave, now the therapist becomes *as if* he has those qualities. This reviewed figure of the actual therapist is less frightening than the transference laden one and so might more readily be engaged as a helpful object. If the relationship to the therapist can become more tolerable, then the patient moves towards being able to tolerate a general heterogenic culture in the group. It was notable in the case study that different points of view were permitted in the group only after the image of the Magpie had been worked through. Vic's comments to Mike were a very useful contribution to the fantasy of escape, which in this group related strongly to escape from the therapist.

Whilst this group managed to find 'the patient', it does happen of course, that some drug and alcohol groups can be so defensive that engagement does not take place. Also, with such damaged patients, once dealt with, the ambivalence about the therapist easily becomes intolerable again. But the value of the art therapy process at these times is that they have recourse to the paradoxical function of the art object as a barrier against relating until a new conception of him can be found. I have found that the work of engaging the patient in this way in art therapy tends to aid their engagement with other groups on the programme. The repetition of this process can offer the patient helpful insight into what goes wrong in their relationships, and this can be a guide to making them more satisfying. The longer term implication of this is that it can signal that life without substance misuse is more tolerable if one can engage one's needs reciprocally in human relationships.

## BIBLIOGRAPHY

Albert-Puleo, N. (1980) 'Modern psychoanalytic art therapy and its implications to drug abuse'. *The arts in psychotherapy*, vol. 17, pp. 43–52.

Arroyave, F. (1990) 'The group analytic treatment of drinking problems'. *Spheres of Group Analysis*, p. 109–17.

Donnellan and Toon (1986) 'The use of 'therapeutic techniques' in the concept house model of therapeutic community for drug abusers. For whose benefit – staff or residents?' *International journal of therapeutic communities*, vol. 7 (3), pp. 36–42.

Foulkes, S.H. (1975) *Group Analytic Psychotherapy. Methods and Principles.* London: Gordon and Breach. Reprinted London: Karnac, 1986.

Freud, S. (1913) 'On narcissism'. *Collected works*, vol. XIV.

Kernberg, O. (1975) *Borderline Conditions and Pathological Narcissism.* New York: Jason Aronson.

Knauss, W. and Freund, H. (1985) 'Group-analytic psychotherapy with alcoholic inpatients'. *Group Analysis*, XVIII/2, pp. 124–30.

Lachman-Chapin, M. (1983) 'Kohut's theories on narcissism: Implications for art therapy.' *American Journal of Art Therapy*, vol. 19, October, pp. 3–9.

Meissner, W. (1980) 'Addiction and paranoid process'. *International Journal of Psychoanalysis*, vol. 8, pp. 278–310.

Miller, A. (1979) 'The drama of the gifted child and the psychoanalyst's narcissistic disturbance'. *International Journal of Psychoanalysis*, vol. 60, pp. 47–61.

Rosenfeld, D. (1971) 'A clinical approach to the life and death instincts: An investigation into the aggressive aspect of narcissism'. *Journal of psychoanalysis*, vol. 52, pp. 169–77.

Springham, N. (1992) 'Short term group processes in art therapy for people with substance misuse problems'. *Inscape*, Spring, pp. 8–16.

—— (1994) 'Research into patients' reactions to art therapy on a drug and alcohol programme'. *Inscape*, vol. 2, pp. 36–40.

Svrakic, D. (1985) 'Emotional Features of Narcissistic Personality Disorder'. *American Journal of Psychiatry*, 142: 6, June, pp. 720–4.

Tahka, J. (1979) 'Alcoholism as a narcissistic disturbance'. *Psychiatria Fennica*, pp. 129–39.

Temple, N., Walker, J. and Evans, M. (1996) 'Group psychotherapy with psychosomatic and somatising patients in a general hospital'. *Psychoanalytic Psychotherapy*, vol. 10, No. 3, pp. 251–68.

Winnicott, D. (1970) *Playing and reality*. London: Penguin.

—— (1986) 'The concept of false self'. *Home is where we start from*, London: Pelican Books, pp. 65–71.

Yalom, I. (1975) *The theory and practice of group psychotherapy*. New York: Basic Books.

# Chapter 8

# Long-stay art therapy groups

*Jane Saotome*

## INTRODUCTION

This chapter will look back at the role of the 'group' within the 'traditional' form of art therapy as it was practised in long-stay psychiatric hospitals and at developments in groups in this rapidly diminishing setting. A small scale M.A. research project which I undertook in the early 1990s indicated a confusion of practice, but one in which some common features were discernible. Some of the findings from this research will be presented. Case material from an on-going (over many years) art therapy group of long-stay residents of a psychiatric hospital who are now awaiting resettlement outside will be discussed. Pivoting uneasily between hospital and 'community care' the group illustrates the difficulties of transition from long-stay patient to long-term client and the parallel transition and changes within art therapy practice in this setting.

The role of the containing art room space and the flexibility of art therapy in institutions to engage a diversity of sometimes anxious, disturbed and confused patients within a group setting, have been vital characteristics of practice. The slow run-down to closure of the hospital where I work has resulted in a reduction, to some extent, of this dynamic containing function. It has been replaced by what I think of as the imperative of the ending. That is, the inevitability of the hospital closure has on varying levels been understood by the few remaining residents and that this factor underlies and has caused changes in the art therapy group to be discussed. The fear, uncertainty and sense of loss surrounding the process of moving into the community after decades of institutional living have been powerfully, if sometimes obliquely, reflected in material brought to sessions. Consequently the group has become more cohesive, intense and focused. At the same time, the group, whose members all suffer from long-term psychotic illnesses, could not function within a formal or rigid model of art therapy practice. It necessarily maintains some features common to the earliest forms of art therapy in large psychiatric hospitals.

## RESEARCH

My research, which was completed in 1993, was an investigation into art therapy practice with groups of long-stay residents in the few remaining large psychiatric hospitals. From the beginning the concept of what constitutes 'a group' and how it is described made research difficult. Even prior to the pilot study, in conversations with art therapists it became clear that descriptions such as 'open group', 'closed group', 'art psychotherapy group' or 'group' itself were confused, not universally defined, and subject to scrutiny from recently qualified art therapists well versed in group dynamics and group analytic theory. Art therapy litera-ture provided a historical perspective and a definition of early practice in the 'Studio Based Open Group' (Case and Dalley, 1992), together with descriptions of later development into more formalised models of practice. These formed a useful base from which to proceed.

Art therapy groups in long-stay psychiatric hospitals have their origins in the 'Studio Based Open Group' which evolved in this setting in the 1940s. Considered the traditional or 'classic' form of art therapy practice (Case and Dalley, 1992) it developed out of art studios opened in psychiatric hospitals mainly for recreational use (Waller, 1992). Since its origins are located before the establishment of art therapy training, practice was largely informed by individual therapists' experience of art schools, colleges, etc., and any experience of therapy they may have had (Case and Dalley, 1992; Waller, 1992).

The essential definition of the 'Studio Based Open Group' is that work is on an individual basis but within a group setting. The role of the 'group' appears unclear and is presented in the art therapy literature as being of secondary or little importance. The suggestion is that the dynamics operating within these groups, though sometimes acknowledged are not utilised. Case and Dalley describe this kind of group: 'art is regarded as the medium of treatment rather than the group. The therapist relates to each member individually and will probably talk to each one in turn, sometimes at length' (Case and Dalley, 1992: 196). Approaches to individual work within these sessions differ, encompassing wide variations of theoretical and idiosyncratic practice. Early examples of this are Adamson working in the late 1940s and early 1950s, believing in the 'inherent healing' nature of art but with a structural research based medical brief (Waller, 1991), and Lydiatt in the 1950s with a developed Jungian perspective (Thomson, 1989). My research suggests that comparable diversity remains evident in the 1990s (Saotome, 1993).

Although the group setting in this model of practice might then be viewed as primarily the context for individual work, the ethos which was actively fostered from the earliest art therapists working in psychiatric hospitals indicates that senses of containment and commonality in a social context might be considered significant features of practice.

I suggest that although these early 'groups' might not be considered groups from a group psychotherapy perspective, these factors pertain to more formalised and psychodynamic models of practice. They were a vital and necessary ingredient of sessions and have recurred in the 'community'.

Some characteristics that recur throughout the history of the 'Studio Based Open Group' seem unlikely facilitators of any sense of 'group'. They were none the less utilised by art therapists to engage and accommodate complex hospital populations which contained large numbers of residents suffering the effects of serious psychotic 'illnesses'. Sessions could be 'open' to anybody from various wards or client groups within the hospital or from the whole hospital. There were many self or informal referrals, time boundaries were relaxed (Case and Dalley, 1992), patients moving in and out of sessions and generally there was a sense of informality with refreshments provided and sometimes music would be played (Case and Dalley, 1992; Warsi, 1975). However, this informality, a necessity considering the client group, was used to foster a social context. Warsi, writing in 1975, describes her art therapy department as 'a sort of community in which warm relationships are established and strong social links forged' (Warsi, 1975). Tea breaks might be shared and this obviously promoted a feeling of commonality and introduced some form of structure, however loosely.

The role of the art room as a shared space was (and still is) instrumental in providing a sense of containment. There is an emphasis in relevant art therapy literature on this aspect of the 'Studio Based Open Group'. Popularly the art room has been referred to as 'an asylum within an asylum'. Adamson referred to it as 'an oasis' (Adamson, 1990). It is mentioned by Case and Dalley (1992), Charlton (1984), Thomson (1989), Warsi (1978), and Wood (1992). A letter from Goldsmith quoted by Case and Dalley (1992) described work influenced by Killick (1991) in which the art room is utilised as 'part of the "basic work" and not only as the "frame" or "context" of the work' with 'psychotic' patients in a large psychiatric hospital (Case and Dalley, 1992). Killick herself provides detailed descriptions of her use of the art room environment in a theoretical-based approach to work with psychotic patients (Killick, 1996; Killick, 1997). 'The rules and boundaries structuring the concrete availability and use of space, time, equipment and materials, as well as of the person of the therapist, form points of contact with the reality which psychotic processes attack' (Killick, 1996). Work with long-term clients in the community clearly involves the loss of the containing, specialised art room space. Greenwood and Layton working in the community with long-term clients suggest that this absence means that 'art therapy has to be separated and integrated at a psychic level rather than a physical one' (Greenwood and Layton, 1987).

The ethos and the social context of the early studio based open sessions, together with the sharing of the art room environment, the materials and the therapist, plus the fact that much of the work done would be fairly visible to everyone, points to an interplay between these factors and the individual work made and then related to separately with the therapist. The concept of 'group', though not declared the 'medium' of treatment, was surely evident and of therapeutic value to residents attending sessions.

Some of the characteristic features of the 'Studio Based Open Group' have survived in the hospital setting (Case and Dalley, 1992) and re-occur with comparable groups in the community (Lewis, 1990), but according to Waller and Dalley (1992), there was a gradual development from the early studio based open sessions into a more formalised model with fixed time boundaries and an increased awareness of group dynamics, which was the result of the establishment of art therapy training in the 1970s. There is some evidence of work using themes and group tasks within the hospital population (Charlton, 1984) and in the community (Greenwood and Layton, 1987) which supports Waller and Dalley's suggestion and points to an interest in cohesive or focused groups referring loosely to a framework of group analysis, as opposed to individual work within a group setting.

The findings of my research, although on a small scale, confirmed that some form of the 'Studio Based Open Group' had survived in the retracting long-stay hospitals and that equally some art therapy practice in these hospitals involved more formalised groups. In spite of these differences and in variations of therapists' theoretical and philosophical orientations, most practice was linked by basic similarities. These were that work was on an individual basis in a group setting, a social context and the long-term nature of therapy.

Data was collected from six registered art therapists working in different hospitals with eleven 'groups' comprised of residents from within long-stay populations. It was possible to loosely categorise these groups based on similarities of practice.

Three groups most clearly resembled the traditional 'Studio Based Open Group'. Sessions were unstructured and 'open' to either anyone from within a hospital or an area of a hospital. There was a mixing of clients, a broad range of ages and lengths of time spent in hospital. A high degree of informality was maintained, music could be played, tea and coffee were available for residents to make at any time. The art rooms used for these sessions were the only ones in this study in which large amounts of two- and three-dimensional work were highly visible, and for me they were reminiscent of art rooms in psychiatric hospitals in the 1970s.

Four groups I defined as 'cohesive groups'. They were largely formalised, with a stable number of referred attendees who, in contrast to the 'open groups', tended to come from a shared area of the long-stay population. There seemed to be a clear intention of group identity, although this was little reflected upon. The provision of tea or coffee played an important part in structuring sessions, marking beginnings and middles of sessions. Three of these groups had also some markings of endings with occasional tentative sharing of images.

Two art therapists in this study ran 'groups' that dealt specifically with clients who had a diagnosis of psychosis. They had a shared theoretical base, which affected some aspects of practice. Both cited the influence of the art therapist Killick. There was less interest here in the institutional context than in psychotherapeutic encounters with psychotic processes. The therapists involved would not perhaps consider that they were working with groups as such, although numbers of clients would be working together in the art room.

Two further groups were not easily categorised; one which involved long-stay patients on a medium secure unit was fragmented, although in intention it had features of a cohesive group. The other group involved long-stay patients, together with elderly admission clients being assessed. It was structured so that clients arrived at fifteen minute intervals, otherwise the sessions were unstructured.

Similarities between the 'groups' in this study tended to outweigh differences, suggesting some fundamental characteristics of work with long-stay clients. In all eleven 'groups' the therapist related separately to clients about their work at different times during sessions. Some therapists moved around the room while others engaged with clients about their work when the clients indicated or requested the therapist to do so. In one 'group' individual sessions were allocated in a side office to which work done in the 'studio' could be brought. There were very few structures to facilitate group processes. There was a fixed start and finish time in all groups and structuring revolving around the provision of tea and coffee in the 'cohesive' groups. Apart from the occasional sharing of images at the end of sessions in the cohesive groups and evidence that spontaneous discussions about work sometimes arose in 'open' sessions, there was no sustained collective discussion or exploration of work.

The question then is, are these eleven 'groups' groups in any psychotherapeutic sense of the word and what is the role of the 'group setting'? Some therapists involved here, as previously mentioned, would not profess to be working with groups. The sense of 'groupness' in these sessions appears to relate to the social context and to the on-going, long-term nature of therapy. What is not clear is perhaps how the social context is integrated with or affects the making of images.

Long-stay residents of psychiatric hospitals are described by Leff as 'a very socially deprived group of people' (Leff, 1991: 31) (a description which equally fits long-term clients in the community). A series of research schedules undertaken in 1988, which involved 770 long-stay residents of two psychiatric hospitals, revealed the extreme poverty of these residents' social networks (NETRHA, 1988), a result of both the stigmatisation and socially disabling effects of their 'illnesses' and of long-term institutionalisation. The schedules showed for example that 20 per cent of residents had no friends whatsoever, three-quarters had no relatives in their network and 90 per cent had no contacts in the community. The median social network was between eight and nine people. Two-thirds did not include any staff in their network. In the light of this, the social context of art therapy 'groups', its long-term prospects and the client–therapist relationship would seem significant features of practice.

All eleven 'groups' in my research ran without a fixed termination time. Nine of the 'groups' had been on-going over many years with a stable core of regular attenders. In fact, some groups could be viewed as a consistent (and shared) part of residents' lives. The long-term aspect of art therapy practice with long-stay clients has clear implications for the client–therapist relationship. What is the nature of therapy that has no clear concept or expectation of end (endings in this setting may now revolve around uncertain dates for hospital closures)? What role does the art therapist have in a relationship which may span many years (one client–therapist relationship in my research spanned nineteen years)? The long-term aspects of therapy with comparable client groups are evident in the community and are commented on by Lewis and Wood both working in community settings (Lewis, 1990; Wood, 1992). Wood reflects on the possible blurring and confusion over therapeutic boundaries (Wood, 1992). Within the research some therapists commented on the familiarity that is built up over years and that they were fairly open with clients, revealing some personal aspects of themselves. This openness is echoed to some extent in the work of Greenwood and Layton (1987), involving a community-based group for clients with serious long-term 'illnesses'. 'The relationship is felt to be an empathic sharing in openness . . . the therapist joining in the art work and being prepared to disclose something of themselves verbally . . . ' (p. 14). They call this the 'side by side' approach. In contrast, the two art therapists in my research, working clearly from a theoretical base concentrating on the psychopathology of psychosis, felt that boundary issues for these clients were fundamental and stressed the maintaining of the boundaries of the client–therapist relationship.

The characteristics of the 'Studio Based Open Group' developed in response to both the needs of long-stay residents of psychiatric hospitals (many of whom were suffering the debilitating effects of psychotic illnesses) and to the nature of psychiatric institutions themselves. That is, art therapists were working with both the problems of long-term mental illness and the effects of institutionalisation. The process of institutionalisation, however, so exacerbates the problems of mental illness that it is almost impossible to distinguish between them. Art therapy literature and my own research indicate that art therapists working in this setting had a developed awareness of the effects of institutionalisation and that countering these effects was a major underlying aim of practice (Charlton, 1984; Case and Dalley, 1992; Goodwin, 1978; Skailes, 1997). Within my research common aims were cited as: the provision of the private 'space', self-motivation, 'fighting' apathy and lethargy and the increase of self-esteem and self-worth. Three therapists stressed the creative 'process' and that the image is somehow a reflection of self and there is the possibility of re-integration. The emphasis here clearly remains on individual work, with the role of the group setting in the background but generally unremarked upon.

The gradual loss of the institutional context in art therapy practice with the long-term mentally ill has already brought about a re-focusing of therapeutic intentions with this client group in the community (Greenwood and Layton, 1987; Lewis, 1990). Clearly the absence of the worst aspects of institutionalisation will further affect practice, allowing a more psychodynamic approach within group settings. The continued moves within art therapy training towards more clearly defined psychotherapeutic intentions appear to include an increased interest in looking at approaches to clients suffering from serious psychotic illnesses. Recent literature is indicative of these developments (Killick, 1996; Killick and Schaverien, 1997). However, within this literature there remains an emphasis on individual work.

## A LONG-STAY GROUP

### History of the group

The group which I will discuss has been on-going for more than five years. From the beginning the group had many characteristics of a 'Studio Based Open Group'. At the same time it had some features of a more formalised model of practice, and in this respect the group fits into the category of Cohesive Groups which I defined in my research (see above). During the history of the group, changes occurred as a result of the rundown of the hospital and with the moving into the 'community' of all but the most frail, elderly or 'difficult' residents. There was a gradual and inevitable shift of focus in art therapy sessions from an involvement with countering the damaging effects of institutionalisation to containing the feelings about the loss of the institution as 'home', a known and 'safe' place. This group holds many painful contradictions.

In theory, the 'group' began as sessions open to long-stay residents of the hospital. There was an invitation to anyone interested to attend and referrals were informal. In practice, the same people tended to come every week so that a stable core of eight people was established with about five other less regular attendees, so that the situation became more formalised, although referrals remained informal. There was a growing understanding that this was a 'group' with a recognised membership. Time boundaries were fixed, though not always adhered to by some people. The sharing of tea or coffee, sitting in a circle of chairs, was utilised in sessions to give some form of structured beginning and to emphasise and encourage interaction. This became at times a quite lengthy verbal part of sessions. There was a relaxed and informal atmosphere, music was sometimes played, tea and coffee were available at any time if further required.

There was no formal discussion of work during or at the end of sessions. Partly because most members would have found this difficult, impossible or anxiety provoking and partly because there was no expectation that work would be finished in a particular set time, much work went on over weeks. Most of the work was done on a large central table (although some people chose to work on separate tables). All the images were seen by others and put, when desired, on the art room walls. Everyone had, or developed, highly individualistic and easily recognisable 'styles'. I frequently, but not always, painted during sessions. The images seemed to be a matter of personal agendas and generally I related separately to people. However, since work was easily visible, a real interest in each other's images developed and there was a marked increase in interaction around this. The acceptance and valuing of the images, by myself and the group members began to play a vital role. I thought of the images as a kind of reiteration and re-enforcement of a separate sense of self in the context of a group. In a hospital environment where the forced intimacy of having to live closely with many others is frequently defended against by withdrawal and the abandonment of 'normal' interactions, the group seemed to suggest the possibility that a personal and creative space could exist within a social and intimate context. The images themselves provided a sustaining link between us from week to week.

While maintaining its original format and ethos, changes occurred gradually in the group, the impetus coming from the shrinking of the hospital. The group became smaller as some members left to live in the community; one member died. We moved art rooms twice, the second move involving a situation where conversion work could be heard going on all around us. There was a feeling of siege and a definite drawing together. An increased sense of cohesion developed, with members playing more clearly discernible roles within the group. There was an intensification of the verbal and visual material brought to sessions and a greater interplay and integration between these aspects. The process of resettlement has been protracted over many months and years and the 'goal posts' have continually shifted, so that in a climate of extended uncertainty and anxiety there remained and remains a need for familiarity, almost a maintaining of morale. In this art therapy group the need for familiarity in the making and sharing of images on many levels runs parallel to the powerful undercurrents emerging in the group both verbally and visually.

The small current group now contains some of the last residents waiting to be moved out of the hospital which was once 'home' for nearly two thousand. It seems to carry the whole weight of the process of closure. The possibility of return to the hospital which was available to patients previously will no longer exist. These patients have experienced a slow erosion of their environment. People have 'disappeared' into the community, sometimes quite suddenly, often without a simple marking of transition such as photographs or farewell meals. Much of the hospital is closed, the chapel and social centre are gone, the long corridors lead to empty wards or refurbished offices. The fear and uncertainty evoked by this scenario in people whose grasp of 'reality' can be tentative was graphically bought to an art therapy session via the delusion of one of the group members (David, see below). David was transferred from another hospital when it was completely closed some years ago. He announced that genocide had gone on in that hospital. 'Where had everyone gone?' He had seen the ovens where the bodies were burnt, the same thing was going on in this hospital. This was met by silence from the group and with an acknowledgement from me that it was difficult to imagine where everyone had gone and I gave details of where past members of the group were now living. Later in the session another group member asked me if I knew a certain patient, because that patient was here, in the ashtray. The idea of patients disappearing, being got rid of (or burnt up) and not being wanted is an obvious undercurrent in a retracting hospital. It does also rebound backwards to the original experience of being put into an 'institution', unwanted and abandoned by family and society.

## The Current Group

In discussing the group I will give a brief description of group members (all names and identifying details have been changed) and the images which they make. I will follow this with notes on five consecutive weekly sessions. They illustrate the recurring concerns of group members, the interactions and structure within the group and the relationship between verbal and visual aspects of sessions.

## Group Members

The group is presently made up of four men in their sixties and two women in their forties. Everyone has spent all or the greater part of his or her adult life as a resident of a psychiatric hospital. None have been married, none have children and only two have (occasional) links with relatives outside the hospital. Two people (Tessa and David) have an on-going relationship with each other. Four of the group members (Tessa, David, Doris and Lewis) maintain a regular attendance at sessions, while two members (Charles and Spencer) at times find this more difficult. All have a diagnosis of schizophrenia, most have complicated delusional beliefs which are invariably brought to sessions. Delusions as well as 'odd' behaviour are well tolerated and accommodated in the group.

**DAVID**  David identifies himself as an artist and this role is conceded to him within the group. There is a general acceptance of his authoritative and philosophical comments on everyone's work as well as on things in general. His own images are usually deeply thought out, geometric abstracts drawn in pencil with a ruler. They have a strong spacial element and David's main concern seems to be a struggle to obtain what he describes as 'unbalanced, balanced'. He also says he is trying to achieve perfection. I have come to see David's struggle to achieve 'unbalanced, balanced' as an attempt to come to terms with internal struggles within himself.

David's major contribution to the group is that he brings a focus to the feelings of uncertainty and fear about the future. He sometimes does this with declarations which may contain 'delusional' material or oblique references. These usually make sense in the context of the situation and can mediate experiences and feelings which are shared by the whole group. His ideas about genocide have already been discussed (see above).

**TESSA**  Tessa is David's long-standing girlfriend. A rather child-like character many years David's junior, she is somewhat in his shadow. Their relationship is complex and can involve either of them not attending or not speaking due to some upset between them. A cause of distress for both has been delays and difficulties about moving them into the community together.

Tessa's images are usually tentative and sensitive drawings of items in the art room. At one time David instructed her how to make drawings by copying his own. Unsurprisingly, they looked unlike his and this realisation seemed to give Tessa confidence to make her 'own drawings' as well as emphasising her separateness. Tessa's role in the group is low-key but she occasionally adds to subjects by asking what words mean when the word has not been spoken or by making puns on words.

**DORIS**  Doris, who has mild learning difficulties, has several times in the group expressed her belief that she came into hospital to be changed into a 'new Doris'. A recent drawing shows herself, aged sixteen (thirty years ago) being brought to hospital for the first time by her mother to 'be changed into a new Doris', one which her 'mother will want'. Doris's need to be accepted and wanted as she actually is accounts for much of her behaviour within the group and to some extent the group is able to respond to these needs.

During the early, verbal, part of sessions, Doris is talkative and lively, seeking indulgence and affection. Her absence is always noted and felt. She is sometimes disruptive, sabotaging (or rescuing everyone from) serious discussion by bartering noisily for cigarettes or tobacco. Doris's simple paintings and drawings play an important and highly visible role in the group. She is anxious that all her images are put on the wall. While emphatic that they (and, by association, herself) are 'no good', she continually asks for our acceptance and praise. She in return is extremely liberal with her enthusiasm for everybody else's work.

Over many months Doris has made individual drawings of all of the people who have been, and still are, in the group. This includes myself, herself and any students or visitors who have attended sessions (Figure 8.1). Until recently these were put up prominently on one wall of the art room (and only taken down due to a move to a smaller room). They were a source of shared interest and amusement, they certainly facilitated a sense of unity in the group and provided a visual reminder of people who have left. These bold, black, felt-tip drawings were named by David as 'effigies', and he has referred to them on several occasions in this way. On one level there is a connotation of effigies as things which might be burnt up and got rid of. Another reference, perhaps, to one of the undercurrents in this group. A further connection in David's naming of the drawings as 'effigies' might be that Doris has a history of setting fires in relation to attempts to settle her in the 'community'. A recent incident of fire-setting on the ward in which three other group members (including David) live, resulted in her absence with an uncharacteristic but understandable expression of anger against her. Maybe reflecting the fears surrounding the uncertainty of their own futures, there was a suggestion that she would 'end up' in a 'special' hospital or a prison.

LEWIS   Lewis, a resident of the hospital for fifty-one years is the oldest member of the group. He has had one unsuccessful attempt at living in the community, returning after a few months. He is adamant that he will remain in hospital and is the only member of the group not being actively considered for a move. On return to the hospital he was relocated to a ward with less able patients than himself. Since then, this quiet but sociable and often humorous man has become increasingly

*Figure 8.1*  Some of Doris's 'effigies'

depressed. The possibility that change can be for the better, which might sustain optimism in other group members, is a matter of deep scepticism for Lewis.

At the beginning of sessions Lewis commonly recounts delusional ideas concerning the belief that he is dead, or that parts of him have died, and he expresses a wish to 'pack it all in'. Lewis often introduces some of the recurring themes in the group. For example, he makes repeated references to the passing of time, and he is concerned with his own and others' ages; in reference to the changes in the hospital he often asks 'where will it all end?' His despondency is reflected in his increased reliance on others in the group to provide him with an 'idea' for his drawings. Lewis's rather whimsical drawings of plants, flowers, animals and trees have generally become depleted in vitality.

CHARLES  Charles's involvement in art therapy is spasmodic with weeks of attendance followed by weeks of absence. He experiences high levels of anxiety and it is something of an achievement for him to remain for a whole session. Charles is aloof, suspicious of others and expresses guilt about conflicts between his religious beliefs and sexual matters. A conflict which is echoed in the contrast between his dignified manner and his sometimes 'shocking' sexual revelations. These revelations are generally ignored, the group showing a remarkable level of tolerance. Charles's paintings, however, can on occasions bring everyone together. Charles mainly concentrates on religious themes and one such painting depicted himself being prevented by Jesus from committing suicide. Charles's explanation of this picture had a dramatic effect on the group. It became apparent that everyone in the group had at some point in the distant past attempted suicide. These accounts were shared in an impromptu coffee break.

SPENCER  Spencer attends the group infrequently, often needing a reminder about sessions. A sociable but elusive character, he appears wearing an ever-changing array of head gear, a kind of shifting identity. This elusiveness is apparent in his images. Full of energy, they are a synthesis of abstract and representational elements. Unclear himself about his pictures (as he is about his identity) he readily seeks others' opinions about what they represent. Like Doris he is enthusiastic about having his pictures on the wall. He is happier if his images are grouped together, as if to reinforce each other.

## Sessions

The group necessarily maintains an acceptance of a level of chronicity. As such it does not deal specifically or directly with the psychopathology of 'mental illness'. Ideas of cure or even change are perhaps replaced by struggles of verbal and visual communication for people sharing some circumstances but having disturbed or differing 'realities'. Communication between members can be extremely subtle or inaccessible and the dynamics operating in the group can be difficult to perceive.

In these five sessions most verbal communication, apart from that involving practicalities, was addressed initially to, and then via, myself. It is a familiar pattern that requires a conscious effort to move away from. Group members seem to address me in order to test out and validate the significance of their comments. I am required, in part, to mediate a 'reality' for what at times can be a quite bizarre group. Group members appear to often defend against each other's distress, disturbance and delusional ideas by making no obvious or verbal response. (This, of course, in itself is a response.) The lack of verbal response to Lewis's comments regarding Hitler in Session 2 (see p. 172 below) is typical in this respect.

The relationship between the visual and verbal parts of sessions was at first unclear to me, with almost a divide between them. However, there seemed to develop a collective use of the images which was integrated with the session as a whole and went beyond the description of 'individual work in a group setting'. The sessions described illustrate some of the interplay between verbal and visual aspects of sessions.

The five sessions described here begin at the point of a move to a smaller art room as part of the hospital retraction. The move coincided with ward changes and mergers and these compounded to form what seemed a precursor of the inevitable move into the community.

---

*Session 1*

This session, the first in the new art room, is in the beginning disrupted, fragmented and beset by practical problems. Tessa, David, Lewis and Charles arrive on time (Spencer is absent) and sit in the usual circle of chairs which has been placed, temporarily, directly in front of the door. To me it feels exposed and draughty. We lack a teapot and a key to the kitchen. The small table we usually place in the centre of the circle for ashtrays, cups, etc., is missing: we substitute a chair. Once these issues are resolved we sit, uncomfortably it seems, drinking tea and coffee and there is an unresolved pondering about where is the best place to put the circle of chairs. Tessa suddenly and angrily says that the hospital is a prison and she makes a pun, without the slightest suggestion of humour, on the name of the hospital and a notorious prison. David adds that it is an 'open prison'. Charles goes for a walk and comes back after about five minutes, Lewis goes to the toilets and comes back, Doris arrives half an hour late, making a lively entrance, accompanied by a nurse. She is under continual observation due to a fire-setting incident and the nurse must stay in the session.

Things gradually settle with everyone sorting out materials and beginning to work mainly in silence on the large central table. David draws his usual 'unbalanced, balanced' (see p. 166 above), Tessa draws shakily around some feathers and then attempts to draw them freehand. Charles paints what he calls a 'Spring Picture', a pond surrounded by grass and Lewis makes 'abstract' shapes by filling in areas of a scribble. Doris draws a 'glamourous' picture of the nurse and wants it immediately put on the wall. The nurse joins in: she has just returned from a visit home to the Caribbean. She draws a simple, idealised Caribbean beach picture and talks rather sadly about some of her family who remain there. The end of the session is flat, the time for drawing and painting was short and no comments are made about each other's unfinished work. Some interest is shown in the nurse's picture and explanation, there is perhaps some identification with her situation.

———————

Comment

In this session the anger and restlessness expressed at the beginning of the session was partially alleviated by what I felt was a striving to achieve some equilibrium in an unfamiliar environment by the familiar process of making images together. The acceptance of the nurse into the group was aided by Doris's inclusive gesture of drawing the nurse's portrait and also by the nurse's willingness to be included.

———————

*Session 2*

In this session everyone arrives punctually. Lewis enters, saying he 'wants to die'. We settle quickly, sitting in the circle of chairs, which we have moved to the back of the room, drinking tea or coffee. Most people smoke. Doris is still absent – under observation and being kept on the ward. Her absence is noted but the reason is not discussed. David asks me if I watched the London Marathon on television. He begins to talk about it and I try to draw the others in by asking who else watched it. There is a discussion about how far the marathon is and how long it takes to run. David suddenly says that he was misdiagnosed a schizophrenic forty-five years ago when he was first admitted to hospital and he knew within a week what was wrong with him and this was 'confusion'. Lewis says that Hitler has been at his (Lewis's) brain, 'smashing his brains, hitting them', and he emphasises the hit of Hitler and hitting, making a pun on Hitler's name. I acknowledge Lewis's distress but the group as a whole does not respond. The conversation turns to the length of time spent in hospital. Tessa says, identifying with David, forty-five years (she is forty-eight) and then she changes this to the year of her birth. Charles, clearly upset and angry, remarks that he moved wards at the weekend and that it has not affected him at all because he has decided to leave the hospital next year. He is emphatic but goes on to complain that the man in the next bed kept him awake by shouting all night and then this man accused everybody else of making a noise. I ask the others about the date of their ward move and there are more complaints about the shifting date. Remembering David's sudden change of conversation from the marathon to the length of time spent in hospital I make a connection and say that it all does seem like a marathon. Lewis begins to walk rapidly round the central table. He has often done this in the past but I am now acutely aware of the confined space in the new room and Lewis's difficulties manoeuvring around. Lewis's restlessness initiates a move to the central table with everyone sorting out materials. Tessa chooses some music. There follows about forty minutes of concentration with only occasional interaction between group members and a few brief comments from myself to individuals about their work towards the end of the session. Tessa, David and Charles continue work begun the previous week, Spencer draws a semi-abstract half-figure of a woman with prominent breasts and writes Tessa's name on it (Figure 8.2). He insists that his picture is put on the wall. Everyone else wants their images put on the wall and they are unusually insistent. Once the images are on the wall there is no formal reflection, but there is an informal viewing and uncritical comments. There has been no return to the circle of chairs. Spencer and Lewis leave on time but David, Tessa and

*Figure 8.2* Spencer's picture of Tessa

Charles linger near the door and begin a discussion in response to David announcing that 'it is the battle of the sexes' and that 'women are superior to men', but he will not say why. Tessa laughs but Charles leaves abruptly, saying he wants 'someone to talk to'.

Comment

This session began with the expression of distress relating to the 'marathon'-like quality of the ward and hospital closures, certainly exacerbated by the move of art room. An awareness of the long years spent in hospital was clear. Underlying David's comments about his misdiagnosis might be the question, 'Why has he been in hospital at all?' Being discharged into the community due to a hospital closure collapses the 'acceptable' explanation for being in hospital, that is, one of cure or treatment. The unacceptable explanation is perhaps one of abandonment.

The concentrated making of images in this session seemed to act as a collective defence against this distressing material. The very mundanity of much of the subject matter seemed to provide a necessary familiarity. Significantly, in this current group, the pattern of verbal communication going via myself does not always extend to verbal interactions around the images. Comments about each other's work tends to be comparatively fluid. Frequently it comprises simple remarks, praise and acceptance. The unusual insistence that all the images went on the wall, followed by a 'viewing time' when favourable comments were made, could be seen as a claiming of the new room (the walls were almost bare) and as a case of mutual affirmation.

Occasionally images clearly reflect the dynamics operating between group members which are otherwise difficult to perceive due to the subtle levels of interaction. There is, for example, envy of David and Tessa's relationship. David probably saw Stanley's provocative drawing of Tessa in the session as an affront and accounted for the conversation at the end of the Session. Some weeks later Stanley made another drawing of Tessa in see-through clothes and called it 'The Height of Frustration' (Figure 8.3).

*Figure 8.3* Spencer's 'height of frustration'

*Session 3*

This session proves to be disrupted and difficult. Only Tessa, David and Lewis are present but we have an uninvited 'visitor', Louise, a patient from another area of the hospital who insists on staying and will not be persuaded otherwise. She talks incessantly throughout the session. We sit in the circle of chairs, Lewis notices that I have found the missing table for the cups and ashtrays, saying 'I thought we'd lost that'. He then instigates a conversation about ages and birthdays. David wants to know if mine is 5 May (it's not). Lewis announces that a man and woman from his ward have moved into a community home together. I ask a few questions and it turns out that David and Tessa should have gone to this home. I express some sympathy. David is despondent: he says it fell through because of something he said but adds that everything is nothing compared to what happened to him in the past. There is tension between Tessa and David; Louise tells them to 'kiss and make up'. Lewis asks me if I have noticed anything about him. I'm not sure but suggest 'a good mood'. He says he hasn't gone walking about, he is feeling better.

During the time for painting and drawing David sits alone, smoking by the window, shoulders hunched. Tessa draws some paint brushes and occasionally calls over to David, trying to engage him in conversation. Lewis leaves the room, coming back after ten minutes saying he's 'had a wash'. Louise keeps up a continuous monologue about her own problems and cuts out pictures of exotic places from magazines.

---

## Comment

In this session the usually silent time for making images was taken over and dominated by Louise. David and Tessa's distress felt uncontained. Lewis in contrast was unusually cheerful. It was Lewis who first mentioned the loss of David and Tessa's community placement. In view of his own unsuccessful attempt at living in the community, I wonder about his envy of David and Tessa's relationship and their prospects of living together outside the hospital, as well as the relief he perhaps feels now that their departure has been delayed.

---

*Session 4*

David, Tessa, Lewis and Charles are already sitting in the circle of chairs when I arrive. I make the tea and coffee. Doris arrives with a nurse, but the nurse agrees to wait outside until the session ends. It appears that David, Tessa and Doris should be moving wards soon but the date has been changed. Doris disrupts any discussion of this by asking Lewis for cigarettes. Charles declares that he has never sexually abused anyone and he elaborates. This is ignored by the group, but acknowledged by me. There is silence and Tessa refuses to have any tea. Lewis goes to the toilet and when he returns he complains that he doesn't know what to draw. I remind him of Agnes, a group member who left a hospital few months previously and who used to suggest 'subjects' for him. Lewis says 'she was alright, was Agnes', and David agrees. There are no questions about where or how Agnes is, but I provide some information.

Tessa sits at the long table but does not paint or draw. David half-heartedly draws a roof shape which he says he once saw in an art book. Doris cuts up bright cellophane paper and puts it on a small window pane. (Other panes have been decorated by another group.) As soon as the session finishes Doris calls in the nurse to admire it. Charles attempts the same thing as Doris but becomes agitated and anxious and he leaves early.

———————

## Comment

It seems to me that in this session what is not said is what the session was about: the anger about the ward changes, the discomfort about Charles's declarations, the loss of Agnes, who was a long-standing and articulate member of the group. It is difficult to address issues in any depth with the group and generally the best way to deal with issues is obliquely over long periods of time. In this session the group, with the exception of Doris, found it impossible to make images and this certainly reflects the feelings from the verbal part of the session.

———————

## Session 5

Tessa, David, Lewis and Doris are present for this session. Spencer has not attended for two weeks. Charles, who had been anxious the previous week, informed me that God had told him not to come this week, a 'euphemism' for his anxiety.

We sit in the circle of chairs and drink tea or coffee. I enquire about the date of the move of ward for Tessa, David and Doris, linking with the conversations of previous weeks. David is angry, saying 'it's been put off again, it'll be July, then August, it goes on and on'. He then begins to recount at great length and in detail a suicide attempt he made by walking amongst traffic and how he was eventually knocked down. Doris cuts across this monologue by persistently begging Lewis to give her a cigarette. I mention that we have talked about suicide before and Doris recounts again her own suicide attempt as a young woman. Lewis gets up and goes to the toilet, coming back after a few minutes. When Lewis returns David gets up to sit at the central table and the others follow. Tessa quickly draws two feathers, and Lewis draws four tulips in the centre of a large sheet of paper. David begins drawing, but soon tires of this and returns to the circle of chairs. He sits alone smoking. Doris makes two rapid drawings with a black felt tip pen. The first shows a young woman trying to stab herself, the second drawing entitled 'The Dream of Me, Doris' shows a glamorous woman dressed in 1950s clothes, a bouffant hair style and high heels (Figures 8.4 and 8.5). The first drawing, she says, is her attempted suicide and the second is how she wants to be when she is 'changed'. Doris asks me to put her second drawing on the wall, which I do. Everyone drifts to the circle of chairs, the time for making images has been short and, with the exception of Doris's, the images remain on the table. I join the circle and out of the blue David announces that he knows what he wants said over him when he is dead and this is 'I think he knew something'. Lewis says that he would like said over him 'There's nothing he didn't find out'. I ask Tessa and Doris if they have anything they would like said; Tessa says she would like 'In loving memory' and then adds 'Goodbye York' (the place where she used to live). Doris says she wants 'Thank God she's dead'. In the silence that follows Lewis breaks in and says that Doris should put 'she never really set fire to things'. I ask Doris if she wants to think of some more and she says 'Poor Doris, poor me', then adds 'nice thoughts of me'. The session ends with everyone leaving together. I felt there was warmth and intimacy and a clear sense of cohesion in the group.

———————

*Figure 8.4* Doris's 'suicide picture'

*Figure 8.5* Doris's 'dream of me'

Comment

In this session there was a fairly complex integration of verbal and visual material. There were three clear parts of the session with Doris's images providing a link between them. On a symbolic level Doris's two images, one of death and the other of change, were relevant for everyone in the group. They picked up on the initial discussion of suicide and partly facilitated the discussion that followed. The contemplation about death had obvious parallels with, as David called it, 'the dying hospital', the death of the group itself and the idea of the changes that will follow. The concern about how the group members would be remembered by each other and by myself was particularly poignant.

## CONCLUSION

I see my own role in the group as maintaining a balance between informality of interaction and serious therapeutic intent. I utilise the social context to reduce distances of differing realities and differing ways of relating. There is a level of familiarity between myself and the members of the group which has developed over the years. I do reveal some things about myself, I do engage in the making and sharing of images, as well as the making and sharing of tea and coffee!

This group represents for me the possibility of focused work with long-term clients within an informality of approach and flexibility of structures. My experience is that formalised models of practice facilitate against group processes with this client group. This group operates on many levels at once, the traditional 'individual work in a group setting' can be addressed, at the same time some images can reflect group concerns and be integrated into sessions both verbally and visually.

## BIBLIOGRAPHY

Adamson, E. (1990) *Art as Healing*, Boston and London: Coventure Ltd.

Case, C. and Dalley, T. (1992) *The Handbook of Art Therapy*, London and New York: Routledge.

Charlton, S. (1984) 'Art Therapy with Long Stay Residents of Psychiatric Hospitals', in Dalley, T., ed., *Art as Therapy*, London and New York: Tavistock Publications.

Dalley, T. (1984) *Art as Therapy*, London and New York: Tavistock Publications.

Goodwin, M. (1978) 'Art Therapy with the Institutionalised Patient: I Don't Know How To Not Act Crazy', in *The American Journal of Art Therapy*, vol. 18, October, pp. 3–9.

Greenwood, H. and Layton, G. (1987) 'An Out Patient Art Therapy Group', in *Inscape*, Summer, pp. 12–19.

Killick, K. (1991) 'The Practice of Art Therapy with Patients in Acute Psychotic States', in *Inscape*, Winter, pp. 2–6.

—— (1996) 'Working with Psychotic Processes in Art Therapy', in Ellwood, J., ed., *Psychosis. Understanding and Treatment*, London: Jessica Kingsley.

—— and Schaverien, J. (1997) *Art Psychotherapy and Psychosis*, London and New York: Routledge.

Leff, J. (1991) 'Evaluation of the Closure of Mental Hospitals', in Hall, P. and Brockington, I., eds, *The Closure of Mental Hospitals*, London: Gaskell, Royal College of Psychiatrists.

Lewis, S. (1990) 'A Place To Be: Art Therapy and Rehabilitation', in *Art Therapy in Practice*, Liebmann, M., ed., London: Jessica Kingsley.

NETRHA (North East Thames Regional Health Authority) (1988) 'TAPS Evaluation or Reprovision for Frien and Clabury Hospitals'. Progress Report on the Mental Health Services Evaluation Committee, 1985–88, London NETRHA.

Saotome, J. (1993) 'A Study of Art Therapy Practice with Long-Stay Clients in Psychiatric Hospitals', Unpublished M.A. thesis, Goldsmiths' College, University of London.

Skailes, C. (1997) 'The Forgotten People', in Killick and Schaverien, eds, *Art Psychotherapy and Psychosis*.

Thomson, M. (1989) *On Art and Therapy*, London: Virago.

Waller, D. (1992) 'The Training of Art Therapists: Past, Present and Future Issues', in Waller, D. and Gilroy, A., eds, *Art Therapy, A Handbook*, Milton Keynes: Open University Press.

—— and Dalley, T. (1992) 'Art Therapy: a Theoretical Perspective', in Waller, D. and Gilroy, A., eds, Milton Keynes: Open University Press.

Warsi, B. (1975) 'Art Therapy in Large Psychiatric Hospitals', in *Inscape*, No. 12, pp. 17–21.

# Chapter 9

# Learning from experience in introductory art therapy groups

*Jane Dudley, Andrea Gilroy and Sally Skaife*

## INTRODUCTION

This chapter describes a method of informing people about art therapy through experiential learning. The model that we have developed works with the evolutionary processes that are common to all groups. It recognises the powerful potential of a whole group to contain the participants, which enables them to learn both experientially and cognitively. In order to demonstrate the potency of the process, and to illustrate some of the basic principles of practice, we give the participants a 'live' experience of art therapy whilst also speaking to the theory. We identify the processes of the group and actively illuminate them through explanation of here and now material which we relate directly to art therapy clinical practice. In this chapter we will describe our approach, setting it in the context of the literature and illustrating it through a description of an introductory group.

Introductory courses in art therapy often include an element of workshop-style experiences which may or may not be theme-centred, plus some kind of didactic teaching which might, for example, describe clinical material. We have been running such courses at Goldsmiths' College, University of London, since 1990. From the outset we were reluctant to include a didactic element in the Introductory Course which, we believed, could lead to learning and participation remaining at an intellectual level. However, we were equally, ambivalent about giving newcomers to art therapy an experience that was, in its entirety, directly parallel to therapy because of the risk of raising participants' defences to a level where they were unable to learn. None the less, we believed that experiential learning was the most effective means of introducing people to the theory and practice of the profession.

Our first framework was to separate the information gathering parts of the course from the small experiential art therapy groups. We encouraged students to enter into the experience of the small groups as fully as possible and considered information-seeking questions as resistance to the experience, referring the questions that were always asked to the whole group discussion and information session that occurred at the end of the course. It soon became clear that this way of working led to the small groups becoming less effective for some people, particularly for the more vulnerable participants and especially if the group leader remained entirely in role as a clinician. A paradox gradually emerged. It became apparent that participants were more open to their personal involvement in the experience if straightforward questions about theory and practice **were** answered within the groups: almost as if the small experiential art therapy groups, at a certain point in the groups' process, felt more like a seminar than a group. However, we learnt to **contextualise** our answers – that is, that whilst questions to the group conductor were related by her to the here and now of the group, questions were also answered with direct reference to, and examples from, the realities of clinical work. Our practice within the introductory course has therefore evolved considerably, not in terms of the structure but rather in our approach as educators, art therapists and group conductors; we, as well as the students, have been able to learn from experience.

We developed a procedure which draws participants' attention to the beginning of their learning in the introductory large group, emphasises its development within the small experiential art therapy groups and concludes with the final plenary session, again of the large group. We learnt that it was important to emphasise that the learning process was a continual one and to speak to the concept of an individual, internalised learning process which continues for the duration of the two days, including overnight. We came to emphasise that participants learn from each other, as well as from us, through social contacts and informal discussion (during the breaks) of their pre-course and on-course experiences. We also realised that the first meeting with all of the participants had an important containing function, and we began to pay more attention to establishing the whole, large group before we moved into its smaller constituent parts. In this first whole group we give a general description of the course and of the small experiential groups, distribute the timetable and facilitate introductions. After this session we spend the rest of the day and most of the following in the small art therapy groups, working intensively in a loosely structured, but strongly boundaried, way. We gather everyone together again in the whole, large group towards the end of the second day and invite questions about the profession, training and other issues that may have arisen during the course. Thus we formalise the structure of a beginning, a middle and an end to the course.

In order to guide participants through the two days, and to enable them to be open enough to allow personal experience to emerge and subsequent learning to occur, we, as group conductors and teachers, have found it essential to keep not only the students' but also our own anxiety at a manageable level. It is our experience that a certain amount of regression is inevitable during the groups, which we have to be able to contain. We also need to hold and accept strong projections, and extreme transference and countertransference feelings. We monitor these closely as it is our cognitive awareness of the developmental process of all groups, which also occurs over the duration of the introductory course, which allows us to stay with the feelings and to articulate them within an **educational** frame, which in turn enables both the students and us to live through the experience. None the less, we have also found that the learning experience is most effective when an unconscious group process is allowed to develop. We found that we could predict the anger that often emerged during the first afternoon and that if we stayed with it then the groups worked through something very important. It is our belief that these two factors together – allowing a group process to develop whilst speaking to the issues that emerge on a cognitive level – prevent participants becoming casualties of the experience (with a distressed and defensive response to the group as described by Lieberman, Yalom and Miles, 1973). This is especially important given that the course is often the first experience of psychodynamic work for the majority of participants and is therefore likely to be quite anxiety provoking.

This is particularly significant as research has demonstrated that the occupational motivations of people who enter the 'caring professions' in general (Dryden and Spurling, 1989), including art therapy (Gilroy, 1992) are mixed. They may arise from a generalised interest in the subject area and work experiences in the field but are usually coupled with a conscious or unconscious wish for self-exploration, which is a consequence of stressful experiences in childhood and early adult life. One can expect that there might be some similarities in motivation found within the participants of an Introductory Course in Art Therapy. We have found that alongside wanting to learn about art therapy as a profession there are likely to be more personal needs that participants hope, albeit unconsciously, will be addressed. Sometimes people come to the Introductory Course apparently in order to rediscover themselves as artists: they often seem to have left behind a childhood playfulness and enjoyment of the creative process or been dominated by the critical superego of art education; others have been steered into 'sensible' professions and away from an active engagement with art. There are also students who are either overtly or covertly exploring the possibility of entering personal therapy and come to the course to have a 'taster' of the experience. Naturally participants also want straightforward information about the theory and practice of art therapy and about art therapy education, but there are often people who come to the Introductory Course hoping to learn about art therapy 'techniques' that they may use in their present work. We directly address the issue of unqualified personnel or members of allied professions working with clients using art materials in a quasi-art therapeutic manner as we think it is important to delineate the parameters of art therapy clinical practice. We make the distinction between this and the more general, activity-based use of art with patients, thus enabling participants to understand that whilst art is a valuable and powerful therapeutic tool it is not possible to become skilled in its use during a two day introductory course.

In order to give the Introductory Course in Art Therapy a theoretical context we will explore the literature on the developmental processes of groups and experiential learning. The description of the usual pattern of the Introductory Art Therapy Course we run, with an example, shows the educational process in action, and we conclude the chapter with a discussion of the issues that arise in this approach to initial art therapy education. We should emphasise, however, that the overall pattern we describe here underlies the process of most Introductory Courses and experiential groups that we run. Naturally not all conform exactly to the timing and developmental process we outline – some small groups develop with greater or lesser speed, or go into greater depth than others. The example we give describes a group that we documented in some detail as part of an evaluation procedure, the results of which we will discuss later on in the chapter.

## LITERATURE REVIEW

Despite the fact that many art therapists conduct experiential art therapy workshops and groups as an introduction to the profession, either for colleagues or the general public, the processes of such groups are considered by only a few authors. Discussion of experiential learning in art therapy groups usually addresses them within the specific context of post-graduate art therapy education (e.g., Lachman-Chapin, 1976;

Wadeson and Allen, 1983; Robbins, 1988; Waller, 1993; Gilroy, 1995), while short-term art therapy groups have been considered within the context of acute psychiatry (Waller, 1993) and with particular patient populations (Springham, 1994). Waller (1993) considers experiential art therapy groups within introductory courses; the groups she describes are usually of one week's duration and for professional mental health workers and may include the use of open-ended projects such as 'self boxes'. She says that it is important that experiential groups within introductory courses be contained by plenty of theoretical and small group discussion so that material can be processed.

Theories about the developmental processes of psychotherapy groups often informs the theory and practice of art psychotherapy groups (e.g., McNeilly, 1983, 1987, 1989; Waller, 1993), although a detailed discussion of its application to art therapy groups and case description has, until this volume, remained absent from the literature. Within the group psychotherapy literature there is a considerable consistency in authors' descriptions of group development. Smith (1980) says that most of the literature on group development describes an early/middle phase of tension and conflict which is usually, but not always, focused on the leader. He says that many authors describe the necessity for some kind of early confrontation to happen within the group which does not destroy it but rather enhances its cohesion and enables harmony within a working group to follow (Smith, 1980).

Yalom (1975) and Agazarian and Peters (1981) describe similar stages in a group's development. The group begins with a period of initial orientation; members search for the goals of the group and are highly dependent on the leader, looking to her for structure, guidance, approval and reassurance. A central theme is that all will be well as long as no-one rocks the boat, the underlying assumption being that the benevolent leader will rescue each individual. The group is concerned with its boundaries and uses flight as a defence, whilst the dynamic force is one of dependence and the wish is for conformity. However, the members of the group soon react against their dependency wishes by going against what they imagine the leader wants of them. There is marked hostility towards the leader arising from unrealistic expectations of him or her and the leader's refusal to 'lead' the group in the expected way. The group's preoccupation with dominance, control and power both amongst members, and between members and the leader, indicate that this phase is one of conflict, disenchantment and anger. Agazarian and Peters (1981) describe a particular 'authority phase' during which the group builds its strength in order to confront the leader. There are oblique references to authority figures but soon the therapist is clearly the target: she is tried and found wanting. Usually there is a confrontation question which, rather than being meaningful in itself, is actually an act of power on the part of the group. Because of the deep underlying conflictual dynamics, resolution of this phase is a potent therapeutic process.

Following this period of conflict and confrontation members feel triumphant and powerful and there are very positive feelings about the group and other members. Yalom (1975) says that a period of cohesion usually follows a period of conflict, evident in the increases in self-disclosure, trust and group morale. However, this is followed by feelings of disillusionment and depression prior to becoming a mature group which turns to more personal, individual experience as it goes again through its developmental phases. This pattern varies from group to group, depending on factors within and external to the group, and has been usefully summarised by Tuckman (1965) as four recognisable stages of 'forming', 'storming', 'norming' and 'performing', i.e., an initial period of confusion, followed by conflict, increasing harmony and then effective work in the group.

The approach of the group leader has provoked considerable debate in the group psychotherapy and art therapy literature; there are those who advocate an active leadership style and those who espouse a relatively passive, 'non-directive' approach to group work. The use of structured exercises in therapy groups has been described as a source of 'heady controversy' (Lieberman, Yalom and Miles, 1973, p. 408); it is interesting that similar disagreement is to be found in the art therapy literature. Some authors find them useful (Fagan, 1970; Levin and Kurtz, 1974; Thornton, 1985; Liebmann, 1986), whilst others criticise themes and exercises as leading to an unproductive, too leader-centred an environment (Argyris, 1967; McNeilly, 1983). Most authors who favour the use of structure in groups associate an active leadership style with the early establishment of an harmonious group. However, Lieberman, Yalom and Miles (1973) demonstrated that it is the timing of harmony and conflict which can promote, or obstruct, learning, concluding that 'a reasonable degree of harmony makes for more learning' (p. 305). They showed that a positive outcome of a group was associated with the development of harmony later on in the life of the group, earlier harmony being likely to reflect the absence of conflict and the gratification of members' dependency needs by the leader.

Ideas vary about which factors contribute to effective learning in groups of all kinds, be they experiential training groups, verbal psychotherapy groups or art therapy groups. However, there is general agreement that therapy education, in whatever context and for whichever kind of therapy, should include a mixture of didactic and experiential learning, which involves some type of process learning where the student studies him/herself, and that learning which is active and involves the person of the student is usually the most significant (Dies, 1980). Experiential learning in a group is a powerful educational and personal experience, described by Aveline and Price (1986) as ' . . . valued by most and forgotten by none' (p. 670).

Woolfe (1992b) also notes the heterogeneity of the group that forms in block training events and the importance therefore of eliciting the expectations of students at the beginning. Several authors in Hobbs' edited collection on experiential training (1992a) note that the varied expectations of the participants may be at odds with those of the teachers/group leaders and that it is therefore important to consider the participants' varying needs. Woolfe (1992a) also speaks to the mixed motivations of those who attend experiential training groups, there usually being both extrinsic and intrinsic factors which motivate at conscious and unconscious levels. Motivation is linked to expectations of the 'course': participants always expect some kind of formal teaching from the 'experts', no matter what information they may have been given beforehand about the experiential nature of the teaching. Because experiential learning actively challenges people at an emotional level, Woolfe states that it is important to make it clear to people what to expect and to acknowledge the explicit goals of the particular course and group at the outset (Woolfe, 1992a).

Hobbs (1992a) describes experiential learning as fundamentally participative and collaborative between student and teacher, involving the taking of risks by all concerned. Elsewhere (1992b) he emphasises the importance of the course leaders establishing the ground rules and a sense of safety early on through introductions and a clear description of the programme itself. He describes the anxiety and uncertainty that is generated at the beginning of a course about what is in store, and adds that these feelings are common to both staff and students! Murgatroyd (1992) notes the likely defensive responses of the students to the prospect of learning in an experiential group. He outlines particular leadership qualities that are necessary and describes the tasks: credibility, authority and competence are important, as is the leader's ability to be open and genuine in the relationship with the participants in the course. Woolfe (1992a) makes the point that in such a teaching environment the teacher/group leader cannot remain emotionally separate from the experience; the countertransference feelings that are aroused can be strong. In order to work with this Woolfe suggests that staff are sufficiently self-aware to be able to disentangle their own needs from those of the students and are able to be 'up-front, aware, exposed, not attempting to defend himself or herself with the structure (or shroud) of expert status' (Woolfe, 1992a, p. 7). He adds that this kind of approach to experiential learning is not about anarchy or abnegation of respon- sibility, but rather is about 'facilitative leadership' (ibid.).

Murgatroyd (1992) suggests that the group leader should operate in such a way as to show that the emergent ideas in the group have antecedents in the work of others and to the theory, research and practice of the subject being studied. The giving of positive feedback and reassurance, and constantly reminding the group about the importance of the learning that is occurring as it happens, builds participants' confidence and demonstrates that their new knowledge is applicable and transferable. Woolfe (1992a) says that it is important for the group leaders to accept the thoughts and feelings of the participants and to make direct statements that endorse people's responses in such a way as to direct the group. He goes on to say that to ignore these issues and the needs and expectations of the learners, and to run an experiential group as a therapy group, is to 'invite disaster' (Woolfe, 1992a, p. 8).

The literature therefore shows that there are clearly identifiable phases of group development and that the approach of the group leader is central to the ability of the participants to learn from their experiences in the group; as this is so in group psychotherapy it is possible to infer that the same will be the case in art psychotherapy groups as well as in experientially based art therapy education. The literature also points to the importance of containment in experiential learning, given the expectations, anxieties and motivations of those attending a dynamically oriented course. In the next section of this chapter we will elaborate upon the basic outline of Introductory Course in Art Therapy that we run, demonstrating the potential of experiential groups as a primary educational tool and illustrating their developmental process through an example.

## THE FIRST WHOLE GROUP MEETING

The introductory whole group meeting usually lasts for forty-five minutes and focuses on describing the course as a whole, the basic boundaries of the small groups and of the course, plus the use of the immediate environment and facilities. In this initial large group our performance is crucial as it sets the tone for the whole two days. It has a dual aspect because our intention is to show our confidence in the subject matter and in our teaching method whilst also allowing an appropriate anxiety to be seen. We sometimes find ourselves enacting this by, for example, asking each other what comes next or whether we have forgotten anything, the purpose being to model an interactive process where uncertainty and playfulness are appropriate.

We aim to give a strong sense of emotional and physical containment to the course from the very beginning. We lay great emphasis on timekeeping and notifying lateness and/or absence, and speak on the physical boundaries of not smoking, etc., immediately relating this to the significance of boundaries in therapy. We emphasise the educational framework by referring to the College facilities and to the Post-graduate Diploma in Art Psychotherapy students, and we encourage partipants to take advantage of the information about the profession that is available so that they may inform themselves about art therapy as fully as possible during the two days. We show that they will be looked after by indicating the provision of tea and coffee and making sure that they know about the various places within the campus and the locality where they may get lunch. This we also demonstrate through attention to the individual; for example, the inevitable latecomer will be introduced and we will describe to him or her what has happened so far, thus actively drawing them into the group and demonstrating to all that similar time and care will be taken with each individual.

During the introductory whole group meeting we give a few indications about the kind of experiences that might occur during the small groups and speak about them as examples of the kind of events and feelings that occur in art therapy. We tell the participants about the nature of 'learning through doing' and the probable anxiety that will be generated that is common to all experiential learning about therapy, but we encourage them to 'stay with it' and to see the process through. Central to this is the notion of the art therapy process as well as the educational process being client-, or in this case, student-led. That is to say, we emphasise the principle of each person taking care of themselves in the small experiential art therapy groups and monitoring what personal material they bring to the encounter. We speak directly to the importance of everyone maintaining an awareness of the course as an **educational** process whilst acknowledging the nature of the groups as an 'as if' experience of therapy.

Participants are asked to talk a little about themselves and their motivations in coming on the course. During this part of the introductory large group we work with their perceptions and experiences of art therapy to date and discuss these in the light of their expectations of the forthcoming two days. We try to highlight the significance of their previous knowledge and experience and the uniqueness of each individual's contribution to the process the whole group is embarking upon. This emphasises the point that they will contribute as much to the experience as we will, and it points to the importance of difference. It is often at this point that participants emerge who have come to the Introductory Course with a wish to acquire 'art therapy techniques' to apply in their work. As stated earlier, our response is always to differentiate between art as a recreational, quasi-therapeutic activity and art therapy as a clinical practice.

By this time the introductory large group is usually nearing the end and it is time for coffee. Although we purchase tea and coffee we make it clear that everyone should help themselves, having told them that the kitchen is small and that they will need to find a way to operate together as a whole group, adding that this usually works out OK! We therefore show the participants that we have confidence in their ability to work things out as a group. We also say that during the first coffee break we will go away and assign everyone to one of the three small groups but that we will return, thus emphasising our continuing presence and availability throughout the course. After the break everyone meets together again and people are assigned to their small groups. Each group conductor then leads their experiential group to the studio they will be working in; this seems to be a useful transition from the large group to the small group and from the information-giving session to the 'learning through doing' experience.

## THE FIRST SESSION OF THE EXPERIENTIAL ART THERAPY GROUPS

At the beginning of the experiential art therapy groups, having formed a circle and sat down, we generally reiterate some of the issues that have been said in the large group. We also say that the studio is the group's space for the two days and so another, physical, container is offered which establishes the new small group. Each group leader then usually describes the nature of art therapy in groups: that the process is not solely about making images and endeavouring to gain some understanding of them but that the group's process is also about whatever might occur in the room, the interactions between group members and between the group and the leader and so on. We each make the point that there is freedom for people to do as they wish with the art materials within the group, but that this is within certain limits and boundaries, as it is within therapy. Parallels are drawn to the freedom they have to talk about what they want, but that here again they have to be careful to respect others and to look after themselves. We equate the art materials to those that would routinely be available in a clinical setting and outline the usual structure of the art therapy process, that is, the basic expectation that each person uses the art materials and that discussion of the work follows. Throughout this we, as the group conductors, are very active in the process of the group and seek to positively reinforce group enhancing behaviour; we also clearly rescue those who either overtly or covertly seem to be in difficulty, and we answer questions that arise from what we have said so far.

These introductory remarks in the small groups are critical as we directly address something fundamental about the educational process in art therapy: that therapy develops through the material that is brought to the group but that this has to be moderated. Herein lies a paradox that we endeavour to work with: we might suggest that participants try to be open and honest with each other and spontaneous with the art materials, yet we also say that the art work can be potent and we tell them to look after themselves. This seems to have the effect of releasing the art-making process as the group then knows that it is appropriate and acceptable to be defensive. Because defences are respected, they are, to an extent that is workable in the setting of an introductory course, circumvented and so participants are able to be relatively free.

At this point we usually suggest that the group begin using the art materials. We suggest that their art work be based around the theme of 'introducing yourself to the group', sometimes adding that whatever is made will serve as an introduction. We say that many art therapists use themes and that they can be helpful, but add that we have reservations about them because some themes can elicit the uninhibited and speedy emergence of powerful personal material, which might be difficult to work with in this context. We say that individuals can use the theme of introducing themselves or not, as they wish, and suggest that the group comes back together to discuss the work at a specified time.

When people have finished making their images we further suggest that a circle be formed and that the images go into the middle. We may speak to the fact of images literally going into the middle of the group and that they are thus physically contained by it. We encourage people to talk about their work but focus on those images that reflect the dynamic of the group. It is at this point that a particularly anxious group member often emerges who seeks information about people's pictures; this we address in terms of individual choice about the discussion of their art work whilst also pointing out that responses to another's image can be as informative about the respondent as it is about the artist. Alternatively, the group's attention may focus on someone who speaks quite freely about their work, or a member may seek to monopolise discussion with personal material. Such dynamics illustrate the group's wish to identify a patient within it in order to explore what art therapy is about, which again we speak to.

We thus actively intervene to structure the group's time and provide an underlying sense of direction and containment. Through maintaining a focus on the individual's relation to the whole group, and by referring to the group's here and now processes and its relation to art therapy clinical practice, we remain within the educational frame whilst allowing the group's spontaneous process to unfold. An example of the first morning of a two day experiential art therapy group follows.

---

## EXAMPLE

The group began quietly and some people looked very anxious. The art therapist introduced the session in the usual way (described earlier). The group was silent; the members introduced themselves by name and the leader suggested that they might use the art materials to introduce themselves to the group in a different way, relating it to clinical matters through description of the client who has no words to introduce themselves or their problems. Elaboration and discussion of this continued for the first twenty minutes of the group, during which time the leader outlined the usual structure of art therapy groups, i.e., the exploration of the physical and emotional space, the division of the time between art-making and discussion, and suggested that this group followed the same procedure. The group decided to divide the remainder of the morning session into one hour's painting and forty minutes of discussion. As the group began work one member approached the art therapist saying that as she had not painted for years she did not know what to do. The leader amplified the issue to the group and suggested that everyone simply do whatever they felt safe with.

As the painting time ended the art therapist suggested that everyone bring their work back to the group and sit together in a circle with the images. She explained about the nature of this part of the group process, describing the triangular relationship in art therapy between person, image and art therapist. She also spoke about the importance of images being seen, although not necessarily discussed, and hence the holding nature of the group itself. The images that had been made were blurred, covered, hiding; a few members said they had been surprised by what they had done, that things had emerged, but few had related directly to the theme of 'introducing yourself'. People had drawn images of their inner and outer selves but in a disguised way so that there was little differentiation. The group leader highlighted the importance of defences, of recognising and respecting them, especially as the group members were beginning to press each other with questions about the meaning of their images. She pointed out how, at this early stage, it was important to simply reflect on the image rather than forcing insight, and the group spent the remainder of the session discussing how 'answers' were not the aim of therapy.

---

This first session illustrates the dependence of the group on the leader. She responds in a way which contains the anxiety whilst teaching something of the uniqueness of the **art** therapy process and of the nature of therapy itself, i.e., that meaning and understanding emerges over time and cannot be grasped immediately.

## AFTER LUNCH – THE SECOND SESSION

In our experience people on the Introductory Course in Art Therapy usually begin to talk to each other in greater depth over lunch and compare experiences inside and outside the small groups. By this point participants have realised that the course really is experientially based and that they will not be told how to 'do' art therapy. It often seems to be the case that participants have not quite realised the nature of the course, despite clear description of its experiential base in the programme's literature, to the extent that we have occasionally felt the need to check again that we really have described the course accurately. The realisation that there will not be any formal 'chalk and talk' sessions, and that the learning process draws on individual and group processes, often elicits angry responses which surface in the latter half of the first day. There are also other disappointments: first, that the course and the small groups will not provide therapy for the participants; and second, within the process of the groups and the development of transference, the realisation that the leaders will not behave as the group members might wish.

So, when the groups reconvene after lunch, there are usually many questions fired at us as the group conductors, some of them quite abrasive and hostile. We used not to answer the questions but would instead interpret the anxiety, staying in role as an art therapist. However, we now answer the questions and function much more as educators, almost as if we were conducting a seminar within an experiential group, although not in such a way as to inhibit the development of a group's process. We allow the hostility to be expressed and appreciate it as an act of power on the part of the group, but we deal with the questions at face value; the session therefore has the feel of being more like a seminar than an experiential group. We describe how the experiences and questions that have arisen from the morning relate directly to the theory and clinical practice of art therapy, illustrating our answers through examples of similar issues in clinical work and emphasising that images are always understood in the context in which they are made. Our answers sometimes elicit personal material from members of the group but it is rarely expanded upon by the individual or the group as a whole. If the disclosures gather momentum we intervene with an empathic, rather than an exploratory, response, which contains the material, and we deliberately lead the discussion back to the group as a whole. This part of the afternoon group can take up to an hour, after which the group is usually able to move back into art-making.

Our belief is that it is at this point that we are most in danger of 'losing' the groups and the individuals in them because of the level of anxiety that has been generated in the morning session. Further, students' responses to the first session can be so strong that it induces countertransference responses in us that are akin to panic (hence the occasional checks to see that we had described the course accurately in our literature). At this particular point in the groups it becomes hard not to retaliate and respond defensively to the aggression, to interpret participants' defences and stay rigidly in role as the clinician. It could be said that we collude with the defences in the small groups through answering questions, but it is our belief that through recognising and indeed supporting the defences by the giving of information that we enable participants to become less anxious and hence able to learn;

because we do not retaliate an unconscious need is satisfied. We have found that a flexible response to the aggressive and fearful attacks that are behind the questions, where we move out of the role of the therapist and clearly into the role of an educator, has the effect of empowering the group and enabling them to engage with the art materials and the processes of the group more fully.

Therefore partipants can learn about the corrective experience art therapy can offer through an experience of it.

## EXAMPLE

After lunch the members of the group discussed the emergence of surprising and frightening material in their images and asked the art therapist how important it was to talk about them. They also asked her how patients coped between sessions if they had not spoken about their work. The questions centred around a concern about whether or not both they and the art therapist would survive the two days. Would she return the next day? Did art therapy have to be 'heavy'? Did it always reveal innermost conflicts, or could it be playful? The art therapist talked about the nature of play and described how it could plunge patients into depth material, but went on to speak about how the process of making art was significant in its capacity to contain feelings. The participants then discussed how to spend the remainder of the afternoon and whether or not they as individuals could really do as they wanted. They decided that they could, so long as an awareness of the group was maintained.

The art-making was then prolonged and very playful with lots of clay work and collage. A difference emerged between individual and group experience that was physically enacted through the art work, which was then discussed and negotiated. In so doing the leader felt that the group members had found their own authority, which enabled them to talk about authority figures such as parents and teachers. At the end the art therapist spoke of the process continuing overnight outside the immediate boundaries of the group through group members' thoughts about the day and through their dreams.

The developmental process of this group during the second session was one where anxiety had provoked a flight from an attack on the leader; this was enacted and revealed through the images that were made and explored in the subsequent discussion. On this occasion the attack on the leader did not materialise on the first afternoon, although strength for it was clearly being built. Answers to the post-lunch questions were dealt with through referring to clinical practice, giving narrative examples of work with patients; in so doing the leader both differentiated between the clinical setting and the experiential group, and drew parallels between them.

## THE FOLLOWING DAY

At the beginning of the groups the next morning we each ask the group members about their thoughts, feelings and dreams about the group that have occurred since the end of the previous day. We thus reinforce the message that therapy and learning continue in the absence of the therapist (and of the teacher), and we emphasise the unconscious nature of the process through our interest in their dreams. However, the intepretations of any dreams are always within the context of the group rather than that of the individual. We address the fact that art therapists are unable to gain an instant understanding of images and dreams but that it emerges over a period of time; in the meantime uncertainty and not knowing is OK. We try to enable the students to realise that art therapy is not magical and is not about the instant interpretation of images, but that it is none the less very powerful and not to be undertaken lightly through the use of simplistic techniques. We encourage the students to be open to learning from each other, demonstrating that they both need and do not need the art therapist and the leader of the group.

After such discussions at the beginning of the second day the small groups often become immersed in the art-making process, getting very enthusiastic and excited about the spontaneity and freedom that can be found in the making of images. Our sense is that at this point the unconscious is allowed. This is because by this time we have usually managed to demonstrate that individual material will not be interpreted but can be generally understood and contained in the context of the group and of the norms of clinical practice. The students begin to discover that art therapy is not a magical, all-seeing, soothsaying sort of experience and the myth is dispelled that imagery can be used in a reductively diagnostic manner.

Often, the entire second day in the small groups is spent contemplating its ending. Usually there is a wish for a happy, collective finish but the reality is frequently of a sad, unsatisfactory end as the groups' wish is for the experience to continue. People sometimes speak of previous losses; again we offer an empathic response but do not encourage individuals to explore the material, relating it instead to the here and now of the group and to endings of therapy in general. Towards the end we usually encourage people to think about what happens next to their art work and draw attention to the symbolic issues surrounding the disposal of images and the holding capacity of art work. Usually the groups end with a sense of anticlimax as they separate from us in the flatness of depression.

---

## EXAMPLE

At the beginning of the second day the group members discussed uncaring teachers. Although this was clearly about the art therapist she did not make an interpretation but encouraged the group to explore it; personal material emerged about making good things, bad. Again, the art therapist responded to the material on a cognitive level, explaining how a group recreates previous experiences within the family and that the exploration of conflict in the group constitutes the therapy. At this point the group decided to explore these issues through art-making. In the subsequent discussion the group members said how they had got to know each other well through their art work and to a much greater extent than would have occurred had the group been simply verbal.

From this point the group really got into making images, energetic almost greedy images. Several people re-worked images from the first day, evoking some strong feelings around patterns of behaviour which might be able to change. At the end the art therapist suggested bringing all of the images together and making a circle around them so that they were physically contained by the group. People discussed how important it had been to simply have the space to make things without being overwhelmed by each other or by the images, and at the end of the day were able to acknowledge their anger towards the art therapist who had initiated the group but who then took it away at the end.

Throughout the second day the art therapist had deliberately brought the group back simply to look at the work prior to any breaks, rather than interpreting group phenomena or personal material. Commentary on group phenomena came in the last discussion period when it was placed alongside a cognitively based description of group processes.

---

In the second day of this particular introductory group there is a veiled attack on the leader in the form of discussion of unsatisfactory teachers, which the art therapist responds to through description of the curative factors in groups, i.e., she circumvented the attack through a cognitively based response; this enabled increased engagement with the art materials, leading to a harmonious group. Towards the end of the small group the participants were able to face its imminent end and hear some of the realities of clinical practice in art therapy.

## WHOLE GROUP DISCUSSION

In the final session of the Introductory Course we return entirely to the educational frame in the large group where all of the course participants and staff meet in a plenary session. Students often come into this session physically holding the art work they have made, enacting the point that something has been gained from the two days. We seek feedback and questions about the profession that may have arisen and give out information about the professional association, entry requirements into post-graduate art therapy education, foundation art therapy courses and so on. We thus address the possibility of the students continuing in another context with whatever has begun for them during the two days. Occasionally the questions reveal some hostility as people return to their previous ideas about art therapy as a profession and as a clinical practice, and criticism is levelled at us as representatives of a profession that has demanding pre-course entry criteria. Equally, we are often questioned about the details of the various courses, the essays required and so forth. We usually finish with encouraging people to read the growing art therapy literature and to look at samples of the professional association's journal, *Inscape*.

## EVALUATION

The small group we use as an example was part of a particular Introductory Course where we conducted a pilot research project in order to evaluate our work. Our feeling was that this had an impact on the processes of the two small groups that were conducted on that occasion; they seemed to become rather split, and both art therapists felt that their groups' processes were rather different to those which we had come to expect.

The group we describe here seemed to be more art-based and cognitively oriented than usual, whilst the other group became more like a therapy group with considerably higher levels of self-disclosure and anxiety than is usually the case. Throughout this second group there had been a strong impetus towards personal revelation that had started in the first moments of the group on the first day. This was coupled with a realisation that the group could not offer sufficient time or safety to discuss personal issues in depth, which made it difficult for the group members to settle and become involved in their art work. By the end of the two days the art therapist felt that the group might have been more contained had she emphasised the cognitive aspects more strongly during the first afternoon, despite the very strong push from some participants to use the group to work on highly personal material. She felt that her group had been a balancing act which had only just worked, and that it had drawn heavily on her skills as a group therapist.

None the less, the evaluation showed that members of both groups had found the course to be a good learning experience. Prior to the first meeting with the whole student group we asked the participants to complete brief questionnaires about their expectations of the Introductory Course; immediately after the end of the final, plenary session they were asked to consider whether their expectations had been met and what they had learned. A large majority of the students said at the beginning of the course that they expected to learn about art therapy as a profession, about art therapy education (in particular about the course at Goldsmiths' College), and about the processes of art therapy in groups. A majority also expected to learn something about themselves and about other people, as well as something about art therapy techniques that could be used with clients. Despite the course literature a large majority expected lectures and case presentations. The participants were anticipating learning about the profession and its practice and, on the basis of the information gained, were hoping to be able to make a decision about whether or not to train as an art therapist – 'to decide whether it suits me'.

In the post-course evaluations almost everyone felt they had learnt about the art therapy process and about art therapy groups, as well as about themselves and others, and had felt experiential learning to be a good way to learn. However, a similarly large number of participants reported that they had not learnt about art therapy techniques, nor about art therapy as a clinical practice, and some would have liked more formal input into the course. However, the qualitative comments revealed that everyone had found the course to be a good learning experience, if an 'intense', 'challenging' and 'tiring' one. The descriptions were of having found it 'scary' to begin with, but of finishing the course having enjoyed it and wanting more. It seems that participants had understood enough of the processes of art therapy to be able to decide whether or not to pursue it further, and on the whole had been empowered to seek more information, experience and training.

## DISCUSSION

Our motivation to write this chapter arose from our interest in the processes and paradoxes that emerged as we gained experience in running the Introductory Course in Art Therapy. We began with a fundamental belief in the group process and in the value of making images within it; from this we have been able to develop a model that provides a sufficient depth of learning for the participants to decide whether or not to pursue their interest in art therapy. A reasonably sound and realistic baseline of knowledge is achieved in which enough has been done, but not too much.

The strength of the developmental process that occurs in the two days of the course is striking. In a sense it is possible to see the entirety of the group process in microcosm, sometimes with considerable intensity. The group's process is one of feeling anxious, then angry, then contained; this is the experience that seems to be valuable as it happens in a manageable way. We have found that our awareness of the group's entire process (directly parallel to that of all groups as described earlier) is what enables us to allow and then work with the phase of tension and conflict so that a reasonably cohesive and harmonious group can develop in which people are able to learn. It is our view that acceding to participants' expectations at the beginning of the course with didactic teaching, and to the dependency needs of the participants in the early stages of the group through provision of a clearly defined task, would introduce harmonious feelings too soon and inhibit the depth of learning on the Introductory Course. It is for this reason that we think it is crucial to speak to the nature of the experience that students are about to have immediately as the course begins, as has been highlighted by other authors in the field of experiential training (Hobbs, 1992a; Woolfe, 1992a; 1992b).

A core issue in this teaching method is the balance between education and therapy that has to be maintained. If the group is too cognitively oriented it will not allow regression to occur and sufficient effect to be felt within it to enable emotional material to emerge. When a personal quality is allowed it can be directly related to what a group is able to achieve and to the nature of the art therapy process, whilst also serving to illuminate actual clinical practice. On the other hand, if the group is not held on a cognitive level, then the anxiety becomes too great and people are unable to learn. A useful analogy can be made with sailing: if there is insufficient wind or the sails are allowed to flap, then the boat does not move along. Equally, too much wind might cause the sails to rip and the boat could capsize. But if there is sufficient wind and the sails are set in order to catch it then the boat can proceed on its way.

For many participants on the Introductory Art Therapy Course it will be the first time that they have heard examples of clinical work. Relating clinical practice directly to their experience in the here and now of the group enables students to identify with clients and to have an 'as if' experience of art therapy. We think that the process of re-enactment that occurs through the group demonstrates the possibility of new and different experiences, such as having a different experience of making art. The potential for change, and the potential of the therapeutic triangle in art therapy, can be felt in the group. It goes without saying that this is one of the important formative experiences of becoming a therapist (Dies, 1980). The (often solely) intellectual involvement that occurs with the more formal presentation of case material is of course needed, but we suggest that at such an early, formative stage as this, the distancing that can occur is unhelpful. Indeed, Hobbs (1992a) states that solely intellectual and passive learning can be inadequate and lead to potentially damaging use of knowledge.

Workshops and groups such as these can evoke cathartic experiences; this has an inherent risk of either being uncontained and remembered too well (as per the 'casualties' described by Lieberman, Miles and Yalom, 1973), or of being an experience that is subsequently found to be unsatisfying and lacking in substance, having been no more than 'a quick fix'. Neither is satisfactory. It seems to us to be more helpful to create ripples of learning that are manageable by the group and so by the individual. It is crucial that the person feels in charge of their experience and hence of their learning, that they feel contained by the tutors but neither controlled nor left too much to discover on their own.

In order to achieve this balance we have had to acknowledge that we are, in this context, powerful figures and that indeed we might desire such power. Projected and real power, as well as positive transference, are all easy to accept; expectations that we will provide are high, and the pull to do just that is sometimes hard to resist! The realisation that we will not fulfil the expectations, and the consequent attacks that follow, can be equally hard to take, but if we accept the power and the positive transference, then the students' own power and potential will find difficulty in emerging, as will their own potential to be a transferential object. If power, authority and transference are acknowledged then the collaborative potential of a group comprising staff and students, and truly student-centred learning, is more likely to be achieved. The emergence of a group as a whole experience and the realisation of its strength allows the possibility of disillusion and depression to emerge, with the accompanying insight that the staff, the Introductory Course, and art therapy *per se*, cannot provide all. In our view it is better that the reality of therapy is faced than that they (and we) leave the course in a blaze of idealised glory.

## BIBLIOGRAPHY

Agazarian, Y. and Peters, R. (1981) *The visible and invisible group: two perspectives on group psychotherapy and group process.* Tavistock/Routledge, London.

Argyris, C. (1967) 'On the future of laboratory education'. *Journal of Applied Human Science*, 3(2), pp. 152–83.

Aveline, M. and Price, J. (1986) 'The Nottingham experiential day in psychotherapy: a new approach to teaching psychotherapy to medical students'. *British Journal of Psychiatry*, 148, pp. 670–5.

Dies, R.R. (1980) 'Current practice in the training of group psychotherapists'. *International Journal of Group Psychotherapy*, 30(2), pp. 169–85.

Dryden, W. and Spurling, L. (eds) (1989) *On becoming a psychotherapist.* Routledge, London.

Fagan, J. (1970) 'The tasks of the therapist'. In: Fagan, J. and Shepert, I.L. (1970) *Gestalt therapy now: theory, techniques, applications.* Science and Behavior Books, Palo Alto, CA.

Gilroy, A. (1992) *Art therapists and their art. From the origins of an interest in art to occasionally being able to paint.* Unpublished D.Phil thesis, Univ. of Sussex.

—— (1995) 'Changes in art therapy groups'. In: Gilroy, A. and Lee, C. (eds) *Art and music. Therapy and research.* Routledge, London.

Hobbs, T. (ed.) (1992a) *Experiential training. Practical guidelines.* Routledge, London.

—— (1992b) 'Skills of communication and counselling'. In: Hobbs, T. (ed.) *Experiential training. Practical guidelines.* Routledge, London.

Lachman-Chapin, M. (1976) 'Training art therapists in group art therapy'. In: *Creativity and the art therapist's identity.* Proceedings of the Seventh Annual Conference of the American Art Therapy Association.

Levin, E.M. and Kurtz, R.R. (1974) 'Structured and non-structured human relations training'. *Journal of Counseling Psychology,* 21, pp. 526–31.

Lieberman, M.A., Yalom, I.D. and Miles, M.B. (1973) *Encounter groups: first facts.* Basic Books, New York.

Liebmann, M. (1986) *Art therapy for groups: a handbook of themes, games and exercises.* Routledge, London.

McNeilly, G. (1983) 'Directive and non-directive approaches in art therapy'. *Arts in Psychotherapy,* vol. 10, no. 6, pp. 211–19.

—— (1987) 'Further contributions to group analytic art therapy'. *Inscape,* Summer, pp. 8–11.

—— (1989) 'Group analytic art groups'. In: Gilroy, A. and Dalley, T. (eds) *Pictures at an exhibition. Selected essays on art and art therapy.* Routledge, London.

Murgatroyd, S. (1992) 'Evaluating change and development through workshops'. In: Hobbs, T. (ed.) *Experiential training. Practical guidelines.* Routledge, London.

Robbins, A. (1988) 'A psychoaesthetic perspective on creative arts therapy and training'. *Arts in Psychotherapy,* vol. 15, No. 2, pp. 95–100.

Smith, P.B. (1980) *Group processes and personal change.* Harper and Row, London.

Springham, N. (1994) 'Research into patients' reactions to art therapy on a drug and alcohol programme'. *Inscape,* vol. 2, pp. 36–40.

Thornton, R. (1985) 'A critique'. *Inscape,* 1, pp. 23–5.

Tuckman, B.W. (1965) 'Developmental sequences in small groups'. *Psychological Bulletin,* 63, pp. 386–99.

Wadeson, H. and Allen, P. (1983) 'Art-making in clinical training for conceptualization, integration and self-awareness'. *Leonardo,* vol. 16, No. 3, pp. 241–2.

Waller, D. (1993) *Group interactive art therapy.* Routledge, London.

Woolfe, R. (1992a) 'Experiential learning in workshops'. In: Hobbs, T. (ed.) *Experiential training. Practical guidelines.* Routledge, London.

Woolfe, R. (1992b) 'Coping with stress'. In: Hobbs, T. (ed.) *Experiential training. Practical guidelines.* Routledge, London.

Yalom, I.D. (1975) *The theory and practice of group psychotherapy.* Basic Books, New York.

# Index